In the Spirit
of Powys

In the Spirit of Powys

NEW ESSAYS

Edited by
Denis Lane

With a Foreword by
Jerome J. McGann

Lewisburg
Bucknell University Press
London and Toronto: Associated University Presses

Associated University Presses
440 Forsgate Drive
Cranbury, NJ 08512

Associated University Presses
25 Sicilian Avenue
London WC1A 2QH, England

Associated University Presses
P.O. Box 488, Port Credit
Mississauga, Ontario
Canada L5G 4M2

The paper used in this publication meets the requirements
of the American National Standard for Permanence of Paper
for Printed Library Materials Z39.48-1984.

Library of Congress Cataloging-in-Publication Data

In the spirit of Powys : new essays / edited by Denis Lane.
    p.   cm.
    Includes bibliographical references.
    ISBN 0-8387-5173-3 (alk. paper)
    1. Powys, John Cowper, 1872–1963—Criticism and interpretation.
2. Modernism (Literature)   I. Lane, Denis.
PR6031.O867Z736   1990
828'.91209—dc20   89-42925
                                                                          CIP

Contents

6   CONTENTS

Foreword

That John Cowper Powys is one of the great European novelists of this century has seemed evident since 1929, when the first of his "English" novels, *Wolf Solent*, was published. That he has had, over the same period, a number of ardent detractors is also the case.

This controversy, in its earliest (largely nonacademic) phase, should be understood for what it was: part of the struggle of literary modernism, part of that movement's own attempt to establish and define itself. One finds exactly the same sort of cultural struggles in every volatile period of artistic production. The romantic period, to take only the most obvious case, illustrates the situation very well. For one thing, romanticism had to struggle against other cultural and stylistic traditions that made equal claims to authority: Jane Austen, Maria Edgeworth, and George Crabbe are not romantic writers, and Crabbe in particular entered into a polemic with romantic ideas about writing. Within the romantic movement itself, moreover, writers engaged in sharp controversies with each other about what was good and what was bad. The divisions that stand between (for example) Wordsworth and Byron are not simply personal ones, and these struggles are sometimes continued to the present day in the academy.

Similar controversies may be heard, for those who have ears to hear, within modernism. Being so much more an immediate imperative for us, however, modernism's battles can become, paradoxically, less apparent. What I mean is that when the modernist movement (let us date it 1914–39) descended into academic hands, the teachers began an effort to codify and rationalize its activities. Between 1940 and approximately 1970, the schools imagined, studied, and taught modernism in a highly restricted way. Certain writers came to be imagined as central; others were marginalized or neglected altogether. With the coming of gender and women's studies, in the 1960s, some of the fences that had been raised began to be taken apart. For most academic traditionalists of modernism, however, John Cowper Powys remained a figure of the Marches.

Powys's academic fate may be reasonably deplored. More useful, however, would be a concerted effort to understand that fate, to comprehend why it came about when so many of Powys's contemporaries, and so many later figures of great literary eminence, never ceased to perceive, and to declare, the greatness of Powys's achievement.

When that critical effort is made—and this book is itself part of the effort—I think we will begin to see at least this truth about Powys and modernism: that he brought to the movement the one sign of contradiction it could not bear to face. The ideologies of modernism are often founded on a series of literary critiques and cultural repudiations directed at romantic and, more particularly, Victorian traditions. Modernism imagines itself as a new birth of artistic freedom, an evolutionary leap beyond the tired and overused formulas of the nineteenth century. An enthusiast and student of the most important modernist writers—especially of Lawrence, Joyce, Dostoievsky, and Proust—Powys was a modernist who flaunted his (contradictory) commitments and debts to writers who were hopelessly retrograde, so far as the dominant ideologies of modernism were concerned: for example, to Scott, and even to writers like Reade and Harrison Ainsworth.

Powys is often seen as a student of Hardy, and his novels—especially the famous regionalist texts—exhibit a clear Hardyan debt. But from the point of view I have been trying to develop here, Powys's fictions run an aesthetic parallel with Hardy's *poetry* rather than with his fiction. That is to say, Hardy's poetry stands to modernist poetry and poetics much as Powys's novels stand to the fiction generated by important and touchstone modernists like Joyce, Proust, Woolf, or Genet.

The differential that Powys represents is nicely exhibited at the elementary level of his prose style: for instance, in Powys's notorious sentences. Denis Lane has an acute comment on this essential Powysian textual unit:

> Everything he wrote—and the corroboration is in the manuscripts and letters with their seamless, sprawling lines—suggests that for Powys an English sentence was not an ordered spatial entity at all, but a barely separable unit of narrative energy. (16)

The astonishing paragraph that opens the final chapter of *A Glastonbury Romance* illustrates precisely what Lane calls to our attention.

> The great waves of the far Atlantic, rising from the surface of unusual spring tides, were drawn, during the first two weeks of that particular

March, by a moon more magnetic and potent as she approached her luminous rondure than any moon that had been seen on that coast for many a long year. Up the sands and shoals and mudflats, up the inlets and estuaries and backwaters of that channel-shore raced steadily, higher and higher as day followed day, these irresistible hosts of invading waters. Across the far-stretching flats of Bridgewater Bay these moon-drawn death-bringers gathered, stealing, shoaling, rippling, tossing, waves and ground-swells together, cresting billows and unruffled curves of slippery water, rolling in with a volume that increased its momentum with every tide that advanced, till it covered sand-wastes and sand-dunes, grassy shelves and sea-banks, that had not felt the sea for centuries.

Though just the opening quarter of the paragraph, the excerpt reveals very well the strange beauty of Powys's prose. It is at root an epic style, but Powys works to contaminate and ruin the illusions of its grandeur. "For many a long year" is an upsetting colloquialism, a "false note" all the more perfect for its own paradoxical marriage of a monumental gesture in an everyday idiom. The opening paragraph of *A Glastonbury Romance*, which has outraged fastidious readers, illustrates the same comic and quixotic seriousness in a more absolute form:

At the striking of noon on a certain fifth of March, there occurred within a casual radius of Brandon railway-station and yet beyond the deepest pools of emptiness between the uttermost stellar systems one of those infinitesimal ripples in the creative silence of the First Cause which always occur when an exceptional stir of heightened consciousness agitates any living organism in this astronomical universe. Something passed at that moment, a wave, a motion, a vibration, too tenuous to be called magnetic, too subliminal to be called spiritual, between the soul of a particular human being who was emerging from a third-class carriage of the twelve-nineteen train from London and the divine-diabolic soul of the First Cause of all life.

This is an epic style that has become threadbare without, however, ceasing to be epic. It is the style Powys discovered for maintaining the real presence of the gods in the abysmal residues of a late-empire world.

Two other matters deserve notice. First, though the style is fundamentally periodic in each of these passages, the periodic structure keeps spilling out and leaking away. The effect is especially clear in the second and third sentences of the passage from *Glastonbury's* last chapter. Powys, for example, so loosens the syntax of the participles in the third sentence that the prose begins to eddy and wander.

His language has been so overloaded with repetitive details and structures, however, that it seems to sink and fracture under its own weight. As a consequence, the "building" effect of the periodic form generates its own principle of erosion. The prose thus raises up illusions of ends, destinations, and conclusions, but it does so only to insure that it may ceaselessly and randomly spread and multiply, like some vast rhizomatic system.

Secondly, these two passages evidently call out to each other across the eleven-hundred-odd pages of *A Glastonbury Romance*. The final lunar "flood" is associated with the opening "soul of the great blazing sun," masculine with feminine, great water with primal fire. One wants to observe this because it reminds us of the strange architechtonics of Powysian fiction. Like Joyce and Proust, two of his favorite authors, Powys did not neglect the imperatives of form. But unlike either *Ulysses* or *Remembrance of Things Past*, a work like *Glastonbury* invokes principles of form only in order to generate the thick *materia* of substantive creation. It is, in this respect, much closer in kind to *Finnegans Wake* than it is to *Ulysses*.

This stylistic inertia in Powys founds the "romance" structure of his works, which do not organize themselves by plot so much as by a kind of spreading accretion. Characters multiply and drive each other from the center of attention—or rather they drive each other to their own various centers of attention. The further we proceed into his books the more we realize that we have entered a field full of folk. It is a field whose center is everywhere and whose circumference is nowhere. As for the people themselves, they are odd—as we would expect. That is to say they are singular, diverse, *per*verse.

But these initiating remarks comprise little more than a personal testimony of how I found my way into Powys's fiction more than twenty-five years ago, and why I have never been able to leave it again. The essays in this book will illuminate in depth the extraordinary procedures of Powys's work, and some of its important modernist connections. We will understand modernism much better after we have restored Powys to that context, of course, but—what is perhaps more important—we will have greatly enlarged our sense of the powers of fiction when we have made Powys as essential to our reading as Turgeniev or Austen, Balzac or Dickens.

JEROME J. McGANN
UNIVERSITY OF VIRGINIA

Acknowledgments

On behalf of the contributors to this collection, I wish to thank Laurence Pollinger Ltd. and the Estate of John Cowper Powys for permission to quote from Powys's works. Specific texts and the publishers thereof are cited in the notes to each essay. I am also grateful to John Jay College of Criminal Justice for valuable assistance. And I owe a particular debt of gratitude to Mr. John D. Christie, G. Wilson Knight's literary executor, for his continued support and goodwill.

Introduction

Denis Lane

"Powys Major," as John Cowper Powys was known at Sherborne School, is presently the subject of a renewed and vigorous interest. This is not surprising perhaps for those who take the view that as the author of such books as *Wolf Solent, A Glastonbury Romance, Owen Glendower,* and *Autobiography,* John Cowper Powys wrote some of the finest works of their special, and particular kind in the English language. A gentle, yet steely vision inhabits these works, one that urges compassion, tolerance, and a healing imagination in a disordered world, yet one that offers a voice of caution against the improvidence of denying nature, ritual, and the stoic personality as true sources of psychic serenity. Many today would consider this a vision of utmost importance. Hence, to invoke Powys's Sherborne epithet is to seek not only to distinguish John Cowper from his writer-brothers, Theodore and Llewelyn, but equally to impart the view, collectively held by the critics represented here, that Powys's claim to be seen as a figure of major significance in modern literature is both appropriate and demonstrable.

It is proper, therefore, that our collection should begin with an essay that explores the connections between Powys and James Joyce, the novelist most commonly acknowledged as the exemplar of the modern. The correspondences in their life and work are intriguing and instructive. Both were writers-in-exile, a fact acknowledged more for Joyce than for Powys, even though the greater part of Powys's work was written in America. Exile was self-willed for both, but just as Joyce remained profoundly Irish, so Powys remained profoundly English. Written abroad, their novels were laid in native settings, yet both wrote ultimately not of their homelands but of the inner country of the mind. Their work shares also a willingness, indeed a compulsion, toward experimentation, and this is one of the central connections elaborated here. Moreover, not only was Powys one of the earliest and most ardent of Joyce's supporters—in 1923 describing *Ulysses* as "an organic and thrilling work of genius"—but, argues Charles Lock, Joyce is the one writer whose work best provides the points of reference from which Powys's own achievement may be judged.

No fewer than seven of the remaining essays in the collection deal individually with the "English," or "Wessex" novels: that is, *Wolf Solent, A Glastonbury Romance, Weymouth Sands,* and *Maiden Castle.* Indeed, these are the four novels that have most attracted attention over the years. Sharing unity of time and setting, a common social aura, and protagonists of like temperament and sensibility, the English novels might appear at first glance to comprise a deliberately planned quartet. In actuality, each is a separate work: independent in its conception, self-contained in its passions, and discrete in its legends. To say this, however, does not overlook that all four novels were distilled from Powys's mind during a single decade, those astonishingly productive years from 1925 to 1935 that saw also the appearance of his famous *Autobiography* and his perennially best selling *The Meaning of Culture.* Thus to consider these novels together is to trace the intensity in the growth of Powys's thought and imagination during these years and to be brought into touch with the mind of the artist at its most fertile and energetic. This period marked Powys's attainment of creative maturity, as his mind spawned the huge progeny of its earlier questing. Those writing here on this period of Powys's life are concerned with revealing the complex metaphysical tensions of his novels of that time and with demonstrating how in their creation Powys was engaging some of the chief problems of the modernist aesthetic.

Following these discussions, Richard Maxwell's essay advances a central connection between the longest of the English novels, *A Glastonbury Romance,* and *Porius,* Powys's "Romance of the Dark Ages," over which he labored in North Wales for almost as many years as all the English novels put together. Because many would regard these two books as the twin peaks of Powys's career, there is consonance to the view that as myths of place each is a supreme expression of Powys's continual search for the "Peace paradisic"— the fundamental desire to achieve rest within a frictional world. In this, they also demonstrate Powys's exceptional individuality as a mythologist. A further interpretation of *Porius,* in the essay by Michael Ballin, suggests that the novel is a challenge to Darwinian and Freudian views of the dynamics of history and that—though motivic patterns of death and renewal—it embraces a philosophy of history that falls more compatibly within the speculations of Spengler or Massingham than any others. Often termed a "historical" novel, *Porius* is more appropriately to be recognized as a work that by implication confronts rather than upholds our current perceptions and theories of history. In short, like all of Powys's work, its transcends the usual expectations of its apparent genre.

It is good that G. Wilson Knight's essay—the last that he wrote on Powys—should commence by placing John Cowper's thought within the context of that of his brothers, Theodore and Llewelyn. Although neither was, strictly speaking, a direct literary influence on him, John Cowper nevertheless drew immense psychological support from their presence, their touch, and from their disparate enunciations of a strangely proscribed view of life. *Letters to His Brother Llewelyn*, for instance, shows how John Cowper was always on his best intellectual mettle when in debate with Llewelyn and that he had enormous respect for his younger brother's powers of rational argument. G. Wilson Knight begins by reflecting on the commonality of thought in the work of the Powys brothers. He examines how all three exhibited a perpetual concern with death and the possibility of an afterlife. And finally, he traces this recurrent strand as it is displayed in John Cowper's *Morwyn* and the major poem, "The Ridge." He does this with all the verve and acuity for which as a leading interpreter of English literature in this century he was justly renowned. For those who have watched the interplay between Knight and Powys, there is special interest to be found after fifteen years in Knight's re-formulation of his first views on this topic, as expounded in his contribution to *Essays on John Cowper Powys* (ed. Belinda Humfrey, 1972).

Collectively then, this set of essays is likely to provide a picture of John Cowper Powys's achievement, of his uniqueness and singularity as a writer, and of some of the most pressing problems of his interpretation. In addition, however, they will point to the difficulties and obstacles that, by their very nature, his novels tend to throw in the path of the candid reader. Indeed, it must be allowed that Powys has never entirely been without his detractors, and although this is decidedly less the case now than fifteen or twenty years ago, some of these criticisms linger as undeserved canards on the literary reputation of this extraordinary writer. I should like to address, however briefly, some of these criticisms at this point.

If we look at the history of his critical reception, we see that Powys has primarily been arraigned on two charges: first, that he was an escapist, and second, that he lacked artistic control. Often these charges are combined: that he was possessed of "a huge verbosity," that he embraced "a fake philosophy" (Harry Coombes); or that he was guilty of "an intellectual incontinence," was deficient in his "sense of social reality," had no "theodicy" (Robert Nye);

or that he indulged in "cloudy rhapsody" and was "almost completely without the abilities of an artist" (William Plomer).

Much depends, of course, on the perspective that we bring to a reading of Powys. If our expectations are for the confident structures of nineteenth-century fiction, or for Edwardian complacence, or for Jamesian forcing of pattern and order within a small, tidy, "perfect" work of art, then we are likely to be disappointed by what Powys offers. If, however, one can appreciate the slow growth of story through accretion, complexity seen whole rather than reduced to simple elements, plurality of truths, and daring and breadth of vision, then Powys is likely to evoke a deep response.

In addition, it could be argued that Powys possesses an aesthetic conscience that—although certainly not weak—is singularly his own. He never entirely escaped the conviction, for instance, that one wrote for oneself. "I am a *carp* of aesthetical swallowing," he remarked in a letter to Louis Wikinson, ". . . a lover of *Colossal size* in Poetry and Art, not to mention Novels! You see I write the sort of book I like best to read." We know that among his favorite novelists were Scott, Dickens, Conrad, and Dostoievsky—together with Hardy, whom he knew personally—but did Powys write simply to re-create the pleasures of reading this formidable gallery? Certainly there are times when his diction and prose rhythms seem to suggest Scott, whose writing he cites fondly in *One Hundred Best Books* (1916) for its "large, easy, leisurely manner . . . its digressiveness, its nonchalant carelessness." And sometimes, too, his scenes resemble those of Hardy, his structures those of Dostoievsky. But Powys had his own form to make and his own voice to raise, and he succeeded in doing both in a way that indicates, in the words of Glen Cavaliero, "his complete self-sufficiency as an artist." This self-sufficiency was achieved, I believe, with enormous effort: the product of a powerful imagination working against a current of admiration for his predecessors so forceful and so strong—to judge from his often effusive essays in literary appreciation—as to have overwhelmed any lesser talent.

Everything he wrote—and the corroboration is in the manuscripts and letters with their seamless, sprawling lines—suggests that for Powys an English sentence was not an ordered spatial entity at all, but a barely separable unit of narrative energy. Likewise, on a greatly magnified scale, his entire fictional imagination was too generous and unpredictable to submit to the patterns of aesthetic forms previously tried and found true. From *Wolf Solent* on, to the high point of his career—the creation of *Porius*—we see Powys developing and intensifying a new version of romance (and it is the term he favored); that is, *fables* that incorporate aspects of the miraculous and the extraordinary, that are characterized by imaginative excitement, and that are full of exaggeration and largeness, but not of falsehood or fakery. As narratives, they answer perfectly to that persuasive formula enunciated by Powys in the *Autobiography*, that "a human story, to bear any resemblance to the truth, should advance and retreat erratically."(237) Equally, Powys's link to Scott, Hardy, and the others that I have mentioned seems ultimately to be a question not of imitation but of affinity, of a natural temperamental alignment between himself and writers who see life in melioristic terms, who are aware of cosmic absurdity, who understand human suffering, isolation, and obsession, who are more interested in the fringes and limits than the norm of human experience, who know human beings are grotesque and mean, violent and self-serving, and yet are capable of love, heroism, and self-sacrifice. His endearment to large dimensions, to aggregation, to deliberate dis-order mimicking life, is what many critics have mistaken as Powys's lack of artistry, whereas it expresses a type of artistry that possesses its own inherent logic and that fosters its own dynamic results.

The development of Powys's "self-sufficiency" seems to have taken its most significant turn during the early 1920s. *After My Fashion*, the lost-but-now-found novel of about 1918, contains Powys's only portrayals in fiction of distinctly urban (or for that matter American) life. After this, Powys turned away from any further attempt to create a sustained a view of "mainstream" or conventional society. Increasingly, he set his novels deeper in the hinterland and history of Britain, mostly confining them to realizations of life among individuals and groups of a bohemian disposition and persons of independent means, or, in the case of the novels set in Wales—*Owen Glendower* and *Porius*—to panoramic but putative episodes in Welsh history. Although in this he did not entirely eliminate the social reality of his novels (and I refer readers to Anthony Low's essay in this volume for a discussion of the finer points of Powys's social detailing), he was clearly rejecting a social perspective as a valid fictional medium, at least for himself. Clearly, he sought wider purposes in his work.

Although various contributions to this volume characterize Powys in the roles of polyphonist, configurator, nomad, and phenomenologist, he has been commonly seen—and continues to be seen—as a quester, or at least as the chronicler of the quest. The assorted directions in which critics have seen that quest turning can be indicated by noting the titles of some of the Powys studies that have appeared in the last twenty years or so: *The Saturnian Quest* (G. Wilson Knight), *John Cowper Powys and the Magical Quest* (Morine Krissdottir), *John Cowper Powys in Search of a Landscape* (C. A. Coates). The titles are not redundant: to see Powys in this role is a useful strategy and one that a number of the essayists here adopt to good effect.

My own view is that Powys's novels—certainly the major ones—embody a quest that can justifiably be called religious. I do not, of course, claim that this is their sole or primary preoccupation, but I do suggest that to overlook the patterning of a search for religious significance, in all the varying shapes and dimensions in which this occurs in the Powys novel, would be a serious omission. "What was Religion?" he asks in *A Philosophy of Solitude* (1936). "It was a feeling of wonder, of awe, of fearful joy, of ecstatic and rapturous contemplation in the presence of the mystery behind what we call Nature" (166). To a large degree, Powys's novels may be said to embody this self-same process of "rapturous contemplation," and to the extent that we allow his definition they are confirmed as being religious novels. Certainly, they are concerned with what is "behind" Nature. (As to their power in this respect, George Steiner has written, "Powys is, with Milton and with Blake, one of the foremost imaginers and narrators of the transcendent, of the 'other,' in the language.") But in Powys, the religious impulse is oddly, if finely, honed: he is concerned with the religious instinct but not at all, except to reject them, with the established institutions of religion, which he prefers to call to task for their failure to answer something in us "that craves for the concrete, the tangible, the emphatically simple" (*A Philosophy of Solitude*). Thus his interest is always with the psychological roots of religious awareness, with religion in terms of its spontaneous, non-rational manifestations, rather than with theology or doctrine. "A rational faith," he argues in *The Religion of a Sceptic* (1925), "is a contradiction in terms. The essence of any faith is that it should be irrational. If it is *not* irrational it leaves a certain subterranean craving in us unsatisfied" (9).

An emphasis on the irrational certainly places Powys in the company of other twentieth-century writers, but among them especially we might name D. H. Lawrence, a writer for whom Powys declared a "terrific devotion and admiration" (*Letters to Louis Wilkinson*, 323). Like Powys, Lawrence speaks vigorously of the absolutism of rational thought, of the restorative powers of the passional experience, and of the dichotomy between our submerged, fundamental lives and our overt existences. Yet Lawrence and Powys pursue this conviction in widely differing ways: in Lawrence we witness the pursuit of a psychological integration that leads ultimately to not only a personal but a social vitalization; in Powys, who is undoubtedly the equal of Lawrence as a novelist of psychological insight, there is a more strongly stated assertion of a relationship between the individual and the cosmos, between man in the generic sense and the most elemental source of being. Moreover, the teleology of much of Powys's writing is that the act of advancing one's personality into nature is as much creative as spiritual. He argues that the extent to which man discovers and analyzes the universe around him defines also the extent to which he partakes in its creation. Powys's belief in man's creative power is characteristically advocated through positions that stress intuition and will, at the expense of those that require reason or knowledge. *A Glastonbury Romance* is his fullest fictive expression of this belief, but for a more succinct statement on the subject we can turn to *The Meaning of Culture* (1929) and the following magnificently affirmative passage.

> There is no man or woman in the world who does not experience vague feelings of mystical power, of Cosmic power, bringing him a strange sense of belonging, even in his most miserable objective weakness, to the company of the immortal gods. He does belong to them, he is of that company. Not the wretchedest man or woman but has a deep secretive mythology with which to wrestle his material world and to overcome it and pass beyond it. Not the wretchedest human being but has his share in the creative energy that builds the world. We are all creators. (189)

Powys's novels exist as imaginative efforts to reconcile this faith in individual creativity with the reality of human experience. From Wolf Solent with his "mythologizing," to Porius, with his "cavose-niargizing," he maintains a long line of characters bound up in a state of "deep contemplative tension," each calling upon the will's "unbounded power over secret and private reactions," and each in his own creative manner fulfilling the Powys credo, as expressed in *The Complex Vision* (1925), that the universe is "always capable of being further discovered and further created." It is this principle that provides us with the arduous psychic journey of *Wolf Solent*, with the open-minded antinomy of *A Glastonbury Romance*, with the sanguine force of *Weymouth Sands*, and with the mythopoeic genius of *Maiden Castle* and the Welsh romances.

It is in that self-same spirit of Powysian affirmation that these essays are presented.

In the Spirit
of Powys

John Cowper Powys and James Joyce

Charles Lock

Admirers of John Cowper Powys who are concerned with amending his reputation are faced with a choice of strategies: whether to put yet more emphasis on Powys's eccentricity, his apartness from contemporary cultural forms and concerns, the essential anachronism of his achievement—or whether to resist such comfortable assumptions, and the easy judgments implicit in them, and strive instead to unfold his centrality.

The dilemma arises from the facts of Powys's biography, the disjunction between what he wrote and where he wrote it: there is something eccentric, in both the normal and etymological senses, about a writer trying to make his career in the United States with novels that have not only English settings but an appearance of regionalism. Set in the context of British literature alone Powys is properly eccentric, for in the thirty years of his American residence and "regional novels" he had very little contact with literary figures in Britain. If, however, we acknowledge the American setting of Powys's life between 1905 and 1935, we might see his presence as central. As lecturer, essayist, and—simply—public figure, Powys was a respected and controversial presence in American life.

Powys never met Joyce, nor did Joyce ever visit America. The relationship among these three terms may appear less oblique when *Joyce* is taken metonymically for his works, and especially for *Ulysses*, symbol of the modern. This essay presents the evidence of Powys, in America, as an active and prominent champion of Joyce in lectures and critical writings and in a court appearance; the essay then proceeds to a comparison between Powys and Joyce in respect of their biographical circumstances and artistic intentions, and it concludes with the perceptions of Powys's novels by American reviewers in Joycean terms. When in 1929 Powys published his first major novel, *Wolf Solent*, the reviewers turned to *Ulysses* for an appropriate comparison, a proper yardstick.

In 1934 Powys returned to Britain, and his connections with American cultural life were quickly severed; until his death in 1963 Powys lived in North Wales, and it was assumed by the British literary establishment that he was no more marginal geographically than culturally. Reestablishing Powys in his American context may be of help to his readers today. To assume that Powys's novels might not be hopelessly dwarfed by *Ulysses* is a good beginning. Powys's first readers did not find his novels wanting by that measure, and nor, I think, need we.

They never met, and there is very little likelihood of Joyce's having read any of Powys's books. Joyce certainly knew of Powys, however, as one of the three witnesses for the defense at the "*Ulysses* trial" held in New York in February 1921.[1] The defendants, Margaret Anderson and Jane Heap, editors of the *Little Review*, were charged with publishing obscenity; in April 1918 they had begun to print *Ulysses* in installments, and during the next two years three issues of the monthly *Little Review* were confiscated. It was the appearance of section 13, "Nausicaa" (Gerty MacDowell), printed in the July-August 1920 issue, that prompted John Sumner, secretary of the New York Society for the Prevention of Vice, to initiate legal proceedings. The trial commenced on 14 February 1921, and the next day Powys described it in a letter:

> I had to go to Court—next to the "Tombs" prison—to witness on behalf of Joyce's *Ulysses* for that evil scavenger Sumner is prosecuting Margaret Anderson. I think she will be convicted. . . . The editor of the Dial [Scofield Thayer] who was there too heard Sumner say to a friend of his who asked who's that? "The English Degenerate, John Powys", but I suddenly became aware of real crafty legal blood in my veins; and I wished I could conduct her case in place of her lawyer who I greatly fear will mishandle it. I was, anyway, quite well pleased with the manner in which I kept my head.[2]

Powys's legal craft is revealed in the soundness of his predictions. The lawyer, John Quinn, was less than wholehearted in his defense, and the conviction—with a fine of fifty dollars for each editor—was probably his preferred outcome; his major concern was that *Ulysses* should not be banned as a book. Two of the witnesses chosen by Quinn were not impressively persuasive: Philip Moeller of the New York Theater Guild tried to justify Joyce in terms of Freud, while Thayer admitted that he would not have printed the "Nausicaa" section in his journal, *The Dial*. Powys, however, in Margaret Anderson's words, "declared that he considered it a beautiful piece of work in no way capable of corrupting the minds of young girls."

The trial received extensive coverage in the New York press, which

Joyce himself followed with interest—even detachment—for this was a trial in which Joyce was not personally implicated or at risk. For Powys that publicity made of his testimony much more than a good and honorable deed. As a public commitment—of the three witnesses Powys was much the most outspoken and unintimidated—it was a symbolic act that remained in the public memory and influenced the reception of Powys's novels.

During the years Powys made his base in New York, from 1910, an ideological and artistic struggle was being waged; after the First War lines were drawn with increasing definition, voices and forces were solicited, and impartiality was as unacceptable as opposition. The debate was focused on the role of art, the relative importance of its aesthetic and social functions, and the degree of compatibility between political radicalism and artistic experimentation. In Summer's epitome of Powys, "The English Degenerate," the criticism has a political intention and no reference to creative work; Powys was famous as a lecturer and as yet hardly known as a writer.

The world's Sumners, moralists and philistines, were not involved in the struggle within aesthetic ideologies, and their political force confuses the issues by condemning equally and without distinction Joyce and Dreiser, the aesthete and the socialist. It was with the latter camp—those who would exploit or betray their art for political ends—that Powys had been identified before 1922. In 1915 Powys had been the first person to praise in public Edgar Lee Masters's *Spoon River Anthology*, and in 1916 he wrote, lectured, and protested in support of Dreiser's *The Genius*.[3] In defending "Nausicaa," Powys was given no opportunity to discriminate between his concern for "thematic freedom" in Dreiser and his advocacy of formal experiment in Joyce. Indeed, Powys may not have made any such distinction, but as *Ulysses* became established as the great experimental novel so the association was inevitably made with Powys in those terms.

One could argue that for years before 1922 Powys had been on the side of the Modernist angels—art above politics, technique over content—through his close involvement with the *Little Review*, *The Dial*, and Maurice Browne's Little Theatre in Chicago.[4] It might be more precise to argue that Powys refused to recognize limits or divisions; that, presented with a choice, he took both—along with the responsibility of justifying both. After his public identification with the cause of *Ulysses*, Powys's closest friends among writers remained Dreiser and Masters. In the increasingly embattled world of American culture through the 1920s, Powys can be placed as a mediator and as a scapegoat.

Those familiar with Powys's writings and personality will not be surprised by such an encompassment of options, artistic and political, of Joyce and of Dreiser. The more interesting and perplexing matter is the relationship between Powys's critical opinions and his creative work. Had anything in *Wood and Stone* or *Rodmoor* presaged a sympathy with *Ulysses?* What is the explanation and significance of Powys following his defense of *Ulysses* in 1921—which exposed his reputation and jeopardized his own prospects of publication—with the publication of a novel as unexciting as *Ducdame* in 1925? What sort of refusal to choose is that?

In addressing these anomalies, we should give close attention to Powys's writings on Joyce. There are three substantial essays, on *Ulysses*, on *Finnegans Wake*, and a general survey, none of which Powys chose to collect in his volumes of literary essays. "James Joyce's Ulysses—an Appreciation" was first printed in 1923 in a journal of such limited and provincial circulation that one might say that it was "published" only in the Village Press (London) reprint of 1975. There is a long section on Joyce in the chapter "Modern Fiction" contributed by Powys to the symposium *Sex in the Arts* in 1932, and never reprinted, and a lengthy review of *Finnegans Wake*, published in *Modern Reading* in 1943 and collected in the gathering of Powys's miscellaneous essays, *Obstinate Cymric*, in 1947.

There is advantage in these essays being spread over twenty years, but limitation in the immediacy of their response: Powys is almost invariably at his critical best when writing on books of long acquaintance. Although he often displayed a fine sense of the particular value of the books of his contemporaries (as early as anyone he identified Proust and Joyce as the two greatest novelists of his generation), Powys seldom writes of new books with much persuasion. When one considers the sheer difficulty of Joyce, together with the responsibility of introducing *Ulysses* to a public that had severe problems of access quite apart from those of comprehension, Powys's achievement, sustained over twenty years, is remarkable and needs no extenuation.

That Powys had exceptionally easy access to *Ulysses* may have provided him with the encouragement, if not a sense of obligation, to write about it. In the month in which the *Little Review* proceeded with its serialization, April 1918, Powys, whose personal life was at that time in some confusion, accepted the hospitality of Paul Jordan Smith, then a lecturer in English Literature at the University of California in Los Angeles. In his *Autobiography,* Powys recalled "the extraordinary kindness I received from the Paul Jordan Smiths in California. I stayed a great deal under the hospitable roof of this learned young editor of the *Anatomy of Melancholy* and his magnanimous partner."[5] In return Powys attempted to share with Jordan Smith his enthusiasm for the new work now appearing in the *Little Review*. Powys was not merely a faithful reader of this journal whose role in the history of modern literature was crucial. According to an early editorial, in the issue of March 1915, Powys, "though quite unconscious of it, was one of the main inspirations behind . . . this magazine," and Margaret Anderson describes Powys as "the *Little Review's* godfather."

In 1927, Paul Jordan Smith became the author of one of the earliest books on Joyce, *A Key to the Ulysses of James Joyce,* in which he confesses that he first read Joyce without being persuaded of his worth:

> I read the early and fragmentary chapters that appeared in the pages of the courageous *Little Review*. It is a mistake to read any novel in serial form. . . .[6]

Between 1918 and 1922 Jordan Smith must have succumbed somewhat to Powys's arguments, for he purchased a copy of *Ulysses* shortly after its publication as a book, at some expense and with difficulty. The book was printed in Paris in the summer of 1922 and, despite the seizure and burning of four or five hundred copies by U.S. Customs, some copies were available in America by autumn.[7]

Powys had moved back to New York in the fall of 1918, but in September 1922 he shifted the base of his lecturing activities from New York to San Francisco. In late November 1922, Powys managed to borrow a copy of *Ulysses* and wrote to his brother Llewelyn, in New York, of his good fortune:

> I have been reading a lot of *Ulysses*. I had it for a couple of days and practically read through the whole damned thing, and I really am awfully impressed. I could write an 'article' on it now, I guess![8]

In December Powys was invited to a reading of the "Circe" episode at the home of Colonel C.E.S. Wood and his wife, the poet Sara Bard Field, in San Francisco, and on New Year's Day 1923, Powys managed to borrow a copy of *Ulysses* for the day only.[9] In response to John's letter of November expressing an intention to write on *Ulysses*, Llewelyn urged him to do so. In San Francisco the scarcity of copies was a serious obstacle, but in January Powys moved to Los Angeles, where he remained until the early summer.

From Los Angeles in February 1923 John excused himself to Llewelyn:

As to my writing on *Ulysses* I can't do it till I have the book while
I write, but Paul J. Smith has bought it and whenever I can go to
his house for a day or two I could write it there. It ought to be done.

And the letter continues:

Proust—who is dead you know—will also have to be written of carefully
by me some day, and come with *Ulysses* in a volume of new criticisms,
eh?[10]

That sense of duty, almost an obligation to write about Joyce and
Proust, shows how seriously Powys took himself as a champion of
modern literature, and also how seriously he was accustomed to
having his opinions received.

Powys was able to visit Paul Jordan Smith's house shortly after
his move to Los Angeles, and he alludes in his essay to the hindrance
in the writing of it:

There ought to be a cheap edition of the book. You can't enjoy a thing
like this as you steal hurried glances at it in some sumptuous library,
the owner all the while begging you to 'mind' the precious binding
and the hand-made paper! The thing's a classic. It ought to be handled
like a classic.[11]

Oddly, for all the difficulties of access to the text, essays on *Ulysses*
were flooding the market; at least, more people felt a need to add
their voices to the controversy than there were magazines interested
in promoting such debate. Paul Jordan Smith was himself writing
essays on *Ulysses* and having difficulty getting them published, and
Powys was perturbed to discover that by early March 1923, with
his own essay completed, "*The Dial* says it already has five articles
on Joyce to choose from!"[12]

In his essay, Powys reveals that he is motivated to write not only
in the critical defense of a great book but also in the financial interest
of its author. This was intermittently a period of great financial
difficulty, even poverty, for Powys, and his sensitivity to Joyce's
probable plight augments his sense of the human qualities of *Ulysses*.
Few critics have pointed out as forcefully as Powys the extremity
of the book's conclusion—not Molly's yes but Stephen's no:

One has to have followed the book pretty closely to get the full tragedy
of poor Stephen's refusal to 'stay the night' under his friend's roof.
    Where will Stephen go now?
    God knows!

What is happening now, *very now*, to James-Joyce-Stephen, as we, blundering literati, outrage and insult the terrible humanity of his terrific work?

. . . .

If it should turn out that Mr. Joyce has lacked the "wherewithal" necessary to satisfy his human needs, it will be a bitter commentary upon this generation. . . . (19)

The book's general availability is thus being advocated for the benefit of both the public and the author: luxury editions and collectors' items enrich all but their authors.

Powys begins his critical defense by dealing with the issues for which *Ulysses* was already notorious, obscenity and obscurity. Taking the phrase "agenbite of inwit" as the book's "clue-sentence," Powys on the one hand wants to show how everything in the book is born of pity and remorse, not of any kind of sensual indulgence; on the other hand, he is annoyed with Paul Jordan Smith for having told him that the phrase meant "remorse of conscience." For five long paragraphs, Powys tells us what he had imagined the phrase to mean before the expert put him right. While singling out "agenbite of inwit" as an example of good and justified obscurity—having "a vast aesthetic value by reason of its thrilling suggestiveness"—Powys acknowledges that *Ulysses* also contains examples of "obscurity that is just teasing, tiresome and annoying."

Like obscurity, obscenity is justified for Powys if it is put to the uses of the imagination: "*Ulysses* is wonderful, not because it is disgusting, but because so much of its disgustingness is imaginative." We should note that by saying "so much," Powys concedes that there is some remainder; he does not now need to be quite as defensive as he had been in the trial two years previously.

The few pieces of critical guidance that Powys could have found by February 1923 he tends to ignore or even mock. Of one already fixed assumption he remarks: "It is really absurd to compare James Joyce with Rabelais" (10). Rather, says Powys, Joyce belongs in a thoroughly English tradition, of Sterne, Fielding, Swift, Burton, Browne, Shakespeare, and Chaucer; *Ulysses* is thus "well-bottomed on the broad reassuring pastures of ancient English grossness" (6). As for another critical commonplace, the extent of Joyce's psychological understanding, "there are plenty of modern writers who can psychoanalyse quite as well, if not better. . . ." Powys then savages Arnold Bennett for his claim made in a review in *The Bookman*, August 1922, that "the Marion Bloom monologue at the end of the book reveals the ultimate essence of the psychological content

of the female mind. . . . It certainly may reveal the final essence
of what Bennett will ever discover in the female mind. . . . turn
the worthy matron over, north-north-east, and she will babble of
much less repulsive things!" (4). Joyce's psychology, Powys insists,
owes almost everything to the English comic and satirical tradition,
and very little to Freud and Adler.

As for received opinion about Joyce's relation to Homer, Powys
is almost equally scathing about an unnamed reviewer whom he
quotes:

> 'Joyce had been attracted by the Ulysses myth from his earliest childhood.'
> I daresay he had, good luck to him! So have we all. . . . the book. . . .
> had to be called *something*. . . . You might as well say that the essence
> of Tristram Shandy is in the story of Iseult. (5)

That "so have we all" is revealing: we may suspect, throughout
these comments, that Powys is implying a comparison between Joyce
and himself. He is very willing to praise Joyce, but he is equally
unwilling to concede Joyce's superiority in mythological or psychological matters—especially in understanding the mind of women. Those
who praise Joyce in superlative terms—that is, potentially at the
expense of Powys—are to be defied as strenuously as Joyce's detractors.

Further evidence suggestive of an implicit contest is found in
Powys's speculative picture of Joyce, based largely on intuitions derived from *Ulysses* (Powys had not yet read *A Portrait of the Artist
as a Young Man*):

> obviously a savage anger, a rending or tearing revolt, a poetic afflatus
> transformed into a sort of maniacal cosmophobia.
>   Like a wounded animal the author of *Ulysses* seems perpetually twisting
> round in the dust. . . . (7)

> What Joyce has done is to let his own wounded and lacerated imagination
> play freely, like a vivisected dog turning upon his torturers. . . . It is
> a world-maddened hoax of a deep imagination. . . . It is James Joyce
> himself dancing a furious malice-dance on the dinner-table of the Best
> People. . . . (16, 17)

This is so wide of the mark that we can be confident that Powys
had no knowledge of Joyce's personality: the tenor of his phrasing
suggests that Powys selected Swift as a plausible model. "Malice-
dance" is particularly interesting, because it is the very compound
used to describe that which terminates Wolf Solent's career as a
teacher in London and precipitates the events of Powys's novel.

Wolf Solent was not published until 1929: we can suppose either that an image of Joyce is present in Powys's depiction of Wolf Solent, or, more probably, we can see in Powys's image of Joyce a measure of self-projection, or even identification.

Powys's interest in the author leads him to attend more to Stephen than to Bloom, thus disappointing Joyce's hope that Bloom would hold the center of *Ulysses*. Joyce told Frank Budgen that "Stephen no longer interests me to the same extent,"[13] and he presumably counted on his readers to have satisfied their curiosity about Stephen in *A Portrait*. Powys's unbalanced view of *Ulysses*, then, is attributable mainly to his ignorance of the earlier work. Even this, however, can hardly explain Powys's extraordinary claim, defying all that readers know about Bloom, that the book "is entirely subjective. It reveals only one soul in the world, the soul of James Joyce" (11). And yet one can ask whether a reading of *A Portrait* would actually have enabled Powys to appreciate Joyce's attempt, in Bloom, to move beyond the limiting subjectivity of Stephen. In a later essay on Dickens, Powys makes a severe criticism of the characters of modern fiction; singling out the novels of Lawrence and Joyce, Powys asks whether they contain any individuals or any manifestation of "the mysterious uniqueness of all separate living persons." Proust alone is exempted from his general charge against the characters of modern fiction:

> They do not *stand out*, these dissected perambulatory pathoids. They puke and pine, they mime and mow at one another, they reveal to a wonder their "streams of consciousness"; but their loves and hates are like the loves and hates in fish-ponds and aquariums.[14]

In this 1938 essay, Powys explicitly mentions Bloom as part of the general malaise; in 1923, in giving Joyce his guarded support, he finds it more convenient to treat Bloom as a minor character. Powys is evidently guarding himself against competition, defending his own creative territory, and sustaining his life-illusion of uniqueness among his contemporaries.

On the side of generosity, what impresses one most in this essay is not so much Powys's perception or comprehension of the particular qualities of *Ulysses* as his absolute confidence that Joyce's book is a classic. This confidence is so absolute that there is hardly a hint of polemics or apologetics in Powys's tone. Whether the book is literature at all would seem to be a matter long settled in Powys's mind: he has contrived to take for granted the most controversial book of the era. This judgment is a singular tribute to Joyce, but in paying it Powys elevates himself above all those who find such things worth discussing. In that elevation there is only one writer to keep company with Powys, and that is Proust. Proust had died on 18 November 1922; in the months following, Powys refers to that death frequently, almost obsessively, as if it were of personal significance. With Proust's death, Joyce became Powys's only rival and peer. By 1923, at the age of fifty, Powys had written nothing of the first importance, but his self-confidence appears not to have been troubled by lack of evidence.

Unfortunately for Powys's reputation—although of no consequences for his self-esteem—"James Joyce's Ulysses—An Appreciation" was not published in any major journal. When it was at last printed in October 1923 in *Life and Letters*, the company broadsheet of Haldeman-Julius (the publisher for whom Phyllis Playter, Powys's companion, was working), it was consigned to fifty years of oblivion.

By 1932, the date of his essay on "Modern Fiction" in *Sex in the Arts*, Powys had been keeping abreast with *Work in Progress*, printed in *transition* and other periodicals from April 1927 onwards, and he had read *A Portrait of the Artist as a Young Man*. Powys had also, by this time, published *Wolf Solent* and *A Glastonbury Romance*. In "Modern Fiction," Powys discusses the treatment of sex in the novels of four contemporaries, Proust, Joyce, Dreiser and Lawrence, and he hints at regret that "it is Joyce and Lawrence, rather than Proust or Dreiser, who are the masters of our younger contemporaries."[15] In writing about Joyce, Powys combines the theme to be addressed, sex, with the attitude to and treatment of language. *A Portrait* "deals with the onanistic cerebralism of a passionate and learned youth. All is ingrown, all is introverted, all is charged with imaginative semen." Powys explains Joyce's concern with sex as "a reaction from Seminarist suppression," and argues that behind that concern, in all Joyce's books, "smokes that appalling Sermon upon Hell's torments." The sermon is juxtaposed by Powys with Joyce's rejection of English culture and his uneasiness with the English language. Powys quotes Stephen on the English dean and the "words" *"home, Christ, ale, master"*: "And just as the soul of the young Dedalus frets 'in the shadow' of our English tongue, so does the soul of James Joyce fret 'in the shadow' of our English gentility, *and especially of this gentility in relation to sex."*[16]

Powys links this insight derived from *A Portrait* to the "savage contempt" that he had found in *Ulysses*, and he suggests that the "Circe" episode is the expression of Joyce's contempt for both English gentility and the English language:

["Circe"] is one of the most powerful scenes in our English tongue—our tongue thus twisted to his own wild use by this man who hates it with such deadly hatred![17]

By taking so literally Stephen's detachment from the English language, Powys is able to draw a contrast between himself and Joyce: even in his most Celtic and Cymric moods, Powys has no quarrel with and no sense of alienation from the English language.

In seeing sex and language as equally problematic, in an obsessive relation in Joyce's work, Powys finds nothing entirely original or surprising in *Work in Progress:*

> in all these books there is the mingling of that almost ecstatic sense of word-play—word-implications, word-conjuring, word-coining, word-marrying, word-murdering, word-melting, word-apotheosizing, word-hypostatizing—which takes up the basic facts of sex and perpetually ravels them and unravels them, with passages of almost Shakespearean imagination. The mischief is that the obscurity—for the average person— of the *Work in Progress* retards and perplexes us in our approach to this amazing *tour de force* where a superhuman and inspired scholarship is so evidently at work, melting down the obdurate vertebrae of many languages in order to forge, like Hephaestus, inviting beds of love where the sons of the gods can embrace the daughters of man. . . .[18]

In Powys's writings and correspondence through the 1930s, there are many references to *Work in Progress*, all favorable, all asserting its superiority over *Ulysses*. His considered judgment is given in a five thousand word essay (not a review), commissioned by the English periodical *Modern Reading*, written in the fall of 1942 and published in 1943. This essay was then reprinted, with a couple of Welsh allusions added, in *Obstinate Cymric*, Powys's collection of essays on vaguely Welsh themes, published by the Druid Press of Carmarthen in 1947. The occasion of Powys's essay is less the publication of *Finnegans Wake*—4 May 1939—than the death of Joyce on 13 January 1941. So firmly associated was Joyce with Powys—in Powys's mind at least, and presumably in that of the editor of *Modern Reading*—that Powys finds himself obliged to begin with an extended disclaimer:

> I can claim no authority in the matter of *Finnegans Wake* save what naturally accrues to an industrious and fascinated, though often completely nonplussed reader.[19]

By 1942 there was a relative abundance of critical and biographical
material that Powys does not disdain to use or recommend. He
tells the reader of the particular value of Harry Levin's recently
published study and acknowledges much help from Frank Budgen's
essay on *Finnegans Wake*, "Joyce's Chapters of Going Forth by Day,"
published in the September 1941 issue of *Horizon* and now appended
to Budgen's classic *James Joyce and the Making of "Ulysses"*:

> Frank Budgen speaks with the weight of one who not only knew Joyce
> and had discussed the book with him, but who also knows Dublin.
> I never met Joyce, and have never been to Dublin. . . .[20]

However, in a manner reminiscent of his treatment of Bennett's
review of *Ulysses*, Powys's debt is no sooner acknowledged than
briskly qualified. Powys will not accept that *Finnegans Wake* is based
on a dream, in spite of Budgen, even in spite of what Joyce told
Budgen. For Powys, sleep and dreams are as important to *Finnegans
Wake* as Homer is to *Ulysses:*

> I still remain totally unconvinced that *Finnegans Wake* deals with anything
> else than that normal human life with which all great writers deal. I
> daresay he *meant* and *intended* to base it on dreams, but I am convinced
> that it ran away with him! And the same thing is true of the Homeric
> element in *Ulysses*. . . . He naturally talks a lot about these precious
> "patterns" to sympathetic and admiring friends. What the devil else should
> he talk about?[21]

Thus "Jack the Dream-Killer," as Powys sometimes signed his letters,
took on in *Finnegans Wake* his most formidable opponent.

Despite the usefulness of Budgen, Levin, and others, Powys is
quick to assure us that this "infatuated admirer and most methodical
reader of *Finnegans Wake*" can manage very well on his own:

> I am not going to pretend that my industrious and I daresay laughably
> serious study of *Finnegans Wake* doesn't give me that delicious sensation
> of difficulty overcome. . . . But conceit of this sort is, I am sure, one
> of the most harmless aspects of mental snobbishness. . . .[22]

Powys goes on to provide an account of the book that few readers
in 1943—and how many today?—would have felt confident to challenge. This tone of unusual self-satisfaction develops into a claim
of some affinity between Powys and the book:

I am, I confess, not a little proud—snobbishly? well, perhaps; but again, perhaps not—that the pluralistic Pantagruelian "mélange" of *Finnegans Wake* suits so well that equivocal element in my aboriginal make-up that is at once heathen and christian, atheistical and polytheistic.[23]

From an affinity with the book, Powys goes on to claim sympathy with its author. Predictably, in the light of his concern with Stephen rather than Bloom twenty years earlier, Powys pays great attention to Shem the Penman. Remembering the very phrase that he had applied to two people only, Joyce and Wolf Solent, respectively twenty and thirteen years earlier, Powys labels him "the malice-dancer Shem—who is the author himself."[24] In this description of Shem/Joyce, the mystery of the "malice-dance"—Powys's own strong sense of identification—is illuminated:

> the ferocious self-humiliations of Shem the Penman, with whose self-abasement I can identify myself with more lively intensity and more christian-malicious satisfaction than with any other self-abasement I have ever met in literature outside St. Paul and Dostoievsky.[25]

Powys suggests that he is *Finnegans Wake's* interpreter by right. It is his British readership's complete ignorance of Powys's honorable and exceptional record as a champion of Joyce that provokes the uncharacteristic vanity and self-regard of his tone. That right of intimacy and identification having been established, Powys delivers his verdict: *Finnegans Wake* is superior to *Ulysses* because it displays "a moral advance." The development that Powys sees between Joyce's two books could be an image of his own development as a novelist. *Ulysses,* we are asked to recognize, contains "a thousand ill-suppressed personal grudges, vicious self-pity and vindictive aesthetic vendettas": this is more properly a description of Powys's own *Rodmoor* or his *After My Fashion.* In contrast is the *Wake's* "large, ample, mellow, mischievous acceptance of all human obliquity," an assessment that likewise well fits the great novels of Powys's maturity.[26]

The importance of Proust's death to Powys has been mentioned; we have seen Powys's explicit identification with Joyce. In his last essay on his great contemporary, written with the entire shape of Joyce's career in view, Powys hints mythopoeically at some form of parallel development: as Joyce grows beyond *Ulysses,* beyond the comprehension of even sophisticated readers, so Powys—as reader—follows, superbly confident, to be neither outdone nor outrun.

More remarkable, in some respects, than what is said by Powys

about Joyce is what is not said. In setting up a comparison between
these two writers, certain obvious similarities and points of connection
offer themselves. Yet Powys makes no mention of their shared Celtic
background or shared condition of exile, and speaks only briefly
and with detachment of Joyce's use of myth and the relation of
myth to story.

Powys's failure to acknowledge the first of these, even in a book
entitled *Obstinate Cymric*, is curious. Each writer was conscious of
himself as an uprooted Celt and, presumably as a consequence, both
were intensely aware of racial qualities and differences. Powys's recurrent treatment of the Celtic-Roman-Saxon-Norman sequence of British history, and his own personal fantasies of Jewish and Negro
ancestry, are significantly matched by the play in *Ulysses* of Greek
and Jewish, Norse and Celtic polarities, and by the artist's chosen
name of Stephen Dedalus. As Glastonbury lies close to the Saxon-
Celtic border that divides Britain longitudinally and is a battleground
of Celtic, Danish, and Norman forces, so Dublin is a city founded
by Vikings and now inhabited by Celts and their Anglo-Saxon over-
lords. The tragedy that Powys stresses in Stephen's refusal to stay
the night is, symbolically, the failure of racial synthesis—of a Greek,
a Jew, and an Anglo-Saxon—and the end of Stephen's aspirations
to "Hellenise the island."

Neither Joyce nor Powys was committed to any sort of political,
cultural, or nationalistic Celticism; the racial concern of each had
an effect centrifugal and isolating rather than centripetal and gathering. Like Stephen, Joyce tried to "fly by those nets" of nationality,
language, and religion, and created a self-imposed and entirely voluntary exile, reinforced and jusified by a creatively healthy form of
paranoia. Powys's motivation, or excuse for exile, is harder to fathom.
Never, in print or in correspondence, does Powys discuss a reason
for spending thirty years outside Britain. Local factors, financial
and marital, can explain his initial move to America in 1905, and
arbitrary circumstance can explain much of his exile's continuance.
What is not explained is Powys's complete refusal to offer any explanation or justification of his exile. Although he has his versions of
contrived exclusions, more willed than suffered, Powys never suggests
that Britain had rejected him or that British life was intolerable.
Powys's neglect of this circumstance that likens him to Joyce may
be part of his general silence on the topic of exile.

In one vital respect their exiles differed: Powys was in an English-
speaking country while Joyce was always surrounded by speakers
of foreign tongues. For Joyce, English was increasingly the language
of his writing only; Powys's style, however, with its exclamations,

clichés, and oratorical periods, seldom lets the reader forget that English is the language of Powys's speech, whether lecturing or buying a ticket for the peepshow. It is not necessarily a paradox that Joyce's linguistic exile enabled him to treat all language as fit for literature, not to distinguish between the formal and the slang. Powys appreciated that Joyce

> is one of our leaders in the modern attempt to scoop up into art all the slang, all the steam-shovels, all the advertisement signs, all the vulgar catch-words. . . . But the modern machine-made slang, so hard-boiled and so cynical, in which Joyce makes his god of Love utter vulgar cock-crows, blends and fuses, in this amazing Panurge of Philology, with a lilting and rhythmical humour which is almost Falstaffian.[27]

"One of our leaders," writes Powys, thus including himself in that endeavour. And seen in the light of Joyce, Powys's style assumes a new complexion: what John Bayley has called "Powys's curiously resonant use of cliché"[28] may be the very ground of his stylistic virtue.

A second aspect of exile worthy of attention and comparative study is its creative use. Here we touch on the provisioning of the imagination, a matter of such magnitude and fragility that even the most self-conscious artist is wary of reflection. Let us assume— without documentary evidence and without hope of finding any—that Powys chose to perpetuate his exile because it was good for his imagination. It is probable that Joyce had a similar motive: what else but an intimation of the sacred untouchability of the subject of all his art kept Joyce out of Ireland from 1912 until his death? Powys's novels, although set in England, were written in America, with only two exceptions; when he returned to Britain in 1934, he turned to historical settings, thus replacing the spatial distance by the temporal. The two exceptions, *Maiden Castle* (written in Dorchester) and *After My Fashion* (written in Sussex), are telling.

To both Joyce and Powys, exile certainly gave one common gift, a passion for accuracy that not only made of memory a dedicated discipline but insisted that memory be restrained by fact. The directories, maps, guidebooks, and newspapers that Joyce drew on for his re-creation of 16 June 1904 are famous; they represent an unprecedentedly strong-willed and thorough submission of memory and imagination to fact in a terminal, ironic contortion of Zolaesque naturalism. Powys's ambition for accuracy is evident in a series of letters sent to Littleton, his brother closest to the spot, during the writing of *A Glastonbury Romance* from 1930 to 1932:

any pamphlets you may pick up about Glastonbury or Wells or those parts do 'ee let me have them! I have two Ordnance Maps of Somerset. I hope there won't be any mistakes! What I find difficult as I talk of twilights so often is to remember *when* twilight *begins* in March—in April—in May etc etc etc. I am worst at that than even at the order of plants which is also a somewhat weak point!
O I want 'ee to read it so carefully & meticulously with all your wits clear and take note of mistakes. . . . Would for instance anyone see a Clifton Blue at Glastonbury on June 25 . . . ?[29]

With this we can compare Budgen's account of Joyce writing the "Wandering Rocks" episode:

Joyce wrote the *Wandering Rocks* with a map of Dublin before him on which were traced in red ink the paths of the Earl of Dudley and Father Conmee. He calculated to a minute the time necessary for his characters to cover a given distance of the city. . . .[30]

At a slightly lower level of dedication or obsession, and closer to Powys's practice, we find Joyce, when working on *A Portrait*, writing to his father for confirmation that the trees at Clongowes were beeches.[31]

This need for accuracy and fear of mistakes is peculiar in imaginative writers. Hardy, usually mistaken for an expert, is often inaccurate in his descriptions of nature, and his agricultural "facts" are sometimes quite wrong; Dickens did not feel obliged to check his invention of London against a map. No reader of Joyce is ever going to test the timing of the "Wandering Rocks," except out of pedantry or idolatry; given our oblivion or tolerance of errors in Hardy, no reader of Powys will be intolerant even if he does spot a late tulip or a rathe primrose. Is such accuracy merely the private obsession of an exile, compelled to create a replica in every detail of that which has been lost or willingly forsaken? Then one must question whether anything has been added to the text, or whether the author's scrupulous labors have been entirely wasted on the reader. There may be some answer to these problems, and indeed a clue to Powys's affinity to Joyce, in the latter's words: "You have to be an exile to understand me."[32]

In turning from shared elements of biography to a comparison of the writings of Powys and Joyce, this essay must be selective and brief. We have already seen Powys disparaging the importance of Homer for *Ulysses* and dreams for *Finnegans Wake;* his irritation with "precious 'patterns'" is matched by Joyce's even-handed fascination with both myth *and* coincidence. To Padraic Colum, Joyce said "Of course . . . I don't take Vico's speculations literally; I use his cycles as a trellis."[33] And as a trellis can be dismantled once a structure stands freely, so the Homeric episode titles used in the *Litle Review's* serialization of *Ulysses* were dropped for its publication as a book. By taking a Greek myth, Joyce was of course collaborating with Stephen in "Hellenising the island," and Stephen's retreat—the failure of his endeavor—is matched by the deliberate incongruity between the Greek myth and the Irish story. Similarly, *A Glastonbury Romance* invites mythological parallels, challenging the reader to translate its characters into those of Celtic or Arthurian myth. In *Glastonbury* Powys establishes a congruity between myth and setting, but by leaving his myth unspecified he achieves instability and a witty, ironic freedom.[34] Insofar as neither Joyce nor Powys were cultural partisans, each had a freedom in his treatment of myth quite alien to the servile devotion of the writers of, for example, the Celtic Twilight. One could point here to the contrast between the latter group's concern with the accuracy and authenticity of myth and their contempt for hard facts, and Joyce and Powys's obsession with factual accuracy and freedom with myths. For these two, myth is vital enough to be used but not too sacred to be manipulated, or abused.

Modernist bells are ringing, summoning us back to *The Dial*. That journal had rejected Powys's essay on *Ulysses* as it had five already from which to choose. In the November 1923 issue, *The Dial* chose to publish T. S. Eliot's "Ulysses, Order and Myth":

> [Joyce's use of myth] is simply a way of controlling, of ordering, of giving a shape and a significance to the immense panorama of futility and anarchy which is contemporary history. . . . Instead of narrative method we may now use the mythical method. It is, I seriously believe, a step toward making the modern world possible for art. (483)

Given the association of Powys with Joyce in the mind of the American literary public, and given the nature of Powys's novels, it is no wonder that reviewers turned to Joyce when faced with *Wolf Solent*. The *New York Times Review of Books* of 19 May 1929 accorded its front-page review to *Wolf Solent*. Percy Hutchinson doubted "whether Powys would have written 'Wolf Solent' if Joyce had not written 'Ulysses'," and he concluded, somewhat elliptically: "John Cowper Powys is a step, an enormous step, beyond James Joyce, but he falls short of the goal." Hutchinson gives few clues as to the nature of that goal, set so meanly after such lavish praise. If *Wolf Solent* falls short, *A Glastonbury Romance* might make a nearer approach. It is certainly an ambitious extension of that "mythical method," already used in *Wolf Solent*, that originated in *Ulysses*.

Before concluding, a bibliographical detail. The dedication page of Paul Jordan Smith's *A Key to the Ulysses of James Joyce* reads:

To
John Cowper Powys
whose sly machiavellian taunts set me
about the making of this book

That this was one of the very first books ever written on Joyce, and that it was the first book ever to be dedicated to Powys, should not be dismissed as a coincidence.

The earliest, simplest, and most brazen comparison of Powys and Joyce will serve not as a conclusion but as a provocation. In 1923, at the time of writing his appreciation of *Ulysses*, Powys had published just two novels, *Wood and Stone* and *Rodmoor* (both of them unsuccessful then and neglected since), and a handful of shorter works. At the same date, Joyce had published three of his four major books. After reading the manuscript of the essay on *Ulysses*, Llewelyn wrote to his brother:

I regard it as a worthy tribute from one great and abused man of genuis to another.[35]

Those terms of reference and equation are not intended to be the contentious claim of a slack conclusion. Instead, together with the evidence presented in this essay, they point to the basic premises from which serious criticism of John Cowper Powys may, at last, proceed.

Notes

1. On the trial, see Richard Ellmann, *James Joyce* (New York: Oxford University Press, 1959), pp. 517-19; Margaret Anderson, *My Thirty Years' War* (London: Alfred A. Knopf, 1930; reprint ed., New York: Horizon Press, 1969), pp. 219-22; John Cowper Powys, *Letters to Henry Miller* (London: Village Press, 1975), p. 36; and unpublished letter from John Cowper Powys to Frances Gregg, 15 February 1921 (typescript in possession of Oliver M. Wilkinson).

2. Unpublished letter from John Cowper Powys to Frances Gregg, 15 February 1921 (typescript in possession of Oliver M. Wilkinson); see also John Cowper Powys, *Autobiography* (London: Macdonald, 1967), p. 404.

3. Powys contributed to the pamphlet *Theodore Dreiser: America's Foremost Novelist* (New York: John Lane, n.d. [1917?]); for Powys's support of the *Spoon River Anthology*, see Edgar Lee Masters, *Across Spoon River: an Autobiography* (New York: Farrar and Rinehart, 1936), p. 367.

4. See Charles Lock, "Maurice Browne and the Chicago Little Theatre," *Modern Drama* 31, no. 1 (March 1988): 106-16. For a general survey of the period, see Richard Chase, "The Fate of the Avant-Garde," in *The Idea of the Modern in Literature and the Arts*, ed. Irving Howe (New York: Horizon Press, 1967).

5. Powys, *Autobiography*, p. 543.

6. Paul Jordan Smith, *A Key to the Ulysses of James Joyce* (Chicago: Pascal Covici, 1927), p. 59.

7. Ellmann, *James Joyce*, p. 521.

8. John Cowper Powys, *Letters to His Brother Llewelyn*, 2 vols. (London: Village Press, 1975), 1:310 (incorrectly dated December 1922 for late November 1922).

9. Ibid., 1:306-07, 312.

10. Ibid., 1:329-30; Powys wrote on Proust briefly in the *North American Review*, March 1924, and at length in *The Enjoyment of Literature* (New York: Simon and Schuster, 1938).

11. John Cowper Powys, *James Joyce's Ulysses—An Appreciation* (London: Village Press, 1975), 5-6. Subsequent page refrences to this reprint edition appear parenthetically in the text.

12. Powys, *Letters to Llewelyn*, 1:331.

13. Frank Budgen, *James Joyce and the Making of 'Ulysses'* (London: Oxford University Press, 1972), p. 107.

14. Powys, *The Enjoyment of Literature*, pp. 336-37.

15. J. F. McDermott and K. B. Taft, eds. *Sex in the Arts—A Symposium* (New York and London: Harper, 1932), p. 36.

16. Ibid., pp. 45-46.

17. Ibid., p. 47.

18. Ibid., pp. 49-50.

19. John Cowper Powys, *Obstinate Cymric* (Carmarthen: The Druid Press, 1947), p. 19. The common misspelling of Joyce's title (*Finnegan's Wake*), probably perpetrated by the publisher, has been corrected throughout.

20. Ibid., p. 20.

21. Ibid., p. 35.

22. Ibid., p. 26.

23. Ibid., p. 20.

24. Ibid., p. 23.

25. Ibid., p. 32.

26. Ibid., p. 21.

27. *Sex in the Arts*, p. 51.

28. John Bayley, "Life in the Head," *New York Review of Books*, 28 March 1985, p. 27.

29. Belinda Humfrey, ed. *Essays on John Cowper Powys* (Cardiff: University of Wales Press, 1972), pp. 325, 326, 328, 331.

30. Budgen, *Making of 'Ulysses'*, pp. 124-25.

31. Ellmann, *James Joyce*, p. 283.

32. Ibid., p. 706.

33. Mary Colum and Padraic Colum, *Our Friend James Joyce* (New York: Doubleday, 1958), p. 82.

34. See Charles Lock, "Polyphonic Powys: Dostoevsky, Bakhtin, and *A Glastonbury Romance*," *University of Toronto Quarterly* 55, no. 3 (Spring 1986): pp. 261-81.

35. Louis Wilkinson, ed., *The Letters of Llewelyn Powys* (London: John Lane, The Bodley Head, 1943), p. 97 (incorrectly dated 20 March 1924 for 20 March 1923).

Meditative Thoughts on *Wolf Solent* as Ineffable History

Patrick Samway, S.J.

> The spiritual creations of the past, art and history, no longer belong to the self-evident domain of the present but rather are objects relinquished to research, data from which a past allows itself to be represented.
>
> —Hans-Georg Gadamer, *Truth and Method*

> A human story, to bear any resemblance to the truth, must advance and retreat erratically, must flicker and flutter here and there must debouch at a thousand tangents.
>
> —John Cowper Powys, *Autobiography*

History by its very nature is ineffable for the simple reason that synchronic events and relationships in their totality can never be re-trieved, re-produced, and re-presented in the all-too-fleeting present. This does not mean, however, that insights into the past and analyses of past events, even though fragmentary, incomplete, and elusive, cannot be achieved. The past is a construct (of evidence, sources, hypotheses, hearsay, letters, documents, fiction, poetry, books, works of art, and the like) that is always in imaginative suspension, because a prime factor of even considering the past-as-past is that its interpretation must continually be open to change, should new sources be discovered or new evidence emerge. As *historia*, history deals with story, and if a historian is going to understand the dynamics of past events and the personalities involved, whether conceived on a narrow or wide scale, he must re-experience the situations and imaginative axes upon which the story rotated. If a historian remained only with verifiable evidence and did not deal with the underlying imaginative forces, he would take the systole and diastole out of the lived past, because often what is vital, palpable, and essential remains unseen by the human eye; without a good grasp of guiding principles and informing powers, history would lack the ability to speak across generations to a common humanity.

From one perspective, John Cowper Powys's *Wolf Solent* pays over-

whelming tribute to the ineffability of history; while writing the
"History of Dorset," which turns out ironically to be a compilation
of insignificant scandals of the region, never detailed nor fully explained, nor even read for that matter, Wolf Solent learns the authentic, living, undocumented story of his own family, the secret affairs
of his mother and father, and the impact that these affairs have
had on the local community.[1] In writing the somewhat bizarre history
commissioned by Squire John Urquhart, Wolf gradually acquires,
often through a haphazard series both of situational arabesques and
direct questioning, a far deeper awareness of the familial and communal dimensions of his own life history, which, were it to be written
down and become part of the documented history he is engaged
in throughout most of the novel, would never rise above the level
of parody as the "History of Dorset" clearly shows. It is precisely
on this level of parody that there seems to be an overtly apologetic
significance to *Wolf Solent:* history, even when revealed in an absorbing novel, lacks the necessary dynamism to exist on its own and
can remain only a hollow shell. The *para ōidē* of historical, especially
Greek, narration normally receives its brilliance, not in isolation,
but only, Powys seems to be saying, when harmonized with the
ode, although in *Wolf Solent* one may even question whether Powys
goes this far.

In this novel, Powys deals imaginatively with the relationship of
history and the novel and has provided the reader with an expansive,
exuberant, barely restrained exemplum in the form of a novel that
seeks its resolution in stripping away all excesses and accepting a
situation that deals precisely with what is the controlling source of
tension in the novel (and the documented history within the novel):
real or suspected infidelity in marriage and the decision to seek happiness in spite of the circumstances. From such a perspective, Powys
invites the reader to meditate on the strengths and weaknesses of
both historical writing and the novel. To a large extent, *Wolf Solent*
is a trap for meditation and raises some theoretical questions concerning both genres.

Granted that some novelists sketch out a plot in writing a novel
and then proceed to flesh it out, others go through a period of
preparation by putting themselves in an environment whereby they
can both allow some unspecified, inner voice to speak to them and
also allow themselves the time and space to listen. Some write one
draft with few revisions; others feel the need to hone and shape
the words and phrases repeatedly to orchestrate the plot, dialogue,
character development, and imagery and give them their proper struc-

ture. One method is not necessarily superior to another, because a value judgment can be made only after the process has ceased, and in the long run both processes can produce quite extraordinary results. In his fiction, Powys implies that a novelist deals with images and situations that are possible, based on our common awareness of what is probable; like a chess player, he places his characters in certain initial situations and then maneuvers them using logic, foresight, and other highly developed skills. For example, Wolf welcomes his mother back to King's Barton and helps her get settled, although her presence is potentially very unsettling for him, especially as he has difficulty locating lodging for her. To his credit, Wolf does not try to restrain his mother, but allows her the freedom to create what is for her a satisfactory social environment. She is the one who leads Wolf, Gerda, and Jason to see Redfern's grave (365 ff.) and finds herself at the center of the tension in the lives of both Gerda and Wolf. During the novel, Wolf learns that his mother treated his father abominably (593) and that Lord Carfax had become involved at one point with his mother. In spite of this, Mrs. Solent flourishes, largely because of Wolf's cleverly sympathetic manner in dealing with her—a trait that reveals that he can cope with many variables at the same time. In reflecting on his relationship with Gerda and Christie and the countryside before him, Wolf intuitively does so in terms of chess: "It was a queer dalliance of the mind that he indulged in just then; for he felt that this airy wraith, that was Christie Malakite, was in some way the child of that mystical plain down there, that 'chessboard of King Arthur'; whereas the girl at his feet was in league with whatever more remote and more heathen powers had dominated this embattled hill. King Arthur's strangely involved personality, with the great Merlin at his side, was associated with both" (314). For Powys, Dorsetshire has been and continues to be a chessboard on which the games of the past have never stopped being played.

In chess, the pieces move back and forth on the field of action, and their number and type are limited and well-defined, each piece having a specific pattern of motion, both offensive and defensive, as well as blocking motions; as a result, chess manuals often read like psychology books. There are myriad movements possible in chess, many of which cannot be predicted in advance precisely because such moves are determined by the equally calculated moves of one's opponents. Chess is a game of strategy where the precise nature of the game is known, but the specific moves of any particular player cannot be determined with accuracy; in fact, the game can often take an unexpected turn at any point should the players wind up in positions not foreseen by either side. In addition, the element of chance can dramatically alter the fate of the players.

The game of chess is helpful for an understanding of what transpires within *Wolf Solent*, but only to a certain degree. What is missing in a chess game are the words that create the illusion of genuine people in conflict with themselves and one another. Chess is a nonspeaking game. A chess board has 64 squares and 32 pieces; real situations in life are infinitely more complex and often demand more forms of interaction than are possible in chess. Although in both chess and in novels the number of protagonists is limited, no novel begins with opposing, absolutely equal forces, aligned in exactly the same pattern, with figures conceived by a medieval mind. Nor do we expect the chess pieces to have moments of epiphanies, nor to grow emotionally and intellectually. Chess pieces are unthinking instruments in the hands of the players; once removed from the board, they are held in abeyance until the game is over and a new game can begin. Unlike chess, the minor characters in a novel, such as Lord Carfax in *Wolf Solent*, a cousin of Wolf's mother, can become major and vice versa, revealing the level of the unexpected that takes place in life.

The historian, like Wolf himself, on the other hand, engaged in the task of writing history has to go through an exercise of the imagination—call it the historical imagination—that centers not so much on listening to inner voices or in thinking in ways that would be appreciated by a chess player, but of seeing what happened in the past. A historian's mode of discovery—in-vention—is analagous to someone engaged in piecing together a puzzle or reading an unknown or lost script; he presumes there are pieces that will fall into place and achieve an accurate picture if he is patient enough. His finished product, the essay or book, describes the methods he used in obtaining the pieces and shows the chronological steps taken to solve this particular puzzle, one related *pari passu* to an infinite series of other puzzles. Each puzzle points to a *terminus ad quem* (the overall pattern) but does not necessarily account for the complete *terminus a quo*. Every historical puzzle is a palimpsest revealing hidden texts and emendations; one must rely on an interlocking network of internal and external pieces of evidence to begin decipherment. In *Wolf Solent*, Squire Urquhart calls attention to such historical methodology when he says that in composing the "History of Dorset," he and Wolf will isolate a particular part of Great Britain as "if it were possible to decipher there a palimpsest of successive strata, one inscribed below another, of human impression. Such impressions are for ever being made and for ever being obliterated in the ebb and flow of events; and the chronicle of them should be continuous, not episodic" (33). Like François Champollion, Wolf admits that he has to go through such a process of discovery: "'I've got a sort of underlife,' he thought, 'full of morbid hieroglyphics. Something must have died down there, and the blowflies are laying their eggs in it'" (426). Yet at times, the process of reading correctly and discovering what has transpired challenges the historian in ways he had not imagined initially; even when images and words gradually become relatively clear, as in the case of Rosetta Stone, the historian is still left with overwhelming questions that can only be answered when he rises above his particular discipline and relates what he has discovered to other areas of life and investigation.

Yet however helpful the analogies of puzzles or hieroglyphics might be, they are faulty, as is the chess analogy for an understanding of the novel, because the flux of the past can only be suggested in a puzzle or hieroglyph, never captured integrally. What was once active, interrelated, and fleshly is reduced to a few flat pieces of cardboard or symbols on stone that can be analyzed using patience and proper training. What is missing most of all in puzzles and hieroglyphs is the living voice reacting to other living voices to create words and ideas that have motivated people in the past. Although the historian, like the scientist and detective, searches for clues, he must do more: he must enter the scene he is creating and see the relationships that contain many more facets than any pre-shaped pieces of a puzzle or predetermined pictographs; he must use his own wisdom, the culmination of his reading, investigations, and experiences of all sorts; he must energize his sources with a personal depth to explain as fully as possible that which was there. In addition, a historian writes history for a reading public who are not indifferent to the wisdom of the author and who demand not just the verifiable data he has assembled and organized; they want to appreciate the import of what he has done in a way that touches the core of their humanity. At this level a historian's work, and also that of the novelist will be finally tested.

In works of history and in novels, the writer manipulates his protagonists so that they can stay within the bounds of their personalities; in the first instance, he finds them in recorded documents, works of art, film, etc.; in the second, he creates them, although in both cases the protagonists are bound by what the mind perceives as possible human action, reaction, and interaction. Above all, both the historian and the novelist structure words to evoke the images and situations they wish to convey; it is in the configurations of these words, images, and situations that both the historian and the novelist share dramatic kinship. Historians, moreover, who deal with a specific time period or epoch often incorporate into their writing analyses of how the creative imagination has constructed works of art and literature, so essential for a grasp of that epoch; they do this to show not only what has been thought, but how it has been thought out.

In reviewing the Harper Colophon reprint of *Wolf Solent*, John Bayley failed to capture the fullness of the experiences that Wolf goes through as he writes the "History of Dorset" and discovers its significance to his own life:

> Although *Wolf Solent* has the form of a *Bildungsroman*, its hero learns nothing and is not subject to that stock fictive evolution common to both Lawrence's Paul Morel and Joyce's Stephen Dedalus, as well, incidentally, as to the heroines of Jane Austen. In their urban or rural setting Powys's lovers are as timeless in their erotic fixations as Queen Phaedra or Helen of Troy. And his narrative proffers all sorts of metaphysical suggestions only to circumvent them, as trees and plants grow around artificial obstructions; sudden vital 'discoveries,' often emphasized by italics, are soon absorbed back into the leisurely ganglion. Even as it absorbs and compels us the novel seems to be inviting us not to take it seriously.[2]

The novel rests mostly on a dualistic view of the world, as Bayley infers, and is highly intramental, although balanced throughout by an unreserved attachment to Nature, which, when subjected to the magnetic forces operative in life, achieves a calm and acceptance of what is.

Wolf deals adequately with the burden of the past so that problems of the present can be addressed properly and seriously. What Bayley failed to perceive is that Wolf undergoes a titanic struggle of the spirit; he lives in the "symbols of his mental life" and

> the two things which . . . threatened this ecstasy—Urquhart's book and a sly, slender Christie, stripped of her clothes—transformed themselves into the wet uneven bark of this trunk against which he now pressed his hand. . . . With a desperate strain of all the energy of his spirit, he struggled to merge his identity in that subaqueous landscape. . . . For, as he strained his spirit to the uttermost, the landscape before him ceased to be a mere assemblage of contours and colours. It became one enormous water-plant, of vast, cool, curving, wet-rooted *leaves*— *leaves* that unfolded themselves, *leaves* that finally responded and yielded to the outflung intensity of his *magnetic* gesture! "Not dead yet!" he

muttered aloud, as, with an exhausted sigh, he turned to retrace his steps. "Not dead yet!" (414, emphasis mine)

This section contains in microcosm key elements of the novel: the struggle between Wolf's interior and exterior worlds, his solipsistic moments of ecstasy, the tension between the task of writing the history book or being with Christie (thus implying the unspoken relationship to Gerda), the ever-changing landscape finally transforming itself and coalescing into leaves, his "magnetic" gesture, and the awareness that he is not dead yet, but has the capability of dealing with the pang and tether of particular situations. This summary distillation of the novel can be found in other passages, thus reinforcing the centrality of these concepts, as for example in the following:

It was as if he [Wolf] had been some changeling from a different planet, a planet where the issues of life—the great *dualistic struggles* between life and death—never emerged from the charmed circle of the individual's *private consciousness*. Wolf himself, if pressed to describe it, would have used some simple earthly metaphor. He would have said that his *magnetic* impulses resembled the expanding of great vegetable *leaves* over a still pool—*leaves* nourished by hushed noons, by liquid, transparent nights, by all the movements of the elements—but making some inexplicable difference, merely by their *spontaneous expansion,* to the great hidden struggle always going on in Nature between *the good and the evil forces.* (8, emphasis mine)

In this novel, as these passages indicate, Wolf senses within himself the twin powers of association and transformation as he deals with the mystical powers within his soul that reach out and touch the outermost regions of the cosmos. Wolf's mindscape seeks a harmony with the landscape around him; were he to remain entirely attached to his own psychic powers and not blend and change his own personal environment, then what he has discovered about himself, his family, and the people of Dorsetshire would be in vain and useless. "He imagined all these things so intensely, one by one, that he began to feel that he shared those nocturnal movements—that he was no stranger among them, but himself a furtive, lonely earth-life among other earth-lives, drawing as they did, some curative *magnetism* from the dark greenish-black hide of the great planetary body" (426, emphasis mine). Throughout the novel, Wolf goes through a dramatic process of discovery, of piecing information together, of aligning himself with the forces around him with the magnetism of his personality, and finally denying himself the luxury of living with a strictly private mythology, so that the people (especially Gerda, Christie, his mother, Selena Gault, James Redfern, Lord Carfax, Jason Otter, and Squire Urquhart) and the situations (especially the "History of Dorset," his father's ghostly presence, the revelation that he has a half-sister, the attraction of suicide, the image of the figure at Waterloo, his marriage to Gerda, and his love for Christie) are so tempered in his mind that through a gradual process of leveling, he is able to gain control of his life and not be overwhelmed either by any single part of it or even all of it. As in chess, he is able to maneuver himself around situations that might obstruct him or remove opposing pieces that thwart him, and thus make progress in living out his life.

In narrowing down the number of possible situations to deal with, Wolf tries to shed excesses, whether they be of his desire to love two women simultaneously or to lose himself in the sprawling countryside around him. The conclusion of the novel reveals that Wolf is about to make a decisive step, one that had almost check-mated both his parents and that deals with his spouse and their own marital bond. He has reached a moment of decision, a time for honesty when he can bring to bear both the knowledge of his historical research (the intrigues of the Abbotsbury and Evershot families), and the folly that that implies, as well as knowledge of his parents' failings; it is precisely at this point that the historical dimensions of the novel are most called into play. It is also here that Powys does not reveal the future direction of Wolf's life; like the past, the future is also ineffable.

The most dramatic form that this leveling process takes is when Wolf abandons his private mythology. The nature of this mythology is never made explicit, although it seems to have been extremely visceral and unfocused. "In fact, the thrill of malicious exultation that passed through his nerve ends as he thought of these things had a curious resemblance to the strange ecstasy he used to derive from certain godlike mythological legends. He would never have confessed to any living person the intoxicating enlargement of personality that used to come to him from imagining himself a sort of demiurgic force, drawing its power from the heart of Nature herself" (4). He acknowledges from the beginning of the novel, "My 'mythology' has been my real life'" (9). His fear that a "new reality" will smash his "whole secret life" (9) is ironically signalled in the epitaph on his father's tomb: *"Mors est mihi vita"* (17). In his mind, this mythology is linked with the freedom he felt being away initially from his mother and also intrigued by the skeleton of his father in the cemetery; he reverses these feelings at the end of the novel when he is pleased to see his mother take up a new career and says "Good-bye father" (598).

Wolf's arrival in Dorsetshire released initially a new energy, arising from watery depths, one that seemed to counteract his private mythology: "Whatever this mysterious emotion was, it leaped forward now towards the new element as if conscious that it carried with it a power as formidable, as incalculable, as anything that it could encounter there" (27). His secret spiritual vice is, in fact, a *"fetish-worship"* that resides in the souls of all forms of life, in planetary bodies, in inanimate things, and in "strange, chemical groupings" (42), and also is embodied in Jason Otter's Mukalog, the god of rain, and in the "Governing Power of the Universe" (74). The opposite of this object of worship is love, which Wolf saw as being possessive, feverish, exacting, and demanding a response (43). His inability to control the welter of feelings and chaotic emotions is summarized in his views toward his mother: "He kept visualizing the mud-scented darkness in which he seemed to be floating as a vast banked-up aqueduct composed of granite slabs covered with slippery black moss. Out of the spiritual tide that carried him along, there whirled up, in spurts of phosphorescent illumination, various distorted physical aspects of the people he had met these last few days. But these aspects were all ill-assorted, incongruous, maladjusted. . . . All these morbid evocations culminated finally in the thought of his mother . . ." (123). Wolf's affair with Gerda initially begins his transformation—of liberation, of motion towards love: "He looked closely at the manner in which the alder-root dipped so adroitly yet so naturally into the river. Yes! It was a kind of ecstasy he aimed at; the kind that loses itself, that merges itself; the kind that demands nothing in return" (140). This alder-root, sinisterly depicted too as a "smooth phallic serpent" (140), represents the immersion into the Female that he is beginning to experience; through his marriage to Gerda, Wolf will "bring that secret 'mythology' of his into relation with the whole world" (157).

Gradually, Wolf discovers that he can bypass the obstacles that the past and present place in front of him; this gives him the flexibility he needs as he moves in various directions. For example, in beginning to consider Mattie Smith as his "sister" (168) and accepting all that that implies, he widens his horizons and accepts what he cannot alter: "He continued vaguely to *puzzle* himself, as they lurched forward in the darkness, as to what it was in his nature that made his seduction of Gerda, his *encounter* with Jason, his *discovery* of Mattie, thus fall away from his consciousness in comparison with

that feather and that candle; and he came finally to the conclusion
before they reached King's Barton, that there must be something
queer and inhuman in him. 'But there it is,' he finally concluded.
'If I'm like that . . . I *am* like that! We must see what comes of
it!'" (170, emphasis mine). This acceptance of self and the other
is an essential element in the novel; it is most dramatically expressed
in Wolf's realization of the beauty of Christie, a metonym of the
terrible beauty in the world that his mythology could not incorporate:
". . . some essence that was what Christie was to her own inmost
self, the bodiless, formless identity in that slim frame, that in confronting infinite space could only utter the mysterious words, 'I am
I,' and utter nothing else" (311). Mr. Torp also recognizes the world
for what it is when he tells Wolf, "It may be a good world . . .
and it may be a bad world, but *it's the world;* and us has got to
handle 'un with eyes in our heads for landslides" (326). In trying
to formulate a philosophy, one that is neither purely solipsistic nor
completely cosmic, Wolf's conclusion situates itself well within a
philosophia perennis: "I refuse to believe," he [Wolf] said to himself,
"and I never will believe until the day Nature kills me, that there's
such a thing as 'reality,' apart from the mind that looks at it! . . .
The 'thing in itself' is as fluid and malleable as these trees. . . ."
(336). In chapter 17, in particular, Wolf ponders the tenets of plural-
ism, pantheism, and monism in his attempt to discover reality; his
incessant probing at this point, his speculations about reality, occur
at the very moment when he begins to see clearly the two triangular
love relationships that have formed: Wolf "knew perfectly well that
Christie understood his attachment to Gerda. He knew perfectly
well that she would understand his resentment at the intrusion of
Bob Weevil" (348). His knowledge at this point of the way the important women in his life have positioned themselves is very clear, although he has not yet resolved how to act; although the same situation
is still present at the end of the novel, Wolf has grown to such
an extent that he is no longer stymied, but can better position himself
so that he can more clearly understand the options that are open
to him. Although he knows fully well the snakelike qualities within
himself, as in all who followed Adam after the Fall, Wolf is undaunted
by this and is able to utter "I am I" at the exact moment when
he seeks a new direction in his life; like "a drowning man he stretched
out his thoughts for help in every direction. To his mother he
stretched them out. To his father he stretched them out. Feebly
and automatically he carried his thoughts like a basket of dying
fish to the threshold of Christie's room. 'Christie! I must tell you
. . . I *must,* I *must,* tell you!'" (352).

The moments of Wolf's epiphany are heralded to some degree by an incantation to Jesus (359, 605) and a repetition of the Euripidean dirge (589, 591, 606), but they are associated mostly with an overpowering experience of Christie's beauty ("Moments as perfect as this required death as their inevitable counterpoise" [440]), the dramatic rejection of the idol, Wolf's symbolic drowning as a second Redfern in Lenty Pond, and Gerda's miraculous imitation of a blackbird whistling. Wolf's moment of self-understanding fuses expected Powysian images, although now Wolf controls his language rather than being dominated by it: "And I know that my 'I am I' is no 'hard, small crystal' inside me, but a cloud, a vapour, a mist, a smoke, hovering round my skull, hovering round my spine, my arms, my legs! That's *what I am*—a 'vegetable-animal' wrapped in a mental cloud, and with the will-power to project this cloud into the consciousness of others" (574). Although such a death-resurrection motif has all the earmarks of Christianity, Powys has not opted for one philosophic or religious symbolic system over another. Wolf's life has to do as much with Platonic thought as it does with Christianity; in fact, what he found in church was not spiritual renewal but the empty casket of King Aethelwolf (the latter part of the king's name symbolically implies that he is a forebearer of Wolf). Yet, Wolf undergoes a type of death, one that can lead to a renewal of mind and spirit. Like Hamlet, Wolf has to quiet his dead father's voice and also console the living who endured the deaths of Albert Smith, James Redfern, and Old Malakite. He says, in fact, "I have killed my life-illusion. . . . I am as dead as William Solent. I've got no pride, no will, no identity left" (505). After acknowledging that he believes in the "Resurrection of the body; and the Life everlasting" (590), Mr. Stalbridge asks Wolf, "Do *you* believe in a future life, Solent?", and although Wolf is hesitant about answering, he seems to side with Mr. Stalbridge's beliefs because he had "been rather hard worked at the school lately" (591). The death-tug is finally snapped, and the void is finally filled when Wolf hears the reassuring words of his dead father: "*You are allowed to forget*" (598). His release is like an entrance into the "Islands of the Blest": "It was like that figure of the Absolute seen in the Apocalypse. It became a *super-substance*, sunlight precipitated and petrified, the *magnetic heart of the world* is rendered visible" (610, emphasis mine). The magnetic forces of the universe have given an intelligible pattern to human situations, and although Wolf is not revealed as the final victor having vanquished all others, he does know where the others in his life are; he sees that they pose no genuine threat to his existence: "Carfax taking Gerda upon his knee, Urquhart begging Tilly-Valley for the Sacrament, his mother borrowing from Mr. Manley, Roger Monk trimming Redfern's grave—all these human gestures presented themselves to him now through a golden mist, a mist that made them at once harmless and negligible, compared with the difference between being alive and being dead!" (610). Wolf's only remaining options are either to escape or to endure, although we know that when he entered the house to seek a cup of tea he had already decided which way to move.

Wolf's relationships with Christie and Gerda, with Squire Urquhart and James Redfern, with Darnley and Jason Otter, with his mother and the voice of his dead father, and with Selena Gault and Mattie Smith, provide the basic material for a new chapter in any future "History of Dorset." Powys knew that the novel provides the drama to history, because the novel form allows the historical a potential to exist vividly in words that evoke what might have happened. Wolf moves in a number of directions throughout the course of this novel as he tries to fit together the pieces of the past, to decipher the cryptic epitaph on his father's tomb, and to align the dimensions of his own personality so that he can deal adequately with all the other people and situations that confront him. He knows that he will lose if he retreats into his private mythology, and therefore as he rejects both solipsism and dualism, he seeks to find harmony in the world about him, one that at times inundates him with its startling, rapturous beauty. Wolf probably embodies many of the characteristics of the people he wrote about in his history; most likely, he reveals an endurance that few of them exhibited. But we will never know for sure, because history can never be fully known and the novel can only speculate imaginatively about it.

Notes

1. John Cowper Powys, *Wolf Solent* (New York: Harper Colophon Books, 1984). All subsequent page references are to this edition, and appear parenthetically.

2. John Bayley, "Life in the Head," *The New York Review of Books* 32, no. 5 (1985): 28.

The Elemental Image in *Wolf Solent*

Denis Lane

Wolf Solent (1929) was John Cowper Powys's fifth novel, written, as its author records in his 1961 preface, while "travelling all the states of the United States except two."[1] The last product of his years as a public lecturer, *Wolf Solent* is generally regarded as being Powys's first major novel. Among the earliest to recognize its achievement was Conrad Aiken, who found it "brilliant" and "flawless." Theodore Dreiser, commenting at the publishers' request on the galley proofs, wrote that it is a work that "holds speculations so intense, so searching and ennobling as to suggest little less than revelation—at their lowest ebb high poetry." More recently, George Steiner has claimed that *Wolf Solent* is "the only book in the language to rival Tolstoy," while Glen Cavaliero sees it as "one of the supreme novels of introspection."[2] If judged solely on the basis of the repeated reprintings of the novel, these claims to excellence have already been justified.

Wolf Solent is a work of psychological realism. Its chief focus falls upon the protagonist, Wolf Solent, and upon the operations of Wolf's mind, a mind caught in the throes of self-definition. The novel's theme is the conflict between concept and actuality: Wolf attempts to find himself and his place in the world but is constantly caught between the dictates of his own nature and the generally adversary character of the world in which he lives. In brief, this late-blooming *Bildungsroman* (Wolf is thirty-five at the start of the novel and Powys himself was fifty-seven at the date of publication) is a powerful and representative study of man's essential struggle to preserve what Powys elsewhere called "the hard, lonely pebble of the undefeated self."[3] Structurally the novel depends on a third-person central consciousness, through whom all the experience of the novel is filtered to the reader, and whose subjective responses, growing, changing and reaching for understanding are the focus of interest in the novel. *Wolf Solent* is Powys's best use of this technique; whatever it fails to do for other characters in the novel, it permits Powys to draw in the figure of Wolf a character of considerable complexity and introspection whose obsessive habits may, despite the novel's mildly comic resolution, be ultimately judged as tragic.

If we call the novel a work of psychological realism, however, we must also acknowledge that its author brings to the genre his special trademark. Powys works out the problem of psychic self-preservation against a background of tension between Wolf and nature.[4] To distinguish it from other important images—the face on the Waterloo steps, for instance, or the *locus amoenus* that is the town of Weymouth–we might call the pervasive presence of nature in the novel, the elemental image. It is elemental, because it is born clearly of or from the elements of earth, air, fire, and water, and the innumerable constituents and cognates of these found in landscape, season, setting, and vegetation, but also because nature is, for Powys, a first principle for directing the way in which *Wolf Solent* is created. We recognize, for example, how the constant images and descriptions of nature infusing the novel supply both the broad outlines and the detailed ingredients of Wolf's emotional evolution. In addition, because nature provides Wolf with a medium for his habit of persistent self-reference, there is much emphasis on mind in landscape; mind and landscape are often causally linked, one determining the other. Again, it is through the elemental image that we best follow the changing moods of Wolf's relationship with Gerda and Christie and his developing responses to social and economic pressures.

Interestingly, Powys appears to have been aware quite early of the need to control the heady influence of nature as a creative force in his fiction. Writing to Llewelyn in 1918 about a projected third novel *(After My Fashion)*, he had observed, "I think Nature must obtrude itself less, don't you?"[5] Yet, a few years later he is furiously defensive in addressing criticisms for cultivating "sensations of nature" in his writing: "[I]f nature makes a feeling thrilling and lovely to me, why should I try to suppress it because Lulu [Llewelyn] calls it 'aesthetically unpleasing' . . . I wish I could put all of this mania of mine into fine poetry or wonderful prose. Some day perhaps I will and then you will see that you were wrong in calling it 'unauthentic.'"[6]

By the time Powys wrote *Wolf Solent* (and his earliest ideas for the novel appear to have come around 1925), he was able to develop an accommodation between these two positions, to find his "wonderful prose," and to create the work that for the first time would successfully enfold the elemental image within the greater purposes of the novel itself. Behind him were four novels and at least ten years of continuous effort at the art of making fiction. Now, seasoned and increasingly confident, he was able to release "this mania" with assurance. There occurs in *Wolf Solent* a miraculous but consonant exfoliation of the elemental image. What in the previous novels had been latent, scattered, or ill-fitting had now become organic and integral. Much of his elemental imagery remained fundamentally the same—for example, from "the clinging tenacity of the earth" of East Anglia in *Wood and Stone* we are led to the "autochthonous essence" of Wessex in *Wolf Solent*—but, although the old sources remain, the elemental image has become a constructive ingredient in the creative process and a new style, consolidated and consistent, has emerged.

What gave impetus to the dynamic development of Powys's elementalist vision for this novel was his need to answer, for the first time to his satisfaction, the call of place, to express in story his indelible attachment to the corners of Somerset and West Dorset where he and Littleton had conducted explorations as children and where they had undertaken those long Sunday marches from Sherborne School where they boarded, to their Montacute home. This was to be his "novel about Sherborne," as he told Littleton,[7] and to Llewelyn he announced that it would have nearby "Bradford Abbas as its 'locale,'" where, "first out of the womb of M. C. P. [Mary Cowper Powys] I must have vaguely been aware of existence. . . ."[8] By replicating in the wanderings of Wolf Solent those of his own early life, Powys displays the landscape of the novel as a series of charged centers of significance so that it becomes possible to speak of it as a symbolic landscape, with the pattern of topographical symbolism following closely the pattern of Wolf's psychological progress.

Powys invests each of the novel's counties with a separate moral and psychological ambience: Dorset carries reminders of a fetid past and suggestions of a strife-ridden future; Somerset offers views of the "lonely, cone-shaped hill" of Glastonbury Tor, for Wolf a symbol of hope, something distant yet nonetheless finite. Topographical differences, in particular, heighten the distinction: Dorset earth, for example, is unsettling, both in odor and substance; Wolf observes that its indigenous quality is expressed in the form of a "rank, harsh, terrestrial sweat" (175); its primary constituent is clay, an image given frequent reference in the novel, suggesting a land bogged down in a clinging, glutinous medium. Human presence merely heightens this impression by defiling the land with dung heaps and privies—features of rural blight that Wolf would wish to see obliterated (413). In Dorset, the pull of the past is felt strongly in the earth. As the final resting place of William Solent, Wolf's "drifting, unscrupulous" father, and of James Redfern, Wolf's unfortunate predecessor as Urquhart's secretary, the Dorset soil harbors particular reminders for Wolf of past events that remain presently unresolved. He fears that he may himself end up in this Dorset clay as "Redfern Number Two," a title conjured for him by Jason Otter, a man whose own claim that "In this world Truth flies downward, not upward" (48) represents a considerable submission of human identity to the powers of place.

By contrast, the topography of Somerset is rendered largely in aquatic terms. General descriptions emphasize the "shy, watery" meadows of the county (310) that appear as an "ocean of greenness" (388) when seen from the distance; or the focus may fall upon the River Lunt, a "patient, muddy stream" that is marked, in evident admonition to Wolf, by its "coherent personality" (96). Mists and rain are concomitants of the landscape, "tutelary vapours," that give Gerda and Wolf protection from the "very ghosts of the dead" (144). Most of all, the aqueous quality of Somerset provides Wolf with moral and material support for his most introspective habit, a type of mystical daydreaming that he calls his "mythology" and that always comes to him in images of submerged, elephantine leaves. His mythology is something Wolf regards as the one inviolable aspect of his personality, but like all else this resource eludes him when control of his affairs disintegrates. When earth is encountered in Somerset, unlike that of Dorset, it is receptive and comforting, bringing a sense of release or dissolution (388, 414).

The principal influences and preoccupations of Wolf's life are presented then as features of a number of localities in which the action of the novel is centered or to which allusions are frequently drawn. Each of the specific locations carries with it a broad hinterland of association—human and prehuman influences, historic and prehistoric residues, the past and the present, all strongly felt through the various localities of the novel—and these associations contribute toward the tension upon which Wolf's mind is built: the tensions between reality and resemblance, participation and detachment. As a twentieth-century novelist deeply and personally concerned with the notion of psychological dislocation, Powys is suggesting through the elemental image that access to knowledge and self-enlightenment comes from nowhere if it does not come from a rooted, specific place in the real world.[9]

If sense of place is wedded to earth and water, then another pattern, the use of the seasons, is wedded to air and fire. The action of *Wolf Solent* is spread over a period of five seasons—fifteen months to be exact—with the result that Wolf's fall and partial resurrection are tightly fused with the intervals of the year, and his progress is impressively illuminated by the commentary the seasons indirectly make upon it. Although Powys avoids any formal seasonal division, such as that adopted by Hardy in *Under the Greenwood Tree*, the story both ends and begins in the spring and all that occurs between falls naturally into a seasonal design. Accordingly, the general movement of Wolf's fortunes is cyclical, covering an initial and transitory period of optimism (first spring and summer), a period of disenchantment and despair (autumn and winter), and finally, a period of increasing but elusive restoration (second spring).

Powys opens the novel with an account of Wolf's springtime journey by train from London to the West Country. The journey is doubly symbolic in that it is for Wolf both a return to the place of his origins and an expression of his identification with the processes of vernal regeneration, a Powysian adaptation of a traditional romantic convention. A catalogue of spring vitality, reflecting Wolf's high expectations of his new life, controls the entire opening chapter. As he passes westward, Wolf is keenly aware of the "sweet airs," the "great curving masses of emerald-clear foliage," and the "cold primroses" (1, 3, 4) of the passing countryside. He finds an especially inviting representation of his "real self" in a black-budded ash tree, but Powys notes that the tree is "still in the rearward of its leafy companions" (5), suggesting, as proves to be the case, that Wolf may be slightly out of step with the true rhythm of the sequence of events he is about to enter.

As he is driven home at the end of his first day in Dorset, "the enchanted springtime stirring in all [the] leaves and grasses" leads Wolf to make further meditations on the promise of his new life:

> To his left the Vale of Blackmore beckoned to him out of its meadows—meadows that were full of faint grassy odours which carried a vague taste of river-mud in their savour because of the nearness of the banks of the Lunt. From Shaftesbury, on the north, to the isolated eminence of Melbury Bub, to the south, that valley stretched away, whispering, so it seemed, some inexplicable prophetic greeting to its returned native-born.
>
> As he listened to the noise of the horse's hooves steadily clicking, clicking, clicking, with every now and then a bluish spark rising in the dusk of the road, as iron struck against flint; as he watched the horizon in front of him grow each moment more fluid, more wavering; as he saw detached fragments of the earth's surface—hill-curves, copses, far-away fields and hedges—blend with fragments of cloud and fragments

of cloudless space, it came over him with a mounting confidence that this wonderful country must surely deepen, intensify, enrich his furtive inner life, rather than threaten or destroy it. . . .

Wolf felt [his] familiar mystic sensation surging up even now from its hidden retreat. . . . The airs of this new world that met its rising were full of the coolness of mosses, full of the faint unsheathing of fern-fronds. Whatever this mysterious emotion was, it leaped forward now towards the new element as if conscious it carried with it a power as formidable, as incalculable, as anything it could encounter there. (26–27)

For Powys, the fullest apprehension of nature, of season, and of landscape is invariably expressed as a unity, as a sensuous and emotional totality. More aware of the entirety of the landscape—of its actual life as well as its subtle but finite psychic emanations—than of any immediate pictorial qualities, he turns the focus upon a psychosensual interaction between it and man. In this passage we note how the evening landscape suggests an animate presence that, having "beckoned" to Wolf, then participates in a voiceless address to the traveler, "whispering . . . some inexplicable prophetic greeting." Furthermore, Wolf's sense of well-being, and the triggering of his mythology, are identified directly with "this wonderful country," that is, with the region itself rather than with the people or events that it may encompass. The focus at the beginning of the passage is primarily at ground level, and the landscape, although seen at a distance, is apprehended closely (in Powys's usual manner) through a blending of smells, texture, and form. But in the second paragraph, the focus drifts upward to present glimpses of cloud and "cloudless space." This new perspective images the perceiver's own upward current of feeling as he begins to formulate his sense of mounting confidence. In brief, Wolf responds to the landscape rather than observes it: he feels it, almost, rather than sees it; he *is* the season and the region.

With the opening tableau completed, Powys turns his attention to using seasonal effects and rhythms to reinforce the major theme of the novel: the death of Wolf's old self and the birth and survival of the new. Wolf's initial optimism prevails through the spring and carries over into summer, and as his personal and domestic arrangements improve he congratulates himself on his "extraordinary good luck" (214) in coming to the West Country. But a period of intense disillusionment awaits him, intimations of which have already been asserted in the developing stages of the novel, particularly in the scene where Wolf first walks the Lunt meadows with Gerda. Here, the elemental images are reasserted:

> Advancing up this lane hand in hand with his companion, Wolf felt his soul invaded by that particular kind of melancholy which emanates, at the end of a spring day, from all the elements of earth and water. It is a sadness unlike all others, and has perhaps some mysterious connection with the swift, sudden recognition by myriads and myriads of growing things, of the strange fatality that pursues all earthly life, whether clothed in flesh or clothed in vegetable fibre. It is a sadness accentuated by grey skies, grey water, and grey horizons; but it does not seem to attain its most significant meaning until the pressure of spring adds to these elemental wraiths the intense wistfulness of young new life. (94)

This sense of a "strange fatality" and the sadness that accompanies it lies fallow during the summer months, principally because Wolf has arrived at passable if patchwork relationships with his mother and with Mr. Urquhart, and because he has attained the "rarified, poetical glamour" of living with Gerda in a "lath-and-plaster workman's villa" at the "airy confluence of two vast provinces of leafiness and sunshine" (213). But what was once a fleeting recognition in the spring has by autumn translated itself into a condition of permanent foreboding. The close of summer signals also the imminent demise of what Wolf calls his "life-illusion," a belief, arising from his mythology, by which he regards himself as "some kind of protagonist in a cosmic struggle" (318), a struggle where the powers of good and evil are ranged in opposition. As autumn closes in, Wolf's personal relationships fragment in all directions, and mere anarchy is loosed upon his world. A trio of pressures leads to the expiration of Wolf's life-illusion: his inability to make sense or headway in his platonic affair with Christie; his realization that Gerda, increasingly aware of his perfidious nature, is herself lapsing into wayward relationships; and, finally, his growing sense of debasement over his hand in the Urquhart chronicles. Powys gathers together the effects of this formula for Solentian depression in an evocation of autumnal dissolution found at the beginning of chapter 19, "Wine."

> The three autumn months . . . became for Wolf, as the days shortened and darkened, like a slowly rising tide that, drawing its mass of waters from distances and gulfs beyond his reach, threatened to leave scant space unsubmerged of the rugged rock which hitherto he had turned upon the world. Something in the very fall of the leaf, in the slow dissolution of vegetation all around him, made this menace to the integrity

of his soul more deadly. He had never realized what the word 'autumn' meant until this Wessex autumn gathered its 'cloudy trophies' about his ways, and stole, with its sweet rank odours, into the very recesses of his being. Each calamitous event that occurred during these deciduous months seemed to be brewed in the oozy vat of vegetation, as if the muddy lanes and the wet hazel-copses—yes! the very earth-mould of Dorset itself—were conspiring with human circumstances. . . .

How heavily the hart's-tongue ferns drooped earthward under the scooped hollows of the wet clay-banks! How heavily the cold raindrops fell—silence falling upon silence—when the frightened yellow-hammers fled from his approach! He felt at such times as though they must be composed of very *old* rain, those shaken showers; each tremulous globe among them having reflected through many a slow dawn nothing but yellow leaves, through many a long night nothing but faint white stars! (390)

The passage embodies much that is typical of Powys's use of the elemental image. Certainly it is the antithesis of Keatsian mellowness or Hardean fruition.[10] In the first place, there is a subtle admixture of the specific and the general, of actual time and timelessness. There is, for instance, no identifiable panorama as subject, yet the landscape and the processes at work upon it are strongly felt. This note of generality enveloping concrete detail is struck throughout the passage but is captured best in the cadent and majestic final sentence. The rain is a specific notation of autumn, but since it is *"old"* rain, it also gives the suggestion of timelessness, of eternal natural processes, and thus leads Wolf to the important consideration that personal preoccupations are subsumed in a larger, implicitly cosmic rhythm that can be apprehended through the immemorial cycles of "many a slow dawn" and "many a long night."

Internally, the keynote of the passage is dissolution and liquidation. We see how Powys achieves this effect by bringing the sensuous focus to bear upon water and water-imagery—a favorite device. From the initial simile of the "slowly rising tide," to the more fixed images of mud and wet trees, he conveys the sense of a season in which all that once was solid is rendered liquid or amorphous. Furthermore, the process and the contemplating personality are direct reflections of each other so that the sense of universal dissolution pervading the passage parallels, both implicitly and explicitly, the disintegration of the protagonist's will under the pressures of circumstance. In particular, the leaden, heavy tone established by such features as the cloud-filled sky and the soaked earth matches Wolf's inner-felt emotions of apprehension and submission. Hence autumn is both the mirror and the instigator of his mood: like the falling leaves,

Wolf is caught in the season's downward rhythm, is part of the reductive flow that makes of Dorset an "oozy vat of vegetation."

We see also how the force of the passage is strengthened by a vocabulary of doom contained in such words as "darkening," "threat," "calamitous," and "conspired," and in the repetition of the phrase "how heavily." This pattern, which directly overlies the surface imagery, further develops the correspondence that Powys draws between the season and Wolf's mood, and at the same time acts as a prefiguration of later events in the novel—for the sensuous and material qualities of the season are linked to human actions (or, in Wolf's case, inaction), thereby becoming part of the narrative texture rather than digressive ornament.[11]

With the approach of the novel's second spring, there are increasing hints that Wolf has arrived at a new notion of self, at a realization that he is himself the "demiurge of the whole miserable spectacle" (473), as he expresses his life situation after a second betrayal of Christie. At this stage of the novel (chapters 21, 22, 23), Powys places greater stress upon Wolf's customarily close relationship with external phenomena. The signs of spring, for instance, remind Wolf that life moves in "great irrevocable curves" (477). He sees the new season as bringing with it the hope of personal renewal and so responds excitedly to the awakening of "reborn life" (490) throughout the countryside and to the earth's "shivering, restorative poignance" (489). Thus Wolf is on the verge of his own rebirth.

Powys brings the novel and its seasonal pattern full circle in the final chapter, to which he gives the title he had once contemplated for the book as a whole, "Ripeness is All"—an apposite borrowing from *King Lear*. It is the last Saturday in May. Both the color and the spirit of the day hint of the miraculous. Warm sunlight infuses the springtime world. Filtered through "thin, opaque clouds," the sunlight transmutes the countryside into a "mellow spaciousness of watery gold" (586), and bathes Wolf in the "lavish waves of the season's fertility" (587). The chapter's constant references to rebirth and fertility strike mythic reverberations. Special emphasis is placed on vegetative vitality—growth is rampant, flowers are either in bud or bloom, stalks full of "warm, moist sap" (588); in fact, "all Dorset seemed gathered up" (606). These details serve as proleptic images of the regenerative surge Wolf is to feel in his own life. At the end of the "pearl-soft afternoon," Wolf appears to have arrived at last at his moment of resurrection. "The loveliness of this day . . . a gift thrown out to him by Chance, the greatest of the gods . . . seemed to have touched his body with a kind of blind new birth. . . . The immense vegetable efflorescence by which he had been surrounded seemed to have drawn his nerves back and down, soothing them, healing them, calming them, in a flowing reciprocity with that life that was far older than animal life! Ah! his body and soul were coming together again now!" (605–6).

Thus reoriented, Wolf prepares to return from the world of sensuous reverie to the world of personal strife, but Powys refuses to finish Wolf's saga without submitting his hero to one final ordeal. Arriving home, Wolf finds Gerda sitting with evident enjoyment on the lap of the visiting Lord Carfax, her pose an ironic duplicate of a photograph Wolf had once seen of her suggestively straddling one of her father's tombstones. In her way, Gerda also has evidently been reborn. In a state of "vibrant jealousy," Wolf turns once more to the ebullience of the season for the restorative powers he needs in answering this first challenge to his new found self. A setting sun and a field of golden buttercups, between them combining both the symbol and the color of the day, remind him that continual renewal and perpetual endurance will be his only means of achieving stability.

> He began walking to and fro now, with a firmer step. Back and forth he walked, while the sun, fallen almost horizontal, made what he walked upon unearthly. Buttercup-petals clung to his legs, clung to the sides of his stick; buttercup-dust covered his boots. The plenitude of gold that surrounded him became a *super-substance*, sunlight precipitated and petrified, the magnetic heart of the world rendered visible! Up and down he went, pacing that field. He felt as if he were an appointed emissary, guarding some fragment of Saturn's age flung into the midst of Blacksod (610)

In this Mithraistic vision, Powys captures the final phase of Wolf's conversion from idealism to realism. Once a "protagonist," now a mere "emissary," Wolf assimilates himself into the organic energies of the day, the field, and the region. Self, place, and season have become one.

> Then, as he turned eastward, and the yellowness of the buttercups changed from Byzantine gold to Cimmerian gold, he visualized the whole earthly solidity of this fragment of the West Country, this segment of astronomical clay, stretching from Glastonbury to Melbury Bub and from Ramsgard to Blacksod, as if it were itself one of the living personalities of his life. 'It is a god!' he cried in his heart; and he felt as if titanic hands, from the horizon of this 'field of Saturn,' were being lifted up to salute the mystery of life and the mystery of death. . . . Between himself and what was 'behind' the Universe there should now be a new covenant! The Cause up there could certainly at any minute make him howl like a mad dog. It could make him dance and skip and eat dung.

Well, until it *did* that, he was going to endure . . . follow his 'road,' through the ink-stains, and endure! (612–13)

The scene recalls, deliberately I feel, the episode in chapter I that brings Wolf's first day in Dorset to a close. But now the apostrophe has been reversed: the man speaks to the earth, where formerly the earth spoke to the man. There are no longer any palliatives, no longer any sense of pastoral somnambulance. Wolf's "familiar mystic sensation," which once came to him so easily, has gone; only the sheer realities of daily existence remain. Yet in this final movement of the novel, the assertion of endurance, of riding firmly and defiantly on his very own life-force irrespective of "Cause," argues that there still exists for Wolf a valuable life to be drawn from the ego and the will.[12]

Besides bringing the novel and its seasonal movement to a conclusion, the buttercup scene is also the culmination of the pattern of vegetative imagery, particularly images of flowers and trees, with which Powys invests the novel. Part of the broader scheme of metaphorical language that focuses on the natural world, Powys's use of vegetative imagery is an especially important dimension in his presentation of character and narrative. We have seen, for instance, how it conveys Powys's characteristic awareness of seasonal markers. Often part of the evocation of locality or place consists of detailed descriptions of flowers, or trees in flower or leaf: marsh-marigolds, poplars, and willows by the banks of the Lunt, white-flowering blackthorn and hawthorn along the Blacksod lanes, the hyacinths of the Ramsgard public gardens. Christie Malakite (her surname is a homonym for the color of mallow leaves) is seen by Wolf as a "living, breathing plant" (232)—her dress, her eyes are brown, and her "silky brown hair" is like "the drooping tendrils of some sort of wild vegetation" (77). Her apparent indifference to the moral complexities of life around her seems to put her in the premoral order of plants and (later) animals. Gerda is likewise given plant imagery. At first she is seen as "an arum lily before it has unsheathed its petals" or as an "unpicked white phlox" (58, 86), images that capture perfectly her passivity and that point to her imminent seduction by Wolf. Later she is more commonly "a peeled willow wand," a prototypal image of a sylvan deity, and thus an integral part of the cult of trees through which Wolf objectifies his relationships with both her and Christie.

Wolf himself has a particular sensitivity for flowers. As the novel progresses, they gradually assume a psychic value for him; they become concrete and objective manifestations, symbols of the less contentious side of nature through which he escapes from responsibility

and failure in his social world. A border of lobelias and asters seen
through the window of Urquhart's study, for example, softens the
impact of the "lewd preciosities" he is engaged in researching and
brings to his mind the contemplation of "something in nature purer
than anything in man's mind" (317). By the same token, wild flowers
have a greater stimulus on him than cultivated ones. In chapter
10, "Christie," a bowl of wild flowers serves as a centerpiece for
a scene of sexual role-playing between Wolf and Christie.[13] The flowers, remarkable for the "perilous, arrowy faintness of their smell,"
function as an objective correlative of the thoughts and feelings of
the participants. Sexual concerns are uppermost in their minds. At
one point in their conversation, Wolf makes a simple but explicitly
sexual gesture: "Suddenly he found himself risen from his seat and
standing against the mantelpiece. He lifted the flowers to his face;
and then, putting down the bowl, he inserted his fingers in it, pressing
them down between the stalks into the water" (235). Powys suggests
Christie's intuitive understanding of his action and her subconscious
deflection of his desire when, with "deft, swift touches," she corrects
"the rough confusion he had made in her nosegay." Much later
in the novel, when it appears that Christie is threatened by her
father's lust, Wolf regrets his failure to press his love-making with
her, asserting that she would have been as "immune as the flowers
on her mantelpiece" had he done so (500).

Another clear pattern of metaphorical language or reference,
heightening the correspondence between man and nature in *Wolf
Solent*, concerns animals and birds. Here, metaphor, for the most
part, defines character or comments on action. Bob Weevil, the principal rival to Wolf for Gerda's affection, is "water-rat featured" (263);
Selena Gault, a former lover of William Solent and the self-appointed
guardian of his memory, possesses "great wild-horse eyes" set in
a "bestial" face (507); and Squire Urquhart has a look that is "almost
saurian" (176). Wolf (whose own name, like that of the Otters, carries
animalistic references) admits to a "pet-dog spirit" in the face of
his mother's "bird-like" animadversions (462).

References to birds, however, apply almost exclusively to the
women in Wolf's life and provide one of Powys's most effective
uses of the elemental image. Christie is associated with the heron—
an aquatic bird, thereby relating her to Wolf's mythology—whose
feather, delicate and rare like herself, she uses as a bookmark. Gerda,
on the other hand, is associated with the blackbird, scavenger of
hedgerows and thickets, whose song she imitates with an uncanny
ability. "The delicious notes hovered through the wood—hovered
over the scented turf where [Wolf] lay—and went wavering down

the hollow valley. He could hardly believe his ears. It was as if she had swiftly summoned one of those yellow-beaked birds out of its leafy retreat. . . . Over the turf ramparts of Poll's Camp it swelled and sank, that wistful, immortal strain. Away down the grassy slopes it floated upon the March wind" (90, 93). Gerda's blackbird whistling is the expression of her brimming sexuality—it is precisely as a friend had told her, "that my whistling was only whistling for a lover" (146). When Wolf's attachment to Christie becomes evident to Gerda, her whistling skill eludes her, and if solicitation from Wolf revives it momentarily (358), only Carfax's debonair flirtation can restore her to full song. "An entrancing bird's note made [Wolf] stop again and glance up the road to where the great ash tree extended its cool, glaucous green branches. . . . Were Gerda and Lord Carfax listening to this liquid music as they ate their Pimpernel cakes? Fool! Fool! Fool! It was not in the tree at all. Oh, he had known it all the while! In the deepest pit of his stomach he had known. It was the girl herself. The blackbird's notes were issuing from that open window. It was Gerda's whistling. That strange power had been given back to her at last" (607).

Part of the same fabric of imagery is Powys's technique of displacing the respective image of each woman to comment on scenes in which Wolf is, by definition, disloyal to the other. In the prelude to Wolf's first intimacy with Gerda, for instance, there is no direct reference to Christie, but through a variety of symbolic details Powys strongly intimates her spiritual presence at the scene. The lovers are in the Lunt meadows: the gray sky overhead is likened to a "great outstretched wing," the clouds seen as "scattered feathers" (138). Gerda's "sea-grey gaze" recalls the color and the habitat of Christie's symbol, while Wolf's thoughts are described, in a clear allusion to Christie, as "languid-winged herons" that "flapped heavily over the dykes and ditches of his life" (139). (The fact that their juvenile chaperone, Lobbie, has been persuaded by the couple to search for blackbirds' eggs further sustains the bird imagery and its attendant sexual overtones.)

A corresponding sequence occurs the following day at the spring horse fair. In spite of the warning from his prospective mother-in-law that Gerda "bain't one for sharing her fairings" (205), Wolf nevertheless pursues his compulsion for Christie and follows her to some nearby castle ruins where she has gone for peace and quiet. As the two begin to recognize their mutual attraction, the "persistent" whistling of a blackbird is heard close by. For Wolf the connection is explicit: "It was impossible that this bird's voice could fail to bring to his mind the events of yesterday's twilight and that upturned

face at which he had gazed so exultantly in the gathering river mists"
(207). Wolf attempts to suppress this recent memory but a bird's
nest, actually that of a blackbird but inexpertly identified by Wolf
and Christie as being that of a thrush, assumes the focus of their
attention—a further reminder by the novelist of the predicament
Wolf is creating for himself. At the conclusion of the scene, Powys
cannot resist making the laconic comment that "the blackbird flew
off with an angry scream" (207).

Techniques such as these belie the notion that Powys's intuitive
methods of composition necessarily preclude the care and craft we
might usually associate with the more "premeditated" writing of
Thomas Hardy, say, or George Eliot. The figurative use of flowers
and trees, animals and birds, provides important thematic and structural signposts in *Wolf Solent*, enlarging our understanding of the
novel and persuading us to accept the emphasis on the natural world
as meaningful and significant rather than escapist and ornate.

In this essay, I have dwelt partly on Powys's central fictional
method in *Wolf Solent* of integrating landscape and character, nature
and mind. Episodes describing human activity and human thought
set within a milieu of natural objects and natural scenery, and the
elemental character of his metaphorical language, implicitly illustrate
the way nature and mental processes are deliberately related in the
novel.[14] The description of the evening vale in chapter 1, for example,
provides through its various external details a mirror reflection of
Wolf's internal contentment; or we may recall how, in the autumn
passage of chapter 19, Wolf's romantic and psychic misfortunes find
their direct equivalent in the seasonal dissolution of the landscape.
Elemental details again figure as external correlatives of inner release
and reorientation in the buttercup scene of the final chapter, but
on this occasion Powys extends the event into something more: it
becomes a superphysical and extrasensory interaction between man
and nature. In part, such a heightened exchange is made possible
by the exceptional relationship Powys has already established between
Wolf and nature. As the principal extension of the novelist's perspective, Wolf is endowed with Powys's acute sensitivity to natural sights,
sounds, and smells, and to the distinctive habits of earth and sky;
they are a perpetual part of his consciousness. "Nature was always
prolific of signs and omens to his mind; and it had become a custom
with him to keep a part of his intelligence alert and passive for
a thousand whispers, hints, and obscure intimations that came to
him in this way" (274). In short, Wolf can read nature accurately;
he understands nature as nature appears to understand him; they
communicate.

Possibly it is here that Powys most displays his originality and courage as a novelist. It is not an exaggeration, I think, to describe this process as a form of instinctual communion. Wolf's identification with the elemental sources of nature comments on and eludidates the mythic and subconscious strands of human psychology. Certainly Powys displays novelistic courage in the extent to which he is prepared to carry this identification. In addition to the buttercup scene, there are numerous other passages in the novel in which Powys portrays Wolf as engaging in a total psychic involvement with nature or landscape as the visible sign of nature (40, 389, 414, 489, 505). In each, a strong strain of morphological enquiry is written into the passage. Powys is challenging, I think, an established assumption inherent in literature and philosophy alike—that spirit being born of matter must necessarily rise above it. Why cannot spirit coalesce with matter, he asks, and why cannot we arrange the symbolism accordingly? One thinks how often in this and other works by Powys moments of ecstasy, great or incidental, are conveyed in terms of a downward flow of the mind, of consciousness, into matter, be it rock, vegetation, or man-made edifice. This then is startling and unusual, and on the scale adopted by Powys, contrary to archetypes, as commonly accepted. His emphasis on the original importance of instinct, this heightening of the submerged or numinous aspects of man's psychology, speaks to us in images fashioned sometimes consciously and sometimes unconsciously, is the most distinctive feature of Powys's treatment of mind and landscape, and is, by extension, one of the most remarkable characteristics of the novel as a whole.

Even when *Wolf Solent* was completed and being readied for publication, Powys continued to conceive of it in naturalistic terms. "I regard the book as a sort of river" he wrote to Llewelyn, ". . . the waters of which you like to bathe in if you like that kind of water but which you leave, drawing up your canoe, at a great psychic curve of the stream where the 'murmurs and scents' of the sea are most vivid. . . ."[15] If that river can be said to run smoothly and majestically, we can attribute this in part to Powys's skillful and sophisticated use of the elemental image. What *Wolf Solent* lacks in the presentation of a recognizable social world it gains in Powys's imaginative and powerful creation of Wolf's private world and in the integration of that world with setting and season. And if at times there is an overemphasis on individuality and personal disposition, the delineation of emotional conflict—and its resolution at the "great psychic curve" of the book's ending—must nevertheless be judged as full and successful.

Notes

1. John Cowper Powys, *Wolf Solent* (1929; reprint, London: Macdonald & Co., 1961), p. vii. Subsequent references are cited parenthetically by page number. The Harper and Row edition (New York, 1984), with introduction by Robertson Davies, has identical pagination.

2. Sources for these quotations are listed *seriatim*. Conrad Aiken, "John Cowper Powys" (1929), reprinted in *A Reviewer's ABC* (London: W. R. Allen, 1961), p. 328; letter to Simon and Schuster, 26 March 1929, *Letters of Theodore Dreiser*, ed. Robert H. Elias (Philadelphia: University of Pennsylvania Press, 1959), p. 488; George Steiner, *Language and Silence* (New York: Atheneum, 1967), p. 236; Glen Cavaliero, *John Cowper Powys: Novelist* (Oxford: Clarendon Press, 1973) p. 60.

3. John Cowper Powys, *A Philosophy of Solitude* (1936; reprint ed., London: Village Press, 1974), p. 59.

4. This feature has been a starting point for a number of critics. John Brebner has accurately observed that Powys "uses nature as a fundamental rhythm" in the novel, *The Demon Within* (New York: Barnes & Noble, 1973), p. 61. G. Wilson Knight writes that the novel "is very largely an exploration of the human psyche in interaffective relationship with natural surroundings," *The Saturnian Quest* (1964; reprint ed., Hassocks, Sussex: Harvester Press, 1978), p. 30. More specific observations are referred to in subsequent notes.

5. John Cowper Powys, *Letters to His Brother Llewelyn*, 2 vols. (London: Village Press, 1975), 1:215.

6. Powys, *Letters to Llewelyn*, 2:326–27.

7. Letter of 21 October 1927. In Belinda Humfrey, ed., *Essays on John Cowper Powys* (Cardiff: University of Wales Press, 1972), p. 322.

8. Powys, *Letters to Llewelyn*, 2:13.

9. For further discussion of this theme, see Cavaliero, *Novelist*, pp. 45–46.

10. I have in mind Hardy's identification of Giles Winterbourne with autumn in chapter 28 of *The Woodlanders*.

11. One of the fullest examinations of the mind-landscape fusion in Powys's writing is found in C. A. Coates, *John Cowper Powys in Search of a Landscape* (Totowa, N.J.: Barnes and Noble, 1982). Her remarks on the tension between pyrrhonism and dualism in Powys's mind (41–60) are particularly instructive.

12. For a penetrating discussion of this episode in the context of the legend of the fleece and the scapegoat, see Ned Lukacher, "Notre-Homme-des-Fleurs: *Wolf Solent*'s Metaphoric Legends," *Powys Review* 2, no. 2 (1979–80):64–73. Another important interpretation of this section of *Wolf Solent* is offered by Morine Krissdottir in *John Cowper Powys and the Magical Quest* (London: Macdonald & Jane's, 1980), pp. 64–79.

13. For an extended and illuminating discussion of this scene, see Brebner, *The Demon Within*, pp. 64–73.

14. Nature even has a way of invading interior settings in the novel. In chapter 10, the uncertain relationship of Wolf and Gerda is imaged in the unusual combination of scents that come through their bedroom window. "Through their open window came the clear, ringing notes of the thrush in the ash tree along with that curious scent of honeysuckle mixed with pig's dung that was their familiar atmosphere" (227). And in chapter 21, there is the east wind's ironic subversion of Wolf's attempt to burn Urquhart's check (484).

15. Powys, *Letters to Llewelyn*, 2:83.

The "mysterious word Esplumeoir" and Polyphonic Structure in *A Glastonbury Romance*

Ben Jones

Readers of *A Glastonbury Romance* will remember the calamitous events of the day on which Mr. Owen Evans, biographer of Merlin and seeker of a new life, fulfills his dark wish to witness a violent killing.[1] Evans witnesses a killing and finds a new life, but neither of these events marks the transformation for which he longed. This day, which would have transformation as its theme and "Esplumeoir" as its signifying word, begins auspiciously. Owen Evans's "high spirits that morning had been largely due to the fact that he had just arrived, in his Life of Merlin, at the beginning of the final scene where the Magician passed into that State of Being hinted in the mysterious word Esplumeoir" (1001). At this point in my discussion, I only want to note "Esplumeoir" as a clue to a "State of Being": its larger implications will become obvious later. On this particular day, in the time-space of Glastonbury, the configurations of variant human desires will not provide what Evans longed for and expected: a transfiguration, a new state of being not only for himself but for the world. In this essay, I explore this "mysterious" word and the role it plays in the structure of the novel. I also hope to provide some insights into what the word and its nuances offer toward an understanding of Powys's achievement and his poetics. "Esplumeoir" provides a clue to our understanding of the novel's polyphonic structure, and particularly to the occurrence of "doubling" as a narrative element in the text.

The commentaries of Mikhail Bakhtin play a role in this reading of *A Glastonbury Romance*. I shall be concerned particularly with Bakhtin's *Problems of Dostoevsky's Poetics*.[2] There are a number of coincidental affinities between Bakhtin's work and Powys's,[3] as there are deliberate affinities between Powys and Dostoevsky, but this essay concentrates on immediate problems in the structure.

A need has already been stated for an approach to Powys that suits his unique achievement as a novelist, and this need has begun

71

to be realized. Charles Lock both speaks to and begins to answer such a need. In "'Multiverse' . . . language which makes language impossible,"[4] Lock states that "a Powys novel is a multiverse which contains the universes of each of the characters and that of the author himself."[5] This statement sets out the possibilities for a "polyphonic" reading, although it still leaves a place for an "authorial" consciousness, a matter to which we shall return.[6] It will be useful to look at Lock's interpretation in more detail: "*A Glastonbury Romance* is an unfocused unbalanced work, and in that is the heart of its originality and greatness. The reader's attention is absorbed totally first in John Crow, then in Geard, then in Sam, and then Geard again, in a most unsettling way."[7] Powys "rejects" the "prerogative of the traditionalist novelist" because he "recognizes that in the pluralistic multiverse of his creation his own view is as limited and as partial, as much of a life-illusion, as that of Geard or Sam."[8]

This passage advances our reading of the Powys text, but it does not yet bridge the gap between the disparity of "unfocused" and "unbalanced" on the one hand and "originality and greatness" on the other. The unconvinced reader will likely remain unconvinced. Strangely, Lock in this passage leaves out any reference to Owen Evans, whose involvement in the novel takes a place alongside John Crow, Sam Dekker, and John Geard. Evans's particular problem— the irreconcilability of his violent sexual obsession with his longing for magical transformation—is one of the major themes in the novel's polyphonic organization. There are problems, too, in Lock's reference to "his [Powys's] own view," implying that this must be *Powys's* own view, not, for example, the view of a created narrator or a dialogical voice. Lock has not yet confirmed the death of the author. But we cannòt afford to miss the pertinence of the general approach that Lock sets out toward an understanding of Powys's mode of novelistic structuring. It anticipates the realization that the work of Bakhtin will provide an opening to the peculiar genius of the Powysian text. This genius may not be so peculiar after all. My concentration will be on the text and how the idea of polyphony— shown in the configurations of the "double"—solves certain critical dilemmas outlined in Lock's essay, particularly those dilemmas which unresolved result in an assessment of *Glastonbury* as unfocused or unbalanced.

Critical writing on Powys has been based on the presupposition that his novels are "monological."[9] Lock has identified for us such a reader, wanting to know *more* about John Crow, and irritated because Sam is not given a tidy place in the scheme of things. The monological approach, as outlined by Bakhtin, presupposes an essen tial and obvious unity, a presence to be established by a focused perspective and articulated by a single, authorizing voice. This is what is usually thought of as the "traditional" novel. Often this voice is identified as Powys's own voice. Powys *is* the author. For example, Glen Cavaliero who often sees the complicated structures Powys used and whose analyses of the novels are essential reading, says: "The great weakness of *A Glastonbury Romance* lies in the fact that too often what are acceptable as superbly imaginative insights and intuitions of an infinitely suggestive nature are presented as dogmas uttered with a kind of pseudo-gnomic wisdom which lend themselves all too readily to the accusation that John Cowper Powys was a crank."[10] This amounts to a reading of Powys that he is a monologist, presenting authorial statements, standing outside his text. Nevertheless, Cavaliero at times takes Powysian criticism to a point just short of a polyphonic reading, particularly when he notes that Powys's aim in the novel, as stated in the preface to the 1955 Macdonald edition, was to "advocate 'an acceptance of our human life in the spirit of absolutely undogmatic ignorance.' The key words here are 'acceptance' and 'undogmatic.' Not even ignorance is to be asserted as an absolute, and the mind is to be left open to all impressions; and the uncertainty is to be *accepted*."[11] For all this, Cavaliero retains an anxiety that Powys was, after all, vulnerable. The vulnerability was based in the reading of the text as monologue, with the single voice often successful but at times "bombastic and inflated," burdening the book "with a super-abundance of metaphysical comment." He acknowledges Glastonbury's "many and glaring faults," and he accepts that "from a narrative point of view Powys is a formless writer."[12] Powys is formless *if* monological organization is presupposed.

Other critics have placed Powys more conspicuously in the monologist category. Morine Krissdottir gives shape to Powys's whole career by interpreting it as a "magical hunt,"[13] emphasizing his "far-ranging and somewhat curious philosophical system."[14] The singularity of the quest is the organizing core of G. Wilson Knight's seminal *The Saturnian Quest*, and he calls *Glastonbury* "less a book than a Bible."[15] John Brebner in *The Demon Within* emphasizes the "vision" in Powys's work, the "Grail-message," for example.[16] These critiques share a common perspective: that Powys sets out a world-view, and that his characters are created in the context of this world-view. The strengths of the novels are identified according to successes obtained in articulating characters, describing landscapes, and realizing a visionary or magical world-view. Like Owen Evans, they seek in the text an "Esplumeoir." This approach, for all its advantages, presupposes the novels to be "monologically" structured. If it establishes Powys's authorial consciousness, it fails to cope with the problems of narrative organization. The overall assessment can be only that "authorial" urgency outweighs the obvious weaknesses in form. But *are* there weaknesses in form? The idea of polyphony speaks to this question.

In his introduction to Bakhtin's *Problems of Dostoevsky's Poetics* (1984), Wayne C. Booth provides a commentary that both draws Powys and Bakhtin together and sets out clearly what Powys considered his own artistic task to be. In Bakhtin's view, as described by Booth, the artist's task "is indeed the only conceptual device we have that can do justice, by achieving a kind of objectivity quite different from that hailed by most western critics, to the essential irreducible multi-centeredness or 'polyphony,' of human life."[17] He adds: "Polyphony, the miracle of our 'dialogical' lives together, is thus both a fact of life and, in its higher reaches, a value to be pursued endlessly."[18] Powys, in his defense of Dostoevsky, puts it this way:

> But his special greatness as a writer of fiction is to be found in the fact that for these revelations he is not just a mouthpiece, still less a calm and critical interpreter, but a true medium; that is to say we have the curious feeling, as we listen to what his most disturbing characters are uttering, that he himself is as startled, shocked, awed and impressed by what they reveal as are their hearers.
>
> For the truth is that this astonishing writer does not content himself with revealing in his oracular and prophetic outbursts any one coherent vision of life, but several contradictory visions, and for this very reason approaches more closely than any other novelist to that 'real reality' for which, as Goethe hinted, Nature herself finds utterance, expressing herself multifariously, and through many different tongues.[19]

What Powys notes particularly—and he is talking about *himself* here—is that Dostoevsky does not reveal "one coherent vision of life. . . ." This correspondence to Bakhtin's "dialogical" reading of Dostoevsky informs us of Powys's attitude toward his own work. The right reading of Powys will be skeptical of "prophetic outbursts" and this "dialogical" skepticism must be taken not only as an ideological position but as the technical procedure, the imaginative engagement, that informs Powys's fiction.

There are two more passages from Bakhtin that will help us establish the terminology. First, his encompassing statement of what he takes "polyphony" to be in Dostoevsky: "*A plurality of independent*

*and unmerged voices and consciousnesses, a genuine polyphony of fully
valid voices is in fact the chief characteristic of Dostoevsky's novels.*
What unfolds in his works is not a multitude of characters and
fates in a single authorial consciousness; rather, a *a plurality of
consciousnesses, with equal rights and each with its own world,* combine
but are not merged in the unity of the event."[20] Second, the terms
of his rejection of the "monologic" approach:

> From the viewpoint of a consistently monologic visualization and under-
> standing of the represented world, from the viewpoint of some monologic
> canon for the proper construction of novels, Dostoevsky's world may
> seems a chaos, and the construction of his novels some sort of conglomer-
> ate of disparate materials and incompatible principles for shaping them.
> Only in the light of Dostoevsky's fundamental artistic task . . . can one
> begin to understand the profound organic cohesion, consistency and
> wholeness of Dostoevsky's poetics.[21]

These two passages offer a "primer" to Powys; indeed, if we substi-
tute Powys's name for Dostoevsky's we have guidelines for identifying
the inadequacies of the "monological" critical position and for having
a critical approach that suits our subject, an approach that allows
both an elucidation of texts and an identification of tradition, for
recognizing the "organic cohesion, consistency and wholeness" of
Powys's poetics.

The word "Esplumeoir" enters our discussion in this way: the
word itself has monological implications. It offers a singular "vision"
of life, has a magical presence and potency, and in the mind of
Owen Evans it becomes an obsession. Powys, in the tracing of events
connected to Evans's obsession, de-mystifies the word, leaving the
text polyphonically organized. Powys manages this de-mystification
through the figure of a "double," John Crow. This is the narrative
procedure that I shall now attempt to describe.

Already we have seen that "Esplumeoir" is singularly connected
to Owen Evans, although its implications of transformation apply
to all characters in the novel. It is a key word in the polyphonic
design. Powys likely took the mysterious word from Jessie Weston's
commentary in *The Legend of Sir Perceval.* She says, "I do not know
what the 'Esplumeoir' was; I doubt if anyone does," but she adds
later in a note that all those with whom she has discussed the word
"agree that the only meaning assignable to the word, *as it stands,*
is that of a cage, or dark room, where falcons would be kept at
the period of moulting. . . ."[22] The word is introduced early in *Glastonbury,* kept in place with Evans as a motif of transformation (molt-

ing), and used to close Evans's involvement in the narrative. Transformation through the powers of the Grail provides the overall narratorial repetition that gives the text its coherence. Esplumeoir does not establish a subtheme or subtext so much as it marks a continuing and enforcing statement, working through repetition and with varying intensities—casual at first, tense on the day of the killing, quiet, indeed buried, at the end. The longing for transformation identifies the consciousness of the individual actors, each of whom gives such longing unique expression, and in this longing lies the coherence of the novel.

Glastonbury itself—the town and its history—also must be brought into the design. Its history, back as far as the ancient lake village, is marked by a long series of transformations: from lake to village, from pagan to Christian, with Joseph's staff changed into the ever-blooming Glastonbury thorn, the recurrences of floods, the rise and fall of the Abbey (its early destruction by fire, the re-building, and its final destruction by Henry VIII), the attempts to restore the Abbey, to dig up Arthur, and to keep continually in the mind the presence of the Grail.[23] We do not wonder at Owen Evans's conviction that Glastonbury is sacred ground.

Evans, like Geard, is obsessed by the thought of Merlin's transformation, and such obsession provides motifs that contribute to the complicated organization of the novel. As Charles Lock implies, reading the novel as a series of "unsettling" shifts from character to character is inadequate because it does not account for the counter-pointing that takes place as the focus moves from character to character: we do not, hopefully, forget one character when another comes into view. The complicated organization is part of the "defamiliarizing" procedure in the narrative. Each character of any importance in the text is caught up in the process of transformation, each with a difference, although each character struggles with some form of sexual desire that is irreconcilable with their aspirations. If Glastonbury is the ground for Blake's "And did those feet in ancient time / Walk upon England's mountain green," it is also the site for the bitter frustrations of "Ah, Sun-Flower." These internal struggles establish patterns of "doubling," and this is most obviously the case with Evans. But as Glen Cavaliero has noted, patterns of doubling occur not only in characters, but in landscape, ancestry and ideologies as well.[24] It is as if the whole world of Glastonbury, at this point in history, perhaps at every point in its history, is polyphonic. To establish the polyphonic form as it relates to Evans' search for Esplumeoir it will be necessary to see him in relation to his arch-double, John Crow.

Contingency has it that John Crow meets Owen Evans at Stonehenge. Crow has set out from Norfolk to walk to Glastonbury, and he arrives at Stonehenge, exhausted, just at nightfall, to find his opposite. Both Crow and Evans are caught up in the mystery of the place. Both are wanderers, seekers, and their coincidental meeting at Stonehenge becomes a visitation. They have arrived at a place of worship, but their worship takes a different form in each case. For Evans, the stones must signify something other, something signified. It is important for him that the stones have come from certain places, that some stones have special uses, that Stonehenge was a temple: "'the greatest Temple of the Druids,'" he tells Crow (101). Crow, on the other hand, is willing to accept the stones just as stones. He could worship a stone, he says: "'Certainly. *Simply because it's a stone!*'" (100). He acknowledges their awesomeness and even prays to them: "What the instinctive heart of John Crow recognized in this great Body of Stones—both in those bearing-up and in those borne-up—was that they themselves, just as they were, had become, by the mute creative action of four thousand years, authentic Divine Beings" (103). They remain stones, however, and such meaning as they have has been given to them. This meeting at Stonehenge sets out the contradiction, the doubling of the two characters, an attraction and repulsion, that carries on throughout the book. Evans's dark and complicated sado-masochism that urges him toward violence both to himself and others, to arrange his own crucifixion, and to witness a murder, materializes finally in the actual murder scene—the crushing of a skull with an iron bar. John Crow is to be the victim. Evans is drawn to kill—or at least see killed—his double. His choice of a victim is not random, nor was Powys's.

After the meeting at Stonehenge, Evans offers Crow a ride to Glastonbury. During the ride there is an intense interplay of consciousnesses. Crow observes that Evans's conversation is itself doubled, composed of "two levels of intensity." One was pedantic and patronizing, the other "not merely humble and sad but tragically humble and sad. . . . And another thing he noticed about the conversation of this man in the large bowler hat and the tightly black overcoat was that it was always when the conversation returned to Glastonbury that this secondary tone came into his voice" (105). As their familiarity increases, Crow asks, I think tauntingly, "'Do you believe, Mr. Evans, . . . in always struggling to find a meaning to life?'" The Welshman replies hesitantly: "'It's not . . . it never has been . . . in my . . . nature . . . to take life . . . in that . . . way . . . at all. I find my meanings everywhere. My . . .' he hesitated for a long time, 'difficulties,' he went on, 'are entirely personal'"

(107). Crow is delighted with Evans's troubled answer, and he confirms his delight, not without malice, with a victorious: "'I simply cannot understand what people mean when they talk of life having a purpose'" (107). He does say, in the same passage, that he finds meanings everywhere, but he finds them in all living things, hence he has no need to search for some theoretical, symbolic, or magical purpose to life. Crow has no use for the word Esplumeoir. It is precisely on this word that the two characters shadow each other. Evans seeks *special* meaning in objects: in ruins, legends, remnants from the past, words, stories, and especially books. He had read Malory twenty-five times, and there are other books as well. To John Crow, this search for special meaning is a practice to be ridiculed, and he has his chance to do this when he agrees to become Manager for the great Glastonbury Pageant. What Powys skillfully, brilliantly, establishes is the doubling motif that shapes the novel's design. For our concerns here, this is the doubling between Owen Evans's fetishism—his life-illusion and obsessive search of Esplumeoir—and John Crow's skeptical, indeed cynical, materialism.

Evans's life-illusion is an extension of Wolf Solent's. It is based in the mythology of a struggle within the First Cause. As he explains to his wife Cordelia: "'Life's a war to the death . . . between the Spirits of Good and Evil'" (346). Solent at least believed that he was on the side of the Good. Evans cannot say this. He goes on, in his Manichean way: "'These Spirits are everywhere. They are encountering each other in every crevice of consciousness and on every plane of Being. Life springs from their conflict. Life *is* their conflict. If the Spirit of Good conquered entirely—as one day I hope it will—the whole teeming ocean of life would dry up. There would be no more life!'" (349). He believes in a *telos*, an apocalypse. As the conversation continues, he envisages "'the whole pit of Hell in ourselves,'" and he cries out that, although some souls may be protected, other souls have trapdoors in their floor leading down to . . . to places unthinkable!'" (350). Powys will not let this scene end too soon, and so for several more pages the unhappy Mr. Evans tells his story: "'Cordelia, do you think there are forms of evil so horrible that nothing can wash them out?'" Having accepted Nature as violently dualistic, he tries to place Christ outside of Nature (a repeated Powysian tactic): "'Of course,' he murmured, turning his back to her and passing his fingers up and down along the bureau's edge, 'Christ is outside Nature; and *that's* my chance! He's outside, isn't he, Cordelia . . . outside altogether?'" (352). He has just told Cordelia that John Crow has asked him to play Christ in the pageant: "'I thought I'd realise in that way how He really did take such things on Him'" (352). Crow had earlier urged Evans on when he auditioned for the role, but we recall that, for Crow, the whole pageant was to be a sham: "'Seriously, Sir,' he blurted out, 'You'll *have* to play Christ in my Pageant. You will! You will! You're not exactly the *type* . . . but that doesn't matter a bit. Oh, you will! You will! Why, you'll beat the Oberammergau person hollow'" (258). In response to Evans's "'Only you'll have to make it as real as you can,'" Crow, regarding "his friend through shrewd, screwed-up, meditative eyelids," says, with the malice of the Double: "'Oh, we'll make it real enough.'" The two men, opposites in fundamental ways, are drawn together in the peculiar fantasy of the event: even the skeptical John Crow was "too occupied with an imaginative picture of that future scene to care very much what he was promising Mr. Evans" (258).

Evans hopes that the pageant will produce some special event, that a "'new Religion . . . different . . . from any that's ever been . . . will . . . will . . . will make a crack in the world. . . .'" He visualizes that "'Something will break out, through that crack, *that will take away our torment'*" (159). What it is that will break out through that crack is Esplumeoir. Mr. Evans is indeed tied on the cross for the pageant, but the ropes are mismanaged, and the scene changes into what John Crow seems to have had in mind. The crowd watches while two girls dance beneath the cross—coached, we assume, by a cynically erotic John Crow: "they made several sinuous movements with their flexible hips and several swaying movements with their bare arms . . ." (600). While this carnival goes on, Mr. Evans hemorrhages on the cross as he cries out the words of the forsaken Christ. The hoped-for miracle does not take place, and Evans's first attempt to find a crack in Nature fails. John Crow, the shadowy opposite, is connected point by point to Evans's desperate show, and Crow's malice succeeds. The pageant is a thoroughly successful sham, and Mr. Evans almost dies. His imitation of Christ has failed, and his torment has not been purged.

Evans's other hope lies in his quest for Esplumeoir and he hopes it will be realized by the completion of his monumental Life of Merlin. Merlin replaces Christ as the arch-mage. The two allusions— to Christ and to Merlin—are closely connected.[25] Christ disappears after the crucifixion, taken to the tomb provided by Joseph of Arimethea, later of Glastonbury fame. There he awaits transformation. Evans's hope has been that through some miracle his own feigned sacrifice at the pageant might allow him a new life, a release from his torment, a resurrection. As we have seen, that miracle did not take place. But Evans also has his conviction that Glastonbury is the site of the entombment of Arthur and Merlin, the Merlin to which he has devoted his study and his life. Merlin may have the power that Christ—Merlin's counterpart, his double—seemingly lacks. Evans's longing for Esplumeoir parallels his longing for a vision of the Grail: "'If only I could see it once . . . just once . . . with my own eyes . . . what Merlin hid . . . what Joseph found . . . the Cauldron of Yr Echwyd . . . the undying grail . . . this madness would pass from me . . . but . . . but.'" The cadenced pleading breaks down in despair: "'but . . . I . . . I . . . *don't . . . want . . .* to see it!'" (151).

From his scholarly work and his accumulated Grail texts (he has read everything), Mr. Evans is convinced that the Grail will appear wherever Esplumeoir is, and his reading of the texts tells him that Glastonbury is the place. We now know why during the trip from Stonehenge Evans's face turned strange whenever he spoke to John Crow about Glastonbury. Glastonbury as the burial place of Arthur is important to Evans, but it is more important that Glastonbury is the burial place, the waiting place, the Esplumeoir of Merlin. Evans's view of the Grail is that its origins are Welsh, Celtic, pre-Christian. It is Crow who, in the ominous logic of the doubling, explains Evans' view: "'My friend Mr. Evans . . . says that it's neither King Arthur nor Joseph of Arimethea that's the real hidden force still active in Glastonbury. . . . It's my opinion that it has to do with Merlin. But I expect I'm all wrong. When I mentioned Merlin all he did was to quote a lot of Welsh Triads in Welsh. He's a queer character, my friend Evans, but he interests me very much'" (120). Here is the narrator's commentary on Mr. Evans's involvement with Esplumeoir:

> As all Merlin's disciples well know, there is a mysterious word used in one of the Grail Books about his final disappearance. This is the word "Esplumeoir." It is inevitable from the context to interpret this as some "Great Good Place," some mystic Fourth Dimension, or Nirvanic apotheosis, into which the magician deliberately sank, or rose; thus committing a sort of inspired suicide, a mysterious dying in order to live more fully. As he sought for one of his favourite passages—for "Esplumeoir" does not appear in Malory—he kept murmuring that particular invocation under his breath, pondering intently on the occult escape offered by this runic clue from the pain of the world, an escape so strangely handed down from far-off centuries in these thaumaturgic syllables. (178–79)

Here is the key word, and the inference is, as we are told elsewhere in the passage, that it represents all the "Scraps, and morsels and fragments, mythical, historical, natural, supernatural" that have become for Evans the essence of the Grail story. Esplumeoir is the Grail's presence, and it is an "invocation," something murmured, a conglomerate sign that has become for Evans the only hope he has for an end to his torment. As a sign of Merlin's life, a life that Evans has committed himself to write and, through his devotion to Geard, to serve, it is the central sign in Evans's life. Evans's life is marked by dualities, and it is necessary now to identify his own countertext. Earlier I referred to the passage in which Evans talks about certain souls who have "trapdoors in their floors leading down to . . . to . . . places unthinkable." The "unthinkable" place for Evans is the basement of the bookstore where he works occasionally. Located in that basement is the countertext, indeed the subtext, a "theological" work named *The Unpardonable Sin*. It sits on the shelf next to a copy of St. Augustine's *Confessions*, and close by is the manuscript copy of Evans' *Vita Merlini* (245–47).[26] The books provide a polyphony: St. Augustine provides the progress of the transformed soul, *The Unpardonable Sin* the world of Evans's temptation and despair, and the *Vita Merlini* the ground of Evans's struggle to find a way out of this temptation and despair. For whatever reasons Evans visits this cellar, he finds his way to *The Unpardonable Sin*, and, with knees weakening and hands jerking, he reads a passage in that book. In that passage is the image of "a killing blow delivered by an iron bar" (250). This is his countertext. The blow is to be delivered to the head of his arch-enemy, his double, the cynical doubter of Esplumeoir, John Crow.

Jessie Weston, we have seen, relates Esplumeoir to "a cage, a dark room, where falcons would be kept at the period of moulting" (a merlin of course, is a falcon), and molting takes us to the motif of transformation. Glastonbury is, in Evans' mind, the place of rebirth into a new life. His failure—his misreading of the word—is that he seeks verification for the possibilities of this new life in the external evidence of space; he seeks verification in Glastonbury and in its relics, as if there were some special meaning in the site and its debris. He fails to accept the alternative that verification only will be found in his own selfhood, in his being in the world. As we have seen, this selfhood is severely impaired. Evans's quest for Esplumeoir is itself de-mystified by the dire actualities of his being in the world, by his irreconcilable sexual torment. Evans's consciousness is caught up in a world where contingency rules.

As we have seen, there is another force present in Evans as he has been created by Powys's imaginative logic, and that is his obsession with gazing at the killing of his double, the skeptical materialist John Crow. In the "Iron Bar" chapter, Powys works out this confrontation in an astonishingly cohesive way. It becomes cohesive, paradoxically, when we read it polyphonically. Even in this scene, contingency will rule. The confrontation takes place on Glastonbury Tor, the very ground, we assume, of Mr. Evans's Esplumeoir. Evans himself is not directly involved in Mad Bet's plot to kill John Crow, but he arranges to be hidden at the right moment in such a way that he will be able to gaze at the killing blow. The details, the carefully organized complications, and the narrative pacing[27] need not be restated or explicated here, but we do note that it is Evans's wife Cordelia—the name bears out its tragic dimensions—who uncovers his involvement and breaks his obsession. They rush to the scene to warn John Crow. The conventional eradication of the double is now reversed: by *saving* John Crow Evans will possibly free himself from his torment. But the murder is accomplished, and by rule of chance, Crow's closest friend (who provides another figure of doubling in the text) is the victim. Evans views the gruesome scene, is violently sick, and—this *is* a romance—is transformed into "visibly and palpably and in every physical respect, if not an old man, certainly an elderly man" (1055). Evans becomes a "slow-moving, absentminded, white-haired gentlemen, reading a blue-covered book as he walks along or as he leans upon the fence":

> This book, if any passer-by were bold enough to peruse its title, would turn out to be Malory's "Morte D'Arthur," but such a stranger would not be able to guess that what Mr. Evans is searching for there is something not to be found in Malory at all—nor in any Grail Book, since the time of the great Welshman Bleheris—namely the real meaning of the mystical word Esplumeoir. (1055–56)

Mr. Evans did not, we assume, finish his life of Merlin, and Esplumeoir remains hidden from him. We note that what in all the early references has been the "mysterious" word has here, at Mr. Evans' closing, become the "mystical" word. The narrative voice is ironic in this final view of Evans. The change to "mystical" in its ironic context sharply adjusts the word and transforms itself to the demystification that Powys announces throughout *A Glastonbury Romance.*

For Evans, the word, whether mysterious or mystical, has failed, just as the feigned crucifixion at the pageant failed. John Crow is deeply involved in all aspects of Mr. Evans's quest for rebirth. To a considerable degree, each man defines his failure in close proximity to and in the face of the other. We discern a carefully structured coherence in the development of Evans's consciousness and in the relationship between his consciousness and Crow's. This dialogical cohesion is formed from their confrontations of the processes of transformation that occur in Glastonbury. In Bakhtin's formulation as outlined earlier, "plurality of consciousnesses combine . . . but do not merge" in any unity of the Glastonbury event.

Jungian scholars have written on Merlin and his withdrawal from the world.[28] They have added a store of information to the mystery of the word. Esplumeoir fits into the theme of transformation of self that is a central concern of Jungian research. It is tempting to extract Powys's use of the word to fit it into the Jungian scheme, but such extraction would do violence to the controlled intricacy that Powys has created. Esplumeoir de-mystified yet brought into an enigmatic but living presence in *A Glastonbury Romance*, takes its place in the polyphonic structure.

The doubled world of Evans and Crow—on the one hand, a Manichean hunter for an illusory *telos*, and on the other, a skeptical materialist moved often by malice—is not the only narrative interaction in the novel. Polyphony disallows such monological privileging. The patterns of exchange are complicated, as they are in a Dostoevskian narrative, and although I have concentrated on Evans and Crow here, I only have been able to outline their relationship. The novel reveals a deep structure in the various engagements of Geard and Sam Dekker and Evans and Crow, indeed of all the inhabitants of the Glastonbury chronotope. The motif of Esplumeoir, read polyphonically, explains the series of transformations and disappearances, and it provides the narratorial repetition that gives the novel its monumental cohesiveness.

Notes

1. John Cowper Powys, *A Glastonbury Romance* (1932; reprint ed., London: Macdonald; Hamilton, N. Y.: Colgate University Press, 1955). All subsequent references are cited parenthetically in the text by page number. The "calamitous events" are recorded in chapter 29, "The Iron Bar." Powys's preface to this edition provides an important statement on the novel.

2. Mikhail Bakhtin, *Problems of Dostoevsky's Poetics*, trans. and ed. Caryl Emerson, intro. Wayne C. Booth, *Theory and History of Literature* 8 (Minneapolis: University of Minnesota Press, 1984).

3. Both Bakhtin and Powys wrote on Dostoevsky and Rabelais, and they share common interpretations. Bakhtin's theories on "carnival" have close affinities to Powys's, particularly to the pageant in *Glastonbury*. They share views on the earth and the body, particularly on what Powys calls "that incongruous and disgustingly

humorous intermingling of the excremental with the sacramental of which Rabelais makes so much" *(Glastonbury,* p. xvi).

4. Charles Lock, "'Multiverse' . . . language which makes language impossible" *Powys Review* 5 (Summer 1979):63–74.

5. Ibid. p. 72.

6. Charles Lock has presented a much fuller discussion of polyphony in his article "Polyphonic Powys: Dostoevsky, Bakhtin, and *A Glastonbury Romance,*" *University of Toronto Quarterly* 55 (Spring 1986):261–81. He focuses on an extensive range of narrative situations in Powys's stylistic development. In my discussion here, written before Professor Lock's article appeared, I am concerned with a particular occurrence, that is, the relation between Owen Evans and John Crow, within the context of polyphonic representation.

7. Lock, "'Multiverse,'" p. 72.

8. Ibid.

9 I discuss this term below, but for a thorough presentation of Bakhtin's use of the term, see *The Dialogical Imagination: Four Essays by M. M. Bakhtin,* trans. Caryl Emerson and Michael Holquist, ed. Michael Holquist, *University of Texas Slavic Series* 1 (Austin: University of Texas Press, 1981).

10. Glen Cavaliero, *John Cowper Powys: Novelist* (Oxford: Oxford University Press, 1973), p. 67.

11. Ibid.

12. Ibid., pp. 78, 60, 61.

13. Morine Krissdottir, *John Cowper Powys and the Magical Quest* (London: Macdonald, 1980), p. 41.

14. Ibid., p. x.

15. G. Wilson Knight, *The Saturnian Quest* (New York: Barnes and Noble, 1964), p. 41.

16. John Brebner, *The Demon Within* (London: Macdonald, 1973).

17. Booth, in *Problems of Dostoevsky's Poetics,* p. xx.

18. Ibid., p. xxi.

19. John Cowper Powys, *Dostoevsky,* (London: Village Press, 1974), p. 8; first published by John Lane, The Bodley Head, 1946.

20. Bakhtin, *Problems of Dostoevsky's Poetics,* p. 6.

21. Ibid., p. 8.

22. Jessie L. Weston, *The Legend of Sir Perceval* 2 (London: David Nutt, 1909; reprint ed., New York: AMS Press, 1972), pp. 230, 329–30.

23. John Thomas gives an excellent account of the Glastonbury tradition in his review article, "'The King Edgar Chapel Man': Bond, Glastonbury, and the 'Alternative' Theory of Gothic Architecture," *Powys Review* 9 (1981/82):35–43. Thomas reminds us that the pageant had an antecedent in the Glastonbury Festival, launched in 1914 and continuing into the 1920s, that took the form "of Bayreuth-like presentation of Arthurian music-dramas" (40). Susan Rands provides detailed and vivid commentary on the Glastonbury site and its associated traditions in "Aspects of the Topography of *A Glastonbury Romance,*" *Powys Review* 20 (1987):27–40.

24. Cavaliero, *Novelist,* pp. 61–62. He uses "antitheses" and "opposites" rather than the term "doubling."

25. See Helen Adolf, "The Esplumoir Merlin: A Study of its Cabalistic Sources," *Speculum* 21 (1946):172–93. Adolf traces a variety of possible sources, including the connection between Merlin and the falcon of the same name. She is concerned with the images of the Messiah developed in Cabalistic literature and extends the discussion into medieval Christian literature.

26. This particular scene sets out a dialogical occurrence between Evans and "Holy" Sam Dekker. Sam has come to the bookstore to obtain a copy of the *Confessions*. When Evans removes the *Confessions* from the shelf, *The Unpardonable Sin* falls over into the vacated space, filling an absence, as it were. The scene is expertly managed by Powys, especially in the way that *Sam's* theological dilemmas are brought into juxtaposition with Evans's.

27. Narrative organization, particularly in the "Iron Bar" chapter, is the focus of an unpublished master's thesis by James Ryan, "A Paradigm of Knowings: Narrative Control in Selected Works of John Cowper Powys," Carleton University, Ottawa, Canada, 1984.

28. Emma Jung and Marie-Louise Von Franz, *The Grail Legend*, trans. Andrea Dykes (London: Hodder and Stoughton, 1971), esp. chapter 24, "The Disappearance of Merlin."

Rituals of Return

A. Thomas Southwick

At least since the republication of Powys's earlier fiction began in Britain twenty-five years ago, opinion has divided drastically as to the quality and value of his achievement. Unlike T. F. Powys, with his secure minor position as a sardonic fabulist, or Llewelyn Powys, manifestly a poetical essayist of distinct though dated charm and character, John Cowper Powys bids to be taken as a grand master, for all his evident flaws, or dismissed for his pretensions. Conflicting positions were mapped out after Powys's death by two distinguished critics. For George Steiner, *Wolf Solent* is one of the very great novels in the language, *Owen Glendower* superior to Scott, the *Autobiography* a "masterpiece," and *A Glastonbury Romance* Shakespearean in its characterizations and bolder than Lawrence in its exploration of eroticism.[1] For V. S. Pritchett, on the other hand, *Wolf Solent* and *Glastonbury* are the works of an inferior romancer, a mystic embarrassingly deficient in his sense of the comic.[2]

Nor, during Powys's lifetime, were his associates by any means thorough admirers of his books. Louis Wilkinson, who loved him, could not abide the long romances. Dorothy Richardson, grateful for Powys's advocacy of her fiction, derogated his each new novel covertly, presenting her reservations in letters to him as the comments of her husband. Llewelyn Powys thought all of his brother's books carelessly written.

Although an avowed admirer of Powys, I believe a middle position possible, dependent on definition of Powys's strengths and weaknesses, his intentions and technique. Like Dr. Steiner, I recognize the need for a "shared idiom of collaborative dissent."[3] Its absence I believe stems from the nature of Powys's works and the response they evoke. Extreme partisanship and denunciation in his case result not from writing that is initially obscure or whose appeal, ultimately, is quite limited—although Powys is, like any original author, troublingly strange on first encounter and his works do resonate most in a certain kind of reader. Rather, it is the cumulative and, one might say, collaborative effect that Powys's books require that makes detached judgment of them so difficult. His candor and didacticism, his concerns and blindspots are so singular and evident that they distract immediate enjoyment of his writings: seemingly, one knows Powys before one knows any of his books. However, with this knowledge, much of their apparent inconsequence and foolishness becomes meaningful. It is not merely a matter of understanding the books biographically; rather one recognizes that in him imagination and language work in a very personal way, and then, because of the integrity of their operation, is persuaded to share in their effort.

All of Powys's best books improve with re-reading; all remain and develop in memory with the vividness of places long inhabited. The sheer breadth and inclusiveness of his books foster this effect. Henry Miller's comparison of *A Glastonbury Romance* to common nourishment, abundant yet precious, is apt.

> It took me almost a year to read it. I read only a few pages at a time, savoring and re-savoring every single morsel, every tiniest crumb, and dreading to come to the end.[4]

Powys's writings promote and sustain the sort of imaginative escape that is their theme and purpose. But the way to such an escape, because of its privacy and its extensiveness, is not easily accessible. As Steiner notes, Powys's best fiction calls "for patience, for a suspension of disenchantment, for a delight in the sheer prodigality of English speech."[5] It is far easier to dissolve this magic forest by concentrating on the absurd stuntedness of some of its trees.

Admiration for the generosity of Powys's imagination should not bar recognition of his besetting vices: his language can turn windy and slack; preachments intrude upon and obscure all of his narratives; indulgent and addicted to the picturesque and the mythologically resonant, he crowds and diverts the structure of meaning in his tales; some of his characters are unpersuasively drawn and motivated, perhaps most those meant to reflect the author's viewpoint; he often fails to represent persuasively human interaction at the most common, conversational level—here his lack of a conventional comic sense is most damaging; he slights or distorts the social and political dimension; he weakens many of his large scenes of action by excessively static or indirect methods of presentation.

All of this matters to the experience of reading Powys, especially to reading him initially, and to judging him. It is only for the dedicated Powysian, cherishing every morsel of a large romance like *Glastonbury*, that such flaws do not damn him as a resolutely undisciplined amateur. Through familiarity with Powys's intentions and strengths, however, such vices, although never transformed into virtues, do recede in importance and come to seem necessary to the whole accomplishment.

Powys's strengths and accomplishment I would define thus: (1) to tell a story with moment to moment immediacy of sensation and memory, whatever the cost to structural shapeliness and selectiveness; (2) to purvey emotion at its most private and, at times, shameful, in small scenes of confrontation that succeed, despite their strained dialogue, through the deep exploration of feeling; (3) to present in their grand narrative style, with its resources of incantation, metaphor, and allusion and despite the danger of overblown tendentiousness, suprarational forces at work in the locale and action; (4) to suggest, moments of vision and mystery using subtle analogy with naturalistic detail and faithful depiction of internal states; (5) to evoke the displaced and disinherited, their resentment and refuges, against a detailed background of custom and belief; and (6) to portray a range of human habitations in their place in nature and to insinuate, through this interrelationship, racial and communal influences that precede the social and political.

Powys is a writer more difficult than most to represent using short passages; much depends on the atmosphere and premises of his books. However, I will attempt to exemplify through his most characteristic and valuable passages both his distinct gifts and, where relevant, his excesses.

The peculiarly Powysian moment depicts a mind blissfully, self-forgetfully awash with sensations and memories. Powys's conception of "the impersonal" is appropriate to describing this desired state: "The impersonal is an escape, bringing with it a feeling of large, cool, quiet, and unruffled space."[6] His romances exploit this sense of vastness and directionlessness. It may be evoked through the contemplation of nature or, more typically, in contemplation of long human continuity within a particular natural atmosphere. Here Magnus Muir, in *Weymouth Sands*, evokes the essence of the sea-coast town through the interplay of immediate sensations and deep-seated memories.

> . . . as he undressed himself the familiar smell of dead seaweed kept entering his room; and a strange phantasmal Weymouth, a mystical town made of a solemn sadness, gathered about him, a town built out of the smell of dead seaweed, a town whose very walls and roofs were composed of flying spindrift and tossing rain. Lying in bed in the faint glimmer of the grate he could hear the waves on the beach, and a great

flood of sadness swept over him. Human hearts seemed all so pitifully
frustrated! . . .

For a while he floated helplessly on the tide of this feeling, watching
his big red curtains slowly inflate themselves and bulge forward, only
to be sucked back, with the retreat of the wind, into hollow answering
concavities. . . .

Then while he settled down under the bed-clothes, there came before
his eyes once more the spire, the clock, the statue of the king, the
outline of the Nothe, as he had felt them when he sat in the cold opposite
the deserted donkey-stand. And the impression gathered upon him that
these simple things had a significance beyond all explanation; that they
were in truth the outward "accidents" of some interior "substance" that
belonged—by a strange law of transubstantiation—to some life of his
that was independent of the humiliations of his ordinary experience;
independent, for instance, of whether when he went to see Curly tomor-
row she made him feel silly and old. His waking thought turned these
things into a sort of magical abracadabra, devoid of all intelligible meaning, but offering, like some invocation in an unknown tongue, an escape
from all his anxieties and shames! (39–40)[7]

Noteworthy initially is the consonance of the physical presences invoked to the changing temper of the character's thought. The drifting
smell of seaweed and the toss of waves stir his helpless floating
on a "tide" and "flood" of feeling—a responsiveness to external stim-
uli of which the curtains, billowing and then returning to "hollow
answering concavities" are an emblem. Likewise, when Magnus's
mind turns to stationary objects such as the spire and the cliffs
of the Nothe, the permanent background of his life in Weymouth,
they reflect an "independent" existence apart from "his ordinary
experience," a refuge from the flux of his emotions. Second, these
sensations are, quite explicitly, an "escape" from his own identity,
first in generalized contemplation of the human condition (upon
which reflections on the predicaments of the other characters in the
book follow), and then by removing him entirely from his own distressed feelings. The Wordsworth of "Tintern Abbey" and "Resolution and Independence" comes to mind in following the movements
of Magnus's reverie; the difference, a crucial one in defining the
character of Powys's fiction, is that Wordsworth departs from his
intimations of a more profound reality resolved, in the spirit of young
manhood, on a more courageous grappling with the issues of his
life. For Powys's disappointed middle-aged protagonists, such as
Magnus, the experience of "impersonal" moments liberates them
from the distress of their own identities rather than fortifying their
sense of themselves; it offers escape.

Besides marking a distinction between Wordsworth and Powys, this emphasis on escape raises a difficulty in the development on Powys's stories. His "moments" do not reflect on his plots or the action of his characters. (Magnus's reverie, for instance, temporarily rescues him from his place in the story, his relationship to Curly.) The effect of many of the most moving of Powys's scenes is to retard the progress of his story. This can irritate the reader for whom romance consists primarily of vivid narrative and characters, but it supports Powys's intention of evoking a stratum of existence apart from external action and identity. The significance of the moment consists in and of itself.

Impersonal identity supplanting personality, a "transubstantiation" related to his depictions of solitary reverie, marks Powys's fine small scenes of emotional encounter. Such transformations occur under the influence of love throughout his fiction, but also, perhaps more strikingly, where the precipitating emotions are more private—shame and jealousy before an unattainable object of desire. A remarkable example appears in *Wolf Solent*, precipitated by the bitterness of Wolf's mother toward her late husband and now toward her son's marriage, as expressed first through her typically ironic dialogue.

> "It's all right! I can stand it!" she cried. "I had plenty of practice with your father, and now I'm going to have the same thing with you. . . . Oh, it's a cruel thing to be a woman!" (448–49)[8]

Beneath the sarcastic verbalization of Ann Solent's anger, the "impersonal" reality of her emotion emerges. With "remorseful shame," her son recognizes "that this formidable body, so grotesquely reduced, was the actual human animal out of whose entrails he had been dragged into light and air" (450). Powys invokes an "animal" reality beneath human consciousness. This awareness transforms Mrs. Solent. She rises above her son "with that grand convulsed face and those expanded breasts, while her fine hands, clutching at her belt, seemed to display a wild desire to strip herself naked before him, to overwhelm him with the wrath of her maternal body, bare to the outrage of his impiety" (449). The alternation between Mrs. Solent's hysterical sarcasm and her embodiment of outraged motherhood continues throughout the scene until she gives Wolf "a hot, intense, tyrannous kiss," and they sit together at tea in what seems "an obscure reversion to those forgotten diurnal nourishments which he must have shared with her before his flesh was separated from hers" (453). While the plot of the novel and the dialogue of Wolf's quarrel with his mother affirm their separation, the emotional and

imaginative weight of the scene grants Mrs. Solent her desired recla-
mation and Wolf his regression.

"The tragedy of passion often consists in the depths of harsh
unlovableness into which it throws its victims" (638), Powys comments on another scene of shameful desire in *A Glastonbury Romance*.[9]
In such scenes, the writer persuasively conveys the eruptions of passion in suppressed, prosaic individuals. Euphemia Drew, like Ann
Solent, is a woman tyrannously reverent of social convention; in
this light Powys has presented her objection to the love of her em-
ployee, Mary Crow, for her trampish cousin John. Then, on Mary's
wedding night, she refuses to allow her to join her husband.

> . . . the two women confronted each other between the fragile coffee-table
> and the fireless grate. The elder wore her usual black silk garment with
> the heavy brooch securing the old lace frill on her withered neck. Opposed
> to her gaunt figure, Mary's form, in her low-cut white dress and big
> crimson sash, looked very young and soft and girlish.
>
> "I'd like you to . . . I'd like you not to . . ."
>
> Miss Drew was evidently struggling to say something that tore at
> her vitals.
>
> "I'd like—" she gasped again.
>
> "What is it, oh, what is it?" stammered Mary, awed, a litle scared
> and completely bewildered.
>
> "I'd like you not to go to him tonight. I'd like you to stay with
> me tonight . . . our last night . . . as you are!"
>
> "Of course, my dear, if you feel it like that—"
>
> "I mean . . . not leave me at all . . . just this once . . . I mean . . .
> let me hold you . . . all night . . . close to me—"
>
> Mary's face must have expressed such trouble, such pity, such confused
> agitation, that the old woman changed her tone to a quieter one. "It
> would be nothing to you . . . to watch . . . to be there . . . to be near
> me . . . just this once . . . and then—" she swallowed a rasping dry
> sob—"tomorrow . . . you shall go."
>
> "Dear! I must think. He'll be at the gate in a few minutes; I must—I
> don't know *what* to say. For him to go back alone—through the streets—
> to that room—oh, I don't know what to do!"
>
> She flung herself down on a chair, her red sash trailing to the carpet,
> like a great stream of blood from a stab in her side.
>
> Miss Drew leaned one of her long, tight-sleeved arms upon the mantle-
> piece and watched her.
>
> The void of her longing for her, of her losing her, throbbed within
> her like a hollow cave, round the walls of which a bitter stifling smoke
> was whirling, seeking an exit.
>
> The French clock on the mantlepiece ticked on remorsely: *tick-tock,
> tock-tick, tick-tock,* as if there were, behind its hidden wheels, some demon

of the inanimate, that was taking vengeance for all the hammering and tinkerings it had had at the hands of its man-creators (636–37).

Powys sustains the confused movements of emotion in the two women through a series of drastic reversals. Out of pity Mary decides to herself to indulge Miss Drew. Shame and passion mingle in Miss Drew's plaintiveness as she sobs and murmurs to Mary. Then, dragged to her feet, she fatally commands Mary to be gone.

> Miss Drew, by the tone in which she said, "Go up . . . that man is waiting," had done her utmost to destroy the very pity upon which her fate depended. . . .
> "Well . . . have you decided against me . . . against the one thing I've ever begged . . . on my knees . . . of a living soul?"
> Her words seemed to come, not from her mouth, but from some other Miss Drew—a towering image of devastated frustration—that hung in the air between them. (638–39).

In the alternation of passion and coldness, Miss Drew's essential self has come forth; there follows her stammered confession of prejudices and longings before Mary states her decision to stay and comfort the old woman. She leaves to tell the maid her message to pass to John and returns to find Miss Drew in possession of herself and commanding her, with her old dignity, to leave.

Powys traces the flow and ebb of thwarted passion and distressed response not primarily by the exchange of dialogue, which takes on a somewhat stilted, automatic quality—as in Miss Drew's repeated protest, "I'm not a bad woman" and Mary's repeated murmur, "The poor heart!"—but rather in his observation of physical and emotional particularities. Miss Drew erect, in her habitual place with one arm along the mantlepiece, manipulates Mary, coldly cloaks herself in self-pity, gives voice to her desolation, and finally reassumes authority. At Mary's feet or sunk into the sofa where her mother told her it was "weakness" to sit (639), she implores and accepts Mary's comfort. Likewise Mary's commands to Miss Drew, first to "Get up!" and then to lie on the sofa (638, 640), imply the hesitancy and then the release of her sympathy more fully than her otherwise impotent words. Similarly, Mary's response to the setting objectifies the motions of her reaction from shock to indecision to resolved empathy. She first looks "distractedly" at the clock on Miss Drew's mantlepiece "which went on ticking in exactly the same tone as if its mistress had been pouring out tea" for her neighbor, the vicar (637). Later, when Miss Drew rebukes her, Mary opens the window and stares out toward the gate where John awaits her (639). Finally, decisively, she shuts the window "with a violent jerk of her strong bare arms" and rushes to embrace Miss Drew (640). By so full an evocation, Powys's scenes of personal drama persuasively convey intensity and complexity of emotion. He mirrors the feelings of both characters and refuses to imply judgment of either.

Typically, Miss Drew's scene with Mary has no consequence on the plot of *A Glastonbury Romance*. After sending Mary to John, Miss Drew never again takes central importance in the story; having once come memorably to life, she resumes her secondary role. Such are the mysteries of the seemingly directionless progress of episodes in a Powys novel. More consequential to *Glastonbury*'s continuity— but as irritating to some readers as the irrelevance of Miss Drew's revelation—is Powys's embroidery of the scene with implications of its counterparts in the existence of animals and inanimate things. The clock on Miss Drew's mantlepiece seems to take vengeance for its suffering at the hands of men. Moths rush in through Mary's open window to die at the lamp and candles, "little suicides of blind desire" (639)—immolations that recall the "stifled smoke" trapped within Miss Drew and her anguished complaint, "*It's this Love* that's burning my life up!" (638). Powys attempts to populate his fiction with other-than-human consciousnesses and, conversely, to imply other-than-human responses in his characters, as when Mary throws her arms around Miss Drew "as she would have thrown them around a wounded animal" (640). Miss Drew at this point exemplifies pain, aside from her human identity. Such denotations embroider a scene that would function dramatically without them; yet Powys's wont to ascribe universal import to his narratives, either directly or through the comments of his characters, necessitates this generalizing. John Crow, waiting for Mary, hears "the pitiful cry of a beast in pain" and likens it to Miss Drew's suffering at the loss of Mary. "His mind was beating now against the blood-stained wedge of the world's pain" (643).

The effectiveness of universalized reactions such as John's depends on the reasonableness of their correlation to the action. John's conclusion, "that not one perfect day can be enjoyed by anyone without hearing something groan or moan," appears reasonable, given the intensity with which Miss Drew and Mary's emotions have been portrayed and his own role as beneficiary of Mary's escape. The transformation of the quarrel between Mrs. Solent and Wolf into "a struggle between the body of maternity itself and the bone of its bone" (449) is validated by the scene's narrative circumstances and the outsized passions displayed in it. Powys errs, however, when he reaches too quickly and without adequate narrative correlation for universal significance. His ill-considered tendency to do so early in his novels can make the novice reader of them lose credence and patience. In the first chapter of *Wolf Solent*, the protagonist

> seemed to see, floating and helpless, an image of the whole round earth! And he saw it bleeding and victimized, like a smooth-bellied, vivisected frog. He saw it scooped and gouged and scraped and harrowed. He saw it hawked at out of the humming air. He saw it netted in a quivering entanglement of vibrations, heaving and shuddering under the weight of iron and stone. (5)

Nothing in the story thus far of Wolf's dismissal from his job and his flight to Dorsetshire or in his anguished sympathy for the London poor has prepared for this extreme image of a living earth tortured by the domination of technology. Nor will any element of the story develop from it.

A similar and even more costly instance of the tendency to assume an unjustified universal perspective occurs in the notorious first pages of *A Glastonbury Romance*, sometimes cited as instances of Powys's windiness and crankishness. John Crow's memory of his mother upon returning to her home country stirs "one of those infinitesmal ripples in the creative silence of the First Cause"; it brings down the "fire-thoughts" of the sun; it touches the awareness of "the soul of the earth" (21–22). Foolhardy in any case and thankfully infrequent throughout the rest of the romance, such dogmatic assertions challenge trust in the narrator's good sense and misrepresent the skeptical outlook and human concerns of his tale.

Over the course of the romance, however, Powys earns his right to oracular knowledge, most fully displayed in chapter 24, "'Nature Seems Dead'." Here the narrator describes the dreams and night thoughts of Glastonbury's residents gathered above the town in struggle between the believers in its legend and their opponents. This supernaturalism persuades because Powys's description remains true to the individual qualities he has portrayed in his characters and to his evocation of the town's geography and history. The episode rests cunningly on the margin between allegorization of the book's human conflicts and outright declaration of a psychic vision.

> The history of any ancient town is as much the history of its inhabitants' nightly pillows as of any practical activity that they perform by day. Floating on its softly upheaving sea-surface of feminine breasts the island-

city of mystery gathered itself together to resist this wedge of rational invasion. Backward and forward, for five thousand years, the great psychic pendulum has swung between belief in the Glastonbury Legend and disbelief. It is curious to think of the pertinacity of the attacks upon this thing and how, like a vapour dispersed by a wind that refashions itself again the moment the wind departs, the moss-grown towers and moonlit ramparts of its imperishable enchantment survive and again survive. When the king murdered the last abbot of this place he was only doing what Philip and Barter and Red and Dave and Paul Trent and John would have liked to do to the indestructible mystery today. In the most ancient times the same fury of the forces of "reason" must have swept across Glastonbury, only to be followed by the same eternal reaction when the forces of mystery returned. The psychic history of a place like Glastonbury is not an easy thing to write down in set terms, for not only does chance play an enormous part in it, but there are many forces at work for which the human language has at present no fit terms. (747)

For the psychological and historical accuracy of this passage and the aptness of the simile of vapor and wind, the reader will allow Powys to assume a timeless and occult perspective. The language of the passage, like that of other, similar places in the book, seems to derive from a mood of Tennysonian romance, as in the reference to "moss-grown towers and moonlit ramparts"—poetic figures that accord also with *Glastonbury*'s recurrent sexual patterning: the town, upheld by the sleeping feminine supporters of the legend, prepares the author's protest of the inadequacy of his language, "psychic" descriptions such as this have consistency and objectification in the human events of his fiction.

Even more grandly successful are the pages that introduce *Glastonbury*'s final chapter, "The Flood" (chap. 30). Writing of the town's apocalyptic inundation, Powys escapes the slackness and whimsicality of the book's opening by alternating finely between figurative and naturalistic details, structuring his incantatory sentences to echo the motion of approaching onslaught, and gearing his vocabulary to resonate with intimations of timelessness and the novel's pattern of symbols. It is a compellling, full-throttle performance, exemplary of Powys's "oracular" writing at its best.

First one notes Powys's recollection of Old English sea poetry in his use of joined words and alliteration. The Atlantic rises in "moon-drawn death-bringers" rolling upon the "far-stretching flats" of the coast (1063). "Ancient sand-sunk boat-skeletons, their very names forgotten, that had caught for years the blood-reflections of sunset in the pools of dead memories and lost disasters, were now totally submerged" (1064). This present flood blends with ancient memories of its predecessors by reference to the "queer amphibious race, descended from Norse invaders and Celticized aboriginals" who live along the coast; to the "infinitesimal sea-creatures" carried inland to enrich the soil of Glastonbury (1065); and to tales of "Demetrius the Traveller, a hundred years before Christ" (1066). Even more remotely, the approaching waters awaken primeval memories.

> Of all mortal senses the sense of smell carries the human soul back the farthest in its long psychic pilgrimage; and by these far-drawn channel airs and remote sea odours the inmost souls of many dwellers in northwest Somerset must have been roused, during those weeks of March. . . . That hidden wanderer, incarnated in our temporary flesh and blood, that so many times before—centuries and aeons before—has smelt deep-sea seaweed and sun-bleached drift-wood and the ice-cold chill of Arctic seas, sinks down upon such far-off memories, as upon the stern of a voyaging ship, and sees, as if in a dream, the harbours and islands of its old experience. (1067)

The reference to prehuman memories is appropriate not only to Powys's contention that earlier forms of consciousness survive in and shape human responses, but also to his inference that the waters approach to cleanse Glastonbury's legend once again of its human traditions. "A moon more magnetic and potent" beckons them; the moon has been identified through the novel with the impossible and the defeated; she here calls forth a destruction of the temporary triumph of mystery in Glastonbury. The waves rise from the mid-Atlantic, locale of the lost civilization reported by Demetrius—in *Glastonbury* associated with impossible happiness contrary to human nature. The waves reflect the destructive forces in man and nature: "They were like the death mounds of some huge wasteful battlefield carried along by an earthquake and tossed up into millions of hill summits and dragged down into millions of valley hollows as the whole earth heaved" (1063). In a related sense, the waves, "irresistible hosts of invading waters" (1063) that threaten the vegetation of the coast with "ravishment" (1064), embody the masculine opposition to the Glastonbury legend.

For all the universal connotations given to the flood, it remains vibrantly physical and particularized. Series of participles catch its motion: "stealing, shoaling, rippling, tossing"; "rocking, heaving, rising, sinking." Patterns of repeated words and consonants reflect its inevitable progress:

Up the sands and shoals and mudflats, up the inlets and estuaries and backwaters of that channel-shore, higher and higher as day followed day, raced steadily these irresistible hosts of invading waters. (1063),

Wide, wet reaches of sand, over which for years fishermen had walked in the dawn with wavering lanterns and whispering voices, and where decrepit posts, eaten by centuries of sea-worms and hung with festoons of grass-green seaweed, leaned to the left or leaned to the right, as chance willed it, were now changed into a waste of grey water. (1064)

The latter sentence also demonstrates Powys's abundant resourcefulness in specifying human labors as the unchanging background to his catastrophe. Similarly, his reference to place names as he maps the flood's course—Stert Flats, Blue Ben, Mark's Causeway (1066)—evokes the sense of a specific locale shaped by nature and history through the ages.

"'Nature Seems Dead'" and "The Flood" show Powys imbuing his fiction with supernatural overtones by paying close attention to details of narrative, description, and tone. His effort depends on his assuming a position of knowledge not all readers willingly grant, and when he attempts to bully his way across the limits of plausibility, as at the opening of *Glastonbury*, the result is ludicrous and damaging. However, when Powys supports his pretensions with confident realism, he attains his effect. This technique works more consistently in his small, subtle scenes than in the grand, universalizing passages. An instance occurs at the close of the disasterously begun first chapter of *A Glastonbury Romance*. The protagonists are ghosts.

"You ought to have been older than all your brothers, woman, instead of younger." The words emanated from a pale, insubstantial husk upon the air, a husk that resembled the cast-off skin of a snake or the yet more fragile skin of a newt, diaphonous and yet flaccid, a form, a shape, a human transparency, limned upon the darkness above the great chair to the left of the fireplace. The words were almost as faint as the sub-human breathings of the plants in the conservatory. (65)

Powys succeeds because of the startling impertinence of the ghost's words, the appropriateness of the similes for his appearance, and the apt comparison of his speech with plant sounds. The ghosts and their ensuing quarrel play no part in the story; an author primarily interested in evoking the occult would have made more of them. Typical both Powys's gusto and of his somewhat distracting reliance on generalization is the movement directly from the coup of bringing a ghost into the scene to a long catalogue of similes for the ghost's words.

They were like the creakings of chairs after people have left a house for hours. They were like the opening and shutting of a door in an empty house. They were like the whistle of the wind in a ruined clock-tower, a clock-tower without bell or balustrade, bare to the rainy sky, white with the droppings of jackdaws and starlings, forgetful of its past, without a future save that of anonymous dissolution. They were like words murmured in a ruined court where water from broken cisterns drips disconsolately upon darkening stones, while one shapeless idol talks to another shapeless idol as the night falls. They were like the murmurs of forgotten worm-eaten boards, lying under a dark, swift stream, boards that once were the mossy spokes of some old water-mill and in their day have caught the gleam of many a morning sun but now are hardly noticeable even to swimming water-rats. (66)

These similes share with "The Flood" passage abundance, increasing abundance, of descriptive detail and a timelessly old setting. In contrast, however, the tone is quiet and the language free of figurative references. Here is Powys's supernaturalism at its most simply accommodated—by naturalistic detail unassertively linking human dissolution to the dissolution of human artifacts in the further recesses of nature. Such associations with the old, the abandoned, and the slowly transformed by nature are one path by which Powys prepares, specifically, for his presentation of the Glastonbury legend as an independent, vital entity; and in general, for his evocation of a realm of existence hidden from normal human transactions.

Powys describes this secret realm as the refuge of the confined and dislocated. He excels at the portrayal of misfits and daydreamers, unfulfilled in their social roles, thwarted in their desires, and dominated, either in fact or memory, by powerful, competent parents. Their predicaments provide the emotional context for escape into nature and imagination, into moments of vision and release.

As in his scenes of emotional encounter, Powys's depictions of blocked and submissive characters are remarkable for their observation of raging, shameful feelings. They are also disturbing for Powys's emphasis on the impotence and self-mockery of these characters. By closely identifying narrative viewpoint with them, Powys seems to affirm the tendency toward self-humiliation that Louis Wilkinson noted as an important aspect of his personality and also to suggest the role that solitary imagination played in his own life as an escape from the commanding presence of his father. Of Magnus Muir, Powys writes in a note to *Weymouth Sands* "certain characteristics and peculiarities have been taken from the nature of the author himself" (15); in the novel, Magnus views his failings and helplessness by comparison with his steady and fearless father.

He was no honourable and dependable man of the world. He was a hypochondriacal tutor of backward little boys! It came over him, as he struggled against the buffets of the wind, longing for the warmth of his room and the reassurance of his book-shelves, that he would have been a much nobler figure of manhood, and one much more likely for Curly to fall in love with, if he could have had the sort of quarrel with Dog Cattistock that the Jobber had.

He set himself now to think of his father as he walked along, glancing sometimes at the foam of the dark sea and sometimes at St. John's spire. The same fear of his father, he thought, that made his love-affairs come to nothing while the old man lived, was still latent in his mind. *He* hadn't been a coward, though he had been a nervous and not at all an adventurous man. But his nature was so massive, his temperament so four-square, that danger itself seemed to growl like a dog and draw back when he advanced.

It was in this shame-faced mood that Magnus permitted his thoughts about his father to seize him by his shoulders as if he had been a prisoner of war, and march him past the Burdon Hotel towards Brunswick Terrace. It was at Penn House, at the end of Brunswick Terrace, the last house but one of the row, that he had lived with his father all those years. (33)

The echo of Caesar's boast in Magnus's recollection of his father's disdain of fear and the narrator's depiction of Magnus controlled as if a prisoner by thoughts of his father reflect the outsized and confining influence the man's memory has on his son. The refuge that Magnus takes in flight from his self-contempt—surrounded by tokens of his childhood where he "lay back . . . in pious quiescence upon his secure past" (35)—indeed is a prison under his father's continuing domination. Magnus relates his contentment there to "those queer interior fancies with which children transform almost any pattern into 'worlds not realized' where there is no other outlet for their restlessness" (35). He thus suggests the origins of his sense of powerlessness and worthlessness in childhood frustrations never vented.

Another escapist in *Weymouth Sands* is Rodney Loder. The sources of his frustration and resentment are more immediately present than Magnus's. Dominated by his father, an imperious lawyer, and jealous of the old man's closeness to his beautiful sister, Rodney disguises to himself his own desire for the girl as his usual feelings of self-pity and concern for his sister.

In such characters as Magnus and Rodney, Powys reveals the depths of self-contempt and anger that feed the drive to escape. There is a troubling pessimism about these characterizations; Powys allows no possibility for the individuals to confront openly their obstacles and grow beyond them; at book's end, Magnus and Rodney remain isolated and confined.

Instead, Powys links the thwarted personal relations of his characters to their capacity for imaginative power. An impressive instance of a blocked emotional state transformed to a moment of near-supernatural exaltation occurs in *A Glastonbury Romance*. Despite the oratorical and poetical language of this episode, with its echoes of De Quincey and Emily Brontë, it is convincing because rooted in the plausible emotional conflicts experienced by its protagonist, Cordelia Geard. The last words Cordelia hears before beginning her ascent of Chalice Hall recall the suspension between passion and filial piety of the dominated sons throughout Powys's fiction.

> God! how selfish of me to keep old Dad waiting for so long! I must get back at once! (212)

Thus Sam Dekker retrieves himself from thoughts of his wayward love for Nell. Meanwhile Cordelia, hidden, makes an escape from her own confining position as the plain, dutiful daughter of the family.

> Oh let them all want me! I've been considerate to everybody too long! (212–13)

Powys generalizes on Cordelia's escape from her family and implies the power of her thoughts to charge the atmosphere of her refuge.

> There can hardly be a village in England or a small town . . . where there are not certain isolated spots loaded with the wild thoughts of these solitary ones. . . . How those lonely spots must be impregnated with these women's rebellious imaginations! (213)

In following Cordelia's passage up Chalice Hill, Powys specifies its atmosphere and modulates his descriptive language according to the stages of the woman's mood. First, with Cordelia lost and restricted in the darkness and among the trees of the hillside, Powys personifies the abstraction "Darkness" and employs the generalization "woman" to reflect Cordelia's need to shed her restricted personal identity. Abandonment to the chaotic, nonhuman mystery on the hillside wins her release by its subversion of the order and the masculine sexuality associated with her subjugation within the family.

This invasion of the bewildered senses of a day-dweller by the enfolding presence of night is a unique phenomenon in human experience. However frequently it may have been felt it always returns with a shock of disturbing surprise. The darkness becomes a polymorphous amorist, irresistible, not to be stayed. We beat it back with blinded sight, paralyzed touch, confused hearing. But there is nothing of us that it does not invade! When it is a woman who is in its grasp it seems to arouse something in the feminine nature corresponding to itself, so that the recessive mystery of darkness in the woman—that underground tide of the old ancestral chaos that ebbs and flows at the bottom of her being—rushes forth to meet this primal sister, this twin daughter of the Aboriginal Abyss, whose incestuous embrace is all about her! (214)

The description of Cordelia's possession by this nonhuman entity skillfully blends details of sense and emotion with implications of an erotic embrace. Paradoxically, Cordelia's loss of personal identity frees her independent sympathy. She voices concern for her human lover.

He is unhappy; and I know not what it is! I thought I knew him through and through—but oh, I know not what it is! (215)

Rhyme, meter, and the archaic inversion "know not" fit the quality of this exclamation as a seeming magic formula that propels Cordelia out of confused darkness to her refuge on the hilltop. As she achieves the hilltop, Cordelia assumes a heroic identity that foreshadows the role she plays as her lover's savior in the penultimate chapter of *Glastonbury*—when she learns the secret of his misery. Powys's language on the hilltop turns appropriately to poetic sonority and mythological references. The dying Titans imagined here suggest the familial domination Cordelia has overcome; the birth she imagines is that of her own independence from the "incestuous embrace." With this birth, the narrator focuses on particular entities in nature, called into identity by a christening rain. The passage begins with Cordelia's arrival at two large oak trees, representative of her parents, that mark her special "resort": "she knew exactly where she was" (215).

Those enormous branches seemed to have begun an orchestral monotone, composed of the notes of many instruments gathered up into one. It was a cumulative and rustling sigh that came to the woman's ears, as if a group of sorrowful Titans had lifted up their united voices in one lamentable dirge over the downfall of their race. It kept beginning afresh, this solemn moan upon the air—a moan which always mounted up to a certain pitch and then sank down. . . . Then all was absolutely still;

and in that stillness like the terrible stillness of uttermost strain in travail, there came the first cry of birth, the fall of a single drop of rain. The first drop was followed by another and that again by another. Cordelia did not hear them in the same place. One drop would fall upon the roadway beneath her; one upon a dead burdock leaf; one upon a faded hart's tongue fern of last year's growth. Then the sound of the falling drops would be drowned in a reawakening of that orchestral dirge. Then the wind would die down over all the upland, and once more an absolute stillness would descend; and in the stillness again—only now in an increased number—the big raindrops would splash to earth, one falling upon a dead leaf, one upon a naked stone, one upon a knot of close-grown twigs, one upon Cordelia's bare forehead. Her feeling at that moment was that some deep psychic chain had been broken in her inmost being. (216–17)

In the intervals of its "official chant," the tree has seemed to offer "a private secret" to Cordelia. The personal significance of this passage has been Cordelia's attainment of independence. In the gladdening, cleansing rain, with the trees "now totally invisible," Cordelia is free to "make her way back to the town" (217). The episode has had "official" significance for the entire novel as well; Powys's phrase "many instruments gathered up into one" appropriately describes his technique in such "orchestral" passages. The wind and rain that come to the town in this chapter, for instance, signify the revival of the Glastonbury legend, as the flood at the end signifies its annihilation. The imputed origin of the storm, South Wales, reflects the Celtic origin of the legend and foreshadows the later influence of Welsh mythology on the narrative. The association of chaotic, abysmal darkness with the setting of the episode, Chalice Hill, and with Cordelia's "recessive" feminine sexuality implies the creative properties of the symbol at the center of the Glastonbury legend, the Holy Grail. Finally, by offering, two conflicting historical identities for the hilltop oaks through Cordelia, either as former objects of Druidic worship or as memorials of the Viking invasion of Somerset, Powys renders ambiguous the significance of the dying race that the oaks recall. Do they connote Glastonbury's earliest religious traditions or its present, rational usurpers? By allowing a dual significance, Powys implies both the creative and destructive powers of the chaos contained by the Grail. Cordelia's figurative childbirth suggests creation, but returning from the hill she hears Philip Crow the industrialist as he flies his plane in the storm—"travelling like a devil through the black rain" (217).

The Chalice Hill episode suggests why Powys is not only an enthralling storyteller for many of his readers but also a companion and guide. On Chalice Hill, Cordelia escapes her social and familial roles to attain a new identity, independent of them. This renewal enables her return to the town and her home. Transformations of this kind occur again and again in Powys's fiction. He is a poet of human identity, achieved not through personal relationship but through solitary awareness of the forces of nature. He thus describes a path of self-realization and freedom for the humiliated and disillusioned.

The parental figures of Powys's fiction dominate its social settings as fully as they command the memories and family life of his protagonists. They are, publicly, spokesmen for conventional values and objects of traditional deference—lawyers, civic leaders, schoolmasters, and clergymen. The escapists of Powys's fiction live in the shadow of the public authority and secure social identity of the older generation. Inevitably, Powys undercuts the moral prestige of these town fathers by revealing drives for passion and power that lie behind their pronouncements and example; he sets these revelations in the domestic life of his protagonists and their parents. For instance, when Mat Dekker, the vicar of Glastonbury, urges his son Sam to give up the young woman whom he adulterously loves, Powys sympathetically, but frankly, discloses the source of this counsel—which Mat, until the end, obscures to himself—as not in the father's religious beliefs but rather in his sexuality. Reverend Dekker reaches the crisis of his dilemma at a christening party where he witnesses the woman's mistreatment by her vengeful husband.

> The point had come, as he stood there, when he must either tear the priest's mask from him and cover that bowed head with more than religious consolation, or get away from her . . . leave her . . . to get home to his son . . . to his aquarium . . . to his dead wife—to his God . . . The heavily built man stood there panting like a great dog whose mistress has gone down one path and his master down another. His greenish-black trousers remained so still above his square-toed muddy boots that to a whimsical eye—only there was no whimsical eye just then in Whitelake Cottage—they became objects quite distinct from his head and shoulders; objects that hung, like a drowned man's trousers, on a post by the wharf. (863)

As in the portrayals of Mrs. Solent and Miss Drew, desire for a forbidden object here arises. No confrontation can ensue, however. Matt's self-division between his religious and social duties and his sexual longing is described not whimsically but pertinently as the seeming separation of his head and shoulders from his lower body, impaled upon his desire.

A similar but more tyrannous and willful self-division is described in the elder Loder, the commanding lawyer of *Weymouth Sands*, called "the General." He exposes his pain-wracked body to his daughter and doctor to elicit horrified pity from them.

> . . . it was still a comfort for the old man to harrow the feelings of those who yet had feelings to be harrowed. His daughter knew well enough that he had not stripped naked, nor had he stretched himself out like this, *until they began to ascend the stairs.* He could torment and scare little Lettice, the under housemaid, without having to proceed to such lengths as these, but with Ruth and Girodel, he was prepared to let himself go. . . .
>
> Ruth moved to the window while Girodel by a mixture of persuasion and astute muscular pressure got his patron into his white night shirt and into his bed, but when safe under the sheets, the General . . . made it worse for them by launching into so vivid, so revolting, so realistic, and at the same time so emotional a description of his ulcers, that Ruth, with a distressed and angry flush on her white cheek and even a faint spot on her forehead, abruptly left the room. (487)

Description of Mr. Loder's agony derived no doubt from Powys's own years of affliction by ulcers, and the old man's dramatization of his pain perhaps reflects Powys's recognition of his own tendency to emphasize his suffering. The dedication of *Weymouth Sands*, on the other hand—to the sister who left off art studies in London and Paris to care for Reverend Powys in his last years—strongly suggests another original for the dominant fathers in this novel and throughout Powys's fiction: "To Gertrude Mary Powys remembering Her Life with My Father at Greenhill Terrace, Weymouth" (6).

Discovery of the deception and self-division of fathers in Powys's fiction estranges his protagonists from familiar domestic surroundings and from the childhood security they recall. Much of Powys's fiction begins with the mixed experience of homecoming and the sense of dislocation from childhood surroundings that accompanies it. Memory of childhood security is a living refuge become ambiguous and threatened for Powys's protagonists by their changed perception of the fathers who ensured that serenity. Wolf Solent's recollection of continuity and stability as he sits in a home redolent of his boyhood innocence presents the initial rapture of homecoming.

> Wolf had long begun . . . to drink up every peculiarity of the room in which they sat—of the furniture upon which the heavily-globed gasjets of the candelabra shed so mellow a glow. . . . he became aware of a

faint scent of apples. Where this scent originated he could not detect. It seemed to proceed equally from every portion of the apartment. And as he gave himself up to it, it brought to his mind a kind of distilled essence of all the fruit and flowers that had ever been spread out upon that massive brown table; spread out upon former editions of "The Western Gazette"; editions old enough to contain news of the death of Queen Adelaide or of Queen Charlotte! (200–201)

Characteristically Powys's description moves from notice of present objects and atmosphere to the "essence" of genteel nineteenth-century leisure and stability they represent for Wolf. Later, however, a contrasting description of the same setting implies Wolf's separation from the assurances and innocence of his home. The impression of once-familiar objects having taken up a remote existence of their own is common in Powys's protagonists' experience of their old-fashioned settings.

He looked at her as she fixed her eyes on the floor, frowning; and then he glanced away at the mahogany sideboard, where Mr. Smith's heavy pieces of polished silver met his gaze, with the detached phlegm of old, worn possessions that have seen so many family-troubles that they have grown professionally calous, after the manner of undertakers and sextons. (415)

His half-sister has told Wolf of the financial ruin of the master of the house, Mr. Smith; soon he will witness the man's bitterness over a life of care for his wife and children. The "heavy" objects in this description suggest not stability but a burden. The "old" possessions do not allow imaginative return to the past but rather signify the death of the ways that employed them. The likening of these "detached" heirlooms to "undertakers and sextons" anticipates both the death of Mr. Smith and the death of Wolf's social identity with his inability to sustain the security the house had afforded. Attempting to comfort the children of the house, Wolf, in his powerlessness, surrenders consciousness of himself as a person. He is expelled "out of his human skin, out of that old Ramsgard house, out of the confines of life itself." "He had slid away somehow into some level of existence where human vision and human contact meant nothing at all" (418). Powys describes Wolf's emotional displacement, his inability, because of domination and betrayal by his elders, to maintain identity through personal relationship—"human contact."

The thrust of Powys's fiction is to bring his characters to self-awareness apart from the futility of their lives among others. They achieve this through encounter with nature. Taking life on the most elemental terms, simply as a part of nature, with no more pride than a plant or beast and no more need or opportunity than they for religious doctrine or social role to mediate essential consciousness, Wolf reconstitutes his identity independently and prepares to confront the disappointments that await him.

> His body and his soul were coming together again now. Emanating from his lean, striding form, from his spine, from his legs, from his finger-tips, his spirit extended outwards, dominating this forked "animal-vegetable" which was himself. And with this new awareness as his background, he set himself to face in stoical resolution all the years of his life, as he saw them before him, dusty milestones along a dusty highway! (953)

Wolf's experience of his "new awareness" suggests the didacticism that pervades Powys's fiction and dismays some readers, to whom such consolation seems childish. "The mature bore him," V. S. Pritchett has written of Powys.[10] This is true perhaps in that Wolf's story is the prelude to a belated maturity. It inures him to the disillusionment that struggle with other people has compelled and preserves his integrity beyond these conflicts. By identifying his spirit with his body, Wolf hopes to prevent the self-falsification suffered by the social figures in the novel, with their imputed need to maintain authority over other people in order to realize themselves. Wolf's ultimate refuge is a humility fostered by awareness of "animal-vegetable" responses as constituent of his essential consciousness. However difficult it is to assent to Powys's philosophy as a way of life, it is no more esoteric than the teachings of the Tao, with its admonition to conceive life in terms of its most simple and lowly manifestations.

> Turning back is how the way moves;
> Weakness is the means the way employs.[11]

Powys designates all his works of fiction as romances; thus he notes the close association of nature and man in them, with traditions of past strivings with nature invoked as a possible bridge between the two. The characters of romance, Powys writes, "must be penetrated through and through by the scenery which surrounds them and by traditions . . . of some particular spot upon the earth's surface."[12] By assimilating himself to his setting in nature, Wolf becomes, in Powys's definition, a figure of romance. Isolated because of his failure to carry on the ways of his home, Wolf renews tradition, so to speak, at its source. He has lost his social relation to his homeplace but at the same time discovered deeper roots in it. Defining himself in terms of his place in nature, Wolf can survive his loss of social identity and achieve a more secure self-awareness.

Powys most often depicts isolated, socially disinherited characters such as Wolf who turn to nature and there renew an earlier consciousness. At times, however, he asserts the continuance of awareness of nature in the particular life of a community. By discounting social and historical particulars, Powys emphasizes the origin of present habitual responses in traditional accommodations to nature. In this respect, racial consciousness matters to Powys as a medium of instinctual survival by which past awareness of the nonhuman informs familiar gestures. For instance, response to nature as a continuing expression of communal life emerges in the actions of Tilly Crow and her "Perfect Servant" Emma Sly in *A Glastonbury Romance* when they draw blinds and light lamps against the twilight in Philip Crow's house. These gestures reveal Philip's distinguishing traits—his self-discipline and authority—and suggest their source in his childhood and remote forebears. The narrator comments:

> The lights had been lit in both drawing-room and kitchen before the visitors departed. In other houses they would not have been lit! In other houses people would have been too absorbed in talk, too enamoured of the twilight, to have sent for lamps or candles, or thought of closing shutters, drawing curtains, pulling down blinds! This closing out of the twilight was indeed a characteristic Norfolk habit. The great green curtains in Northwold rectory were always drawn close, had been drawn close for years, when twilight began. So no doubt had the old Vikings, when they landed at Wick, gathered round their bivouac fires and turned their backs to the ghostly Druidic light lingering in the West! (198)

Focus recedes effortlessly from this scene to the house of Philip's grandparents to the Vikings who invaded Somerset, with Philip's status as a present-day outlander in the atmosphere of Glastonbury pertinently recalled by this reference. The catalogue of the many means of "closing out twilight" suggests a compulsive quality in this action, while use of the phrase "drawn close" for the rectory's curtains subliminally prepares for their association with the Vikings drawn close around their fires. The anachronism "bivouac" in connection with the Vikings both heightens the suggestion of a response recurring through time and returns the description to its opening, present-day generalization: "In this turbulent universe, . . . ships

at sea, certain soldiers' camps, certain outposts of civilization, conducted under scrupulous authority, become oases of order in a sea
of chaos" (197). Half-humorously the simple domestic action and
its trivial provocation become emblematic of a range of momentous
decisions made in response to nature.

Powys's echo of Conrad in this generalization signifies a shared
concern with defining the human by the quality of his response
to the nonhuman. Willful neglect of historical perspective—in
Powys's tendency to evoke "timeless" settings and use antique similes
and language—allows him to attain an effect similar to that of Conrad's maritime and exotic locales: Powys removes his characters implicitly, as Conrad does explicitly, from their modern social context
and places them in an atmosphere representative of more primitive
struggles and dangers. In this respect Powys's technique resembles
that of the opening of *Heart of Darkness*, with its likening of the
Thames to the Congo by recollection of the Roman invasion and
a savage Britain. But, in other respects, Powys's pursuit of romance
differs from Conrad's pessimistic encounters with nature in fiction.
Powys returns his characters home from cosmopolitan adulthoods.
There, rather than succumbing to the anarchically strange, they re-
sume contact with the reassuringly familiar—for ultimately nature
is, to Powys, not an alien chaos but a home. He emphasizes the
creative rather than disintegrative relationship of human awareness
to the nonhuman—nature as a medium of awareness, as well as
its object. "Sometimes in dreams," remarks John Geard in *A Glastonbury Romance*, "some little inanimate thing becomes terrible to us
. . . becomes tremendous and terrible" (456). From this he reasons,
"Thought is a real thing. It is a live thing" (457). Powys's fiction
upholds the capacity of thought to vivify nature and take emotional
meaning from the seemingly alien. The background of romance "is
laden with old, rich, dim, pathetic human associations" he writes.[13]
His romances strive to renovate those imaginative traditions that
bear the poetry of human associations to the nonhuman background.
His protagonists experience these associations anew and derive from
them awareness of their identity and source.

Thus, in *A Glastonbury Romance* Powys asserts the place of his
modern characters, the cousins John and Mary Crow, in the setting
and traditions of their homeplace. Unlike their cousin Philip, master
of Glastonbury's tin mines, they have no present active relation with
the nonhuman. Rather, typically of Powys's adult orphans, they
return from rootless urban lives to a childhood and ancestral home
in which they no longer quite belong. Their journey on a Norfolk
river, however, renews their association with the land and their inheritance from its customs. In this evocation of romance, characters,

setting, and tradition so interpenetrate that seemingly they coalesce
into some fourth entity, a timeless essence of the experience of the
place.

Powys describes the river itself so as to recall the Viking invasion
of East Anglia, origin of the Crow family in England; he also suggests
a myth of creation by which the people of Norfolk have their immortal
source in the dreamed intercourse of two gods. John and Mary's
journey will recapitulate both the historic invasion and the mythical
sexual penetration. "Every now and then they would come upon
a group of hornless cattle, their brown and white backs, bent heads,
and noble udders giving to the whole scene an air of enchanted
passivity, through which the boat passed forward on its way, as
if the quiet pastures and solemn cattle were the dream of some
very old god into which the gleaming river and the darting fish
entered by a sort of violence, as the dream of a younger and more
restless immortal" (74).

John rowing, Mary guiding, the cousins observe, in the Ruysdael-
like landscape of the shore, a progression of the forms of existence
of Norfolk, from vegetation to animals to representations of human
life.

> Past deep, muddy estuaries the boat shot forward, where the marigolds
> grew so thick as to resemble heaps of scattered gold, flung out for largesse
> from some royal barge, past groups of tall lombardy poplars, their proud
> tops bowing gently away from the wind, past long-maned and long-tailed
> horses who rushed to look at them as they shot by, their liquid eyes
> filled with entranced curiosity, past little farm-houses with great, sloping,
> red roofs, past massive cattle-sheds tiled with those long, curved brick
> tiles so characteristic of East Anglia, past sunlit gaps in majestic woods
> through whose clearings tall, flint church towers could be seen in the
> far distance, past huge black wind-mills, their great arms glittering in
> the sun as they turned, grinding white flour for the people of Norfolk,
> past all these the boat darted forward, rowed, it seemed, by one relentless
> will-power and steered by another. (79)

The progression of descriptive clauses, each introduced by the word
"past," reflects the steady forward motion of the boat and the stages
of the Norfolk past through which the cousins advance. Powys suggests the divine origins of this scene by emphasizing its noble monu-
mentality through his choice of adjectives: "royal, proud, great, massive, majestic." He asserts John and Mary as the inheritors of the
scene by omitting other human figures from it and by contrasting
their "relentless will-power" to the wind-blown or "entranced" movements of the other forms of life. Reference to "the people of Norfolk"
culminates the description and returns the narrator to the cousins,

who through their labor, have become the embodiment of the people. Their "ecstatic toil" joins them in "A sensuality of oneness" and in turn unites them to their predecessors.

> The two of them were alone on that Norfolk river, a man and a woman, with the same grandmother and the same grandfather, with the same grandparents in a steady line, going back to Agincourt and Crecy, going back to all the yeomen of England and all the sturdy wenches of England, to all the John Crows and Mary Crows that fill so many churchyards in the isle of Ely unto this day. (80)

Powys makes this grand historical association rather facilely and conventionally. However, the little action that occurs next consummates the imaginative identification of John and Mary with Norfolk complexly and originally.

> He never reached his second twenty. Disturbed by the appearance of a living javelin of blue fire, flung forth from a muddy ditch, darting like a gigantic dragon-fly, down the surface of the river in front of them and vanishing round a bend of the bank, Mary gave a startled pull to her left rudder-string; and the prow of the boat, veering in midstream, shot with a queer sound, like a sound of snarling and sobbing, straight into the overhung mouth of the weedy estuary, out of which the kingfisher had flown! (81)

Employing similes first of warfare and then of sexual response, Powys links the action to recurrent references throughout the boat journey. He withholds statement of the literal action until the last clause of the first of his two rather long joined sentences, and then delays identifying its literal provocation until the very end. Thus by intentionally obscuring his description of the action, he heightens emphasis on its figurative qualities. The paragraph begins with a simple statement of the result of this action, as John fails to complete the oarstrokes he counts intently. In the next sentence the initially obscure references of the three introductory phrases promote in the reader surprise and disorientation similar to what John experiences. In addition, time references moving backward from the first sentence bring the reader round, at the end, to the moment described at the beginning of the paragraph. The kingfisher and the boat seem caught in some perpetual exchange with the estuary. Through Powys's adroit manipulation of figurative language, past and present and external action and inner emotion have merged into a psychological essence uniting the cousins, the landscape, Norfolk's early history, and the imputed legend of its creation. Although nothing heroic or magical has happened overtly, the boat journey culminates in the cousins' possession of, and possession by, their home.

From the return of Wolf Solent to Dorset to the renewal of the Grail's powers in Glastonbury, from the oceanic comfort won by the outcasts of Weymouth to the wishful reunion of son and father in *Autobiography*, all Powys's narratives move repeatedly to such rituals of homecoming. Not only do his protagonists recover their essential origins, transcending social and familial identity; imagination also returns to the potency of childhood fancy and language to the powers of romance and myth. In Powys's writings, one sees the survival of ancient ways by which men and women have identified the chaotic forces within themselves with the unknowable existence around them. His value to the present time is to suggest that, although the knowledge and distractions that fill modern life increase, its passions and ultimate issues remain unchanged. The wonder and terror that first led to the creation of poetry and ritual remain to merge our days anew with the eternal mysteries around us. In books that audaciously challenge the world of our frenzy and in a life that was itself a kind of quest, Powys strove to seek out these sources of meaning.

Notes

1. George Steiner, "The Problem of Powys," *Times Literary Supplement*, 16 May 1975, p. 541.

2. V. S. Pritchett, "The Mysteries of John Cowper Powys," *New Statesman*, 12 April 1965, pp. 534–35.

3. Steiner, "Problem of Powys," p. 541.

4. Henry Miller, "The Immortal Bard," *A Review of English Literature*, 4(1) (1963), p. 22.

5. Steiner, "Problem of Powys," p. 541.

6. John Cowper Powys, *The Complex Vision* (New York: Dodd, Mead, 1920), p. 46.

7. John Cowper Powys, *Weymouth Sands* (London: Macdonald, 1963), pp. 39–40. Subsequent references are cited by page number.

8. John Cowper Powys, *Wolf Solent*, 2 vols. (New York: Simon and Schuster, 1929), pp. 448–49. Subsequent citations are cited parenthetically by page numbers.

9. John Cowper Powys, *A Glastonbury Romance* (London: Macdonald, 1955), p. 638. Subsequent citations are cited parenthetically by page number.

10. Pritchett, "Mysteries," p. 535.

11. *Tao Tē Ching*, trans. D. C. Lau (Harmondsworth, Middlesex: Penguin Books, 1963), p. 88.

12. John Cowper Powys, "Emily Bronte," in *Suspended Judgments* (New York: G. Arnold Shaw, 1916), p. 322.

13. Ibid., p. 322.

Dry Sand and Wet Sand: Margins and Thresholds in *Weymouth Sands*

Anthony Low

In *Autobiography*, which he commenced writing at Phudd Bottom in August 1933, just after he finished work on the third of his major novels, *Weymouth Sands*, John Cowper Powys describes briefly but memorably the importance to him of his childhood stays at Penn House, Brunswick Terrace, at the home of his "aged relative" in Weymouth.[1] One thing Powys emphasizes will be familiar to anyone who has spent childhood vacations by the sea: a kind of interpenetration between two worlds, indoors and outdoors. "The windows of the drawing-room opened straight on the Esplanade—which was very narrow just there—and on the pebbled bank of the sea, across whose surface to the West you saw Portland, and to the East the White Nose and St. Alban's Head." Yet it was not primarily that view, Powys goes on to say, that lingers in his deepest memory. Rather:

> It was the contents of a curious room that you entered through folding doors from the drawing-room. This room might have been a studied and carefully selected exhibit of Early Victorian bric-a-brac, and its peculiar smell—where no lively tea-drinking disturbed the wistful Sylphs who hover over mother-of-pearl boxes and inlaid lacquer-work trays—that pathetic and beautiful smell of old fragrant carved wood—was wont to mingle with the smells of seaweed and fish and sun-warmed pebbles that came in through those large bow windows.[2]

In this peculiar "ante-room," so named by Powys, though he remarks that it is "behind, instead of in front of" the drawing room, the indoor world mingles with the outdoor world over the dividing and connecting threshold of the open windows. At the same time, the delicate odors of a faded world of "Early Victorian" bric-a-brac, "beautiful" yet "pathetic," mingle with the sturdy, natural, living smells that waft in through the open window off the beach. As one reads, because of the order of Powys's winding sentence, it

112

may seem for a moment as if the shells, pebbles, and seaweed that Powys evokes might have been collected by the visiting children (described on the next page as five-year-old John Cowper and four-year-old Littleton) and actually brought in and put on the tables to rub elbows in pleasant incongruity with the proper Victorian bibe-lots belonging to their "aged relative."[3]

It will be evident to an attentive reader of *Weymouth Sands* that both these vivid images—the view of the esplanade and, stretching out behind it, the beach, the sea, and the familiar icons on the distant coast, seen from within through the bow window, together with the actual entrance of vigorous outdoor smells into the genteel yet still much-loved and beautiful Victorian room—were most likely among the germinal childhood memories that gave birth to the novel.

Perhaps Powys refers to this room, in which the experience or experiences took place that were to prove so enduring in memory, as an "ante-room"—even though architecturally it is just the opposite, a cul-de-sac behind the apparently more important drawing room—because in it such disparate things came together, mingled, and more importantly, formed subterranean connections in the observing con-sciousness of the artist and, through him, of the reader. An ante-room is an entry-way; it is a means of transition between one place or one state and another—outdoors and indoors, natural objects and human artifacts; or it mediates between one condition and another—past and present, old age and childhood, fragility and sturdiness. Finally, an ante-room is that peculiar kind of threshold, at once separating and connecting, within which someone may choose to pause and linger. Together with the window, it joins two distinct worlds as well as two realms of consciousness, and from them it produces something new, a middle region compounded out of both objectivity and subjectivity—neither a single unified thing nor, any longer, two entirely separate things.

Immediately afterward, *Autobiography* recalls still another of Powys's childhood memories: the division of the beach, itself a divid-ing region between sea and land, into two territories, wet sand and dry sand. "In those early visits to Brunswick Terrace," Powys recalls, "it was a considerable event to be taken as far as the 'dry' sand, where the donkey-stand was, and it was a gala-day to be allowed to play in the 'wet' sand, out by the bathing-machines."[4] As Glen Cavaliero briefly remarks, the "wet" and "dry" sands are parts of that central and seminal region that is the "real place of revelation" in *Weymouth Sands*, the curving beach between shore and sea "from which the book takes its title."[5] This particular image, though it recurs from time to time in the novel, appears most emphatically when Powys sets his scene for the chapter that (I would argue) is the novel's major climax and turning point: "Punch and Judy."

> The scene on this particular afternoon, largely because of the warm diffused sunlight which fell from a filmy, feathery sky, and because of the absence of any blustering wind, had an air that resembled the air of Watteau's "Embarkation to Cythera". There was the same ideal atmosphere, as if the whole crowd, both in and out of the shining water, had been removed several degrees from the pressure of daily reality, had been transported, just as they were, to the magic shore of some halcyon sea, where "birds of calm sat brooding on the charmed wave". Nor was the scene devoid of its own inherent aesthetic contrasts. That difference, for instance, between the *dry* sand and the *wet* sand, which had remained in the memory of Magnus as a condensation of the divergent experiences of his life, heightened the way everything looked from the esplanade till it attained the symbolism of drama. On the dry sand sat, in little groups, the older people, reading, sewing, sleeping, talking to one another, while on the wet sand the children, building their castles and digging their canals were far too absorbed and content to exchange more than spasmodic shouts to one another. The free play of so many radiant bare limbs against the sparkling foreground-water and the bluer water of the distance gave to the whole scene a marvellous heathen glamour, that seemed to take it out of Time altogether, and lift it into some ideal region of everlasting holiday, where the burden of human toil and the weight of human responsibility no more lay heavy upon the heart. (456–57)[6]

On the dry sands cluster the adults, "forever limning and dis-limning themselves," "groups and conclaves of a rich, mellow, Rabelaisian mortality, eating, drinking, love-making, philosophizing, full of racy quips, scandalous jibes, and every sort of earthy, care-forgetting ribaldry." On the wet sands play the children, "purer spirits of an eternal classical childhood, happy and free, in some divine limbo of unassailable play-time" (456–57).

For grownups and children alike it is "play-time." Weymouth is, above all, a holiday resort, a sea-side town, created or transformed for that purpose by "the town's historic patron," George the Third (455). In "Punch and Judy" we see the beach at its moment of apogee, very much in contrast with the bleak, wintery scenes with which Powys opens and closes his novel. This is the unique, all-too-brief high summer of the novel's seasonal time-scheme: "a day or two after the August Bank-holiday," and the once nearly deserted beach is now "crowded with visitors" (455). Gathered into the language of this preliminary scene-setting, which is presided over by the Punch-and-Judy show itself, are a whole galaxy of interrelated concepts and images that are familiar in recent psycho-social literary criticism—and also easily recognizable to anyone who has visited the summer beach in childhood or as an adult accompanied by children.

Many key terms are supplied by Powys himself: "holiday," "ideal atmosphere," "removed several degrees from the pressure of daily reality," "magic shore," "free play," "care-forgetting ribaldry," and, above all, the seemingly mystical lifting-up of participants and spectators "out of Time altogether . . . into some ideal region of everlasting holiday," while the children retreat into a "divine limbo of unassailable play-time." To these phrases and images of Powys's, one need add only a few additional terms: *marginality,* a concept that stresses the importance of apparently marginal regions of landscape or of internal experience for the discovery of truths not always evident at the "normal" center of things; *liminality,* the concept of *thresholds* between ordinary regions and states, belonging neither to one thing nor the other—for example, between day and night, land and sea, sleep and waking; *play,* in its way as central to human nature and as important as work or other mundane activities; *carnival* and *festival,* occasions during which the ordinary rules of life are dissolved or suspended in varying degrees; *society* and *community,* two opposing terms for human interrelationships: the first, for people engaged in business and other everyday activities, stratified and rule-bound; the second, for those engaged in various forms of ritual, celebration, and play, free of the usual constraints.[7] Powys himself evokes Rabelais, whom Bakhtin has elevated as a kind of presiding patron over such activities and states of mind. It is a central irony of *Weymouth Sands* that, not only has the modern world relegated holiday and play to the margins of human life, but that nearly all the novel's central characters have become marginal even to this world of play. They are the winter inhabitants—or, rather, the hangers-on—of a summer resort. Marginal to the business and society of everyday England, they are even marginal to the annual festivities that take place on the wet and dry Weymouth sands.

Some of the oppositions between and among which the actions of *Weymouth Sands* take place are: male and female, old and young, master (or mistress) and servant, native and visitor, citizen and gypsy; in the temporal scheme, day and night, winter and summer; in the landscape, sea and land, sea and sky, esplanade and beach, earth castle and scientific institute, town and country, respectable district and slum, pebble and sand, inside and outside, boarding house and bawdy house; in the realm of mind and observation, subjective and objective. Of course, many literary works are built up out of just such dichotomies, and some of the novel's oppositions—love and hate, success and failure, gain and loss, joy and sorrow—may be too obvious or conventional to need much discussion. As I have suggested, however, *Weymouth Sands* treats many of these opposites in a special way that will repay closer attention.

The book opens with a set of major, interlinked oppositions, drawn between sea and land, universal and particular, inhuman and human:

> The Sea lost nothing of the swallowing identity of its great outer mass of waters in the emphatic, individual character of each particular wave. Each wave, as it rolled in upon the high-pebbled beach, was an epitome of the whole body of the sea, and carried with it all the vast mysterious quality of the earth's ancient antagonist.
>
> Such at any rate was the impression that Magnus Muir—tutor in Latin to backward boys—received from the waves on Weymouth Beach as in the early twilight of a dark January afternoon, having dismissed his last pupil for the day and hurriedly crossed the road and the esplanade, he stood on the wet pebbles and surveyed the turbulent expanse of water. (17)

Not only are the three dichotomies I have mentioned evoked in this powerful opening statement of central themes and image-systems, but Magnus is placed, characteristically, at the very threshold and meeting place between opposing elements. He stands on the "wet pebbles" near the boundary between land and sea. Furthermore, he has finished his dreary work, and it is "early twilight": neither day nor night, but that mysterious time of transition, represented by dusk or dawn, during which many of the novel's most transcendent experiences take place.

Other notable oppositions are embodied stylistically in the texture of Powys's language—for example, in the contrast between the long, open vowels describing the outer sea as against the clipped, closed vowels describing the particular waves—and, more broadly, in the contrast in tone between the two paragraphs: the first a romantic reaching out, the second an ironic taking back, as the seemingly objective description by the author John Cowper Powys is reduced, provisionally, to the subjective opinion of the character Magnus Muir. Such a wavelike systole and diastole of romance and irony belongs to the very essence of modernism, which, descending from the infinite longings of the romantics, yet holds itself perpetually on guard against the potential embarrassments of outworn illusion.[8] So, to Stephen Dedalus, also walking along the margins, the sea appears "Snotgreen, bluesilver," its beauty qualified by the requisite modernist irony.[9]

Unlike Joyce, however, Powys does not so much retract as balance and search for new truths in the region of juncture.

The marginality of the scene is emphasized by other imagery. Against the infinite longings represented by Magnus's "broodings by the sea's edge" (17), Powys sets to landward the "Jubilee Clock, that familiar landmark that always made him think of his father, so decently and self-respectingly did it mark the place where the esplanade curved a little" (18). On the cold, January beach Magnus encounters the incongruous spectacle of the Punch-and-Judy show, with its child beggars confronting, from the beach, a "little group of children" who stand watching from the esplanade, "staring at so unseasonable a performance" (19). As the Punch-and-Judy man backs toward the water's edge, trying to catch sight of his daughter Marret and repeatedly crying out her name in his terrible voice, a cockney policeman buttonholes Sylvanus Cobbold as he preaches from the promenade and officially clarifies the distinction between the promenade and the beach. One is a social or civic space that belongs to the town and nation and from which unusual behavior must be excluded; the other is a no-man's-land, where borderline activities of all kinds are permissible:

"If I've told yer once, I've told yer a 'undred times! The beach is the proper plice for these 'ere hexortations. Get out of this! Do you 'ear me? It's all right, lady, . . . No horficer will interfere with 'im if 'e will go down below." (21)

The strong accent—which, appropriately, is metropolitan London rather than provincial—should not obscure the important distinction being made. It is not just Sylvanus's mad sermon that offends society, as represented by its official spokesman, but his persistence in preaching it in the wrong place, too far from the ambiguous margins: namely, on the sober grounds of "'is Majesty's Hesplanade" (21).

Of course, many such rational and official barriers break down, and what looks marginal from one point of view may become central from another. As the beach divides the sea from the esplanade, the esplanade divides the beach from the town. Similarly, from time to time community and play emerge from their assigned spaces to challenge society and invade the workaday world. So much of *Weymouth Sands* takes place in the borderlands between work and play, sea and land, that the distinctions between these worlds seem to dissolve. So too, the sharp lines of demarcation between land and sky, sea and sky, fade and disappear. Typically, in a later scene, as Richard Gaul, the Philosopher of Representation, looks out of

his window between yellow muslin curtains, he sees a sea and a
sky that blend indistinguishably, one with the other:

> Richard derived, as he alternately sipped his tea and inhaled his cigarette-
> smoke, a peaceful and soothing pleasure from the faint contrast between
> the greyness below the horizon-line and the greyness above it. Both
> these expanses were reduced to the lowest possible level of emphasis
> to which any material phenomenon *could* be reduced without actually
> becoming invisible; and sad though these two levels were, with that
> indescribable line of demarcation separating the horizontal perspective
> of the one from the perpendicular perspective of the other, their sadness,
> like two muted notes in a wistful bar of music, was of a kind that
> had more of peacefulness in it than of sorrow. (97–98)

As with so many of the oppositions in the novel, the dividing line
between the subtle grays of sea and sky is nearly impossible to detect;
yet, farther away from this line, the two broad, elementary realms
remain distinct. It is just at the horizon that the ordinary distinctions
break down. The result of gazing at and meditating on this ambiguous
juxtaposition is to produce in the mind of the beholder feelings
both sad and peaceful—an emotional response that might fairly be
said to characterize the reaction of a reader to the novel as a whole.
These opposite and incompatible emotions, like water and air or
water and earth, are opposing elements that cannot coexist; yet as
they can meet at the margins in the natural world, so they can
each share in the responding human consciousness.

The first juxtaposition in the novel of another important pair of
opposites that we have noticed in the *Autobiography*, inside and outside, takes place in Magnus's mind as he sits on the bench waiting
for Perdita's steamer and shivers in the cold night air. He recalls
his father, coming home from a long walk "through the rain to
a candle-lit room and a good tea and a good fire" (24). This handling
of the imagery—by opposition and contrast—is common throughout
the novel, many of whose scenes take place in a variety of rooms
as well as against the open landscape. Related to the opposition
in this image between warm inside and cold outside is a second
opposition between father and son: one is described as confident,
untroubled by doubts, massive in his certainties (see also 18, 27,
32–33); the other as hesitant, insecure, fundamentally a coward.
The father—a representative of what we may call Victorian man
as seen by the children of the Victorians—has the gift of un-self-
questioning faith; his son, condemned to be a modern, must constantly strive to rebuild his life on the foundations of doubt.

The first inside of a room that we see after this cold, outdoor beginning is at Miss le Fleau's: it is her peculiarly reassuring "brown room" (34), which represents for Magnus a genteel, comfortable, motherly, yet doubtfully potent "Victorian" shelter against love adventures, the breaking of class boundaries, endemic modernist doubts, and various other psychically dangerous activities. Yet it also necessarily represents a retreat from living and loving, which, if they are to be real, must take place not (or not only) in the remembered past but in the available present—which is to say in the modern world. Although this rich opening chapter, which begins outdoors, ends indoors, it ends by moving once more into a symbolically marginal space. The comforting but illusory contrasts between inner warmth and outer cold, safe enclosure and threatening exposure, breaks down as Magnus retires to his room for the night.

> He then slowly undressed himself in front of the few crimson coals that remained of his fire, while his candles spluttered themselves into extinction. And as he undressed himself the familiar smell of dead seaweed kept entering his room; and a strange phantasmal Weymouth, a mystical town made of a solemn sadness, gathered itself about him, a town built out of the smell of dead seaweed, a town whose very walls and roofs were composed of flying spindrift and tossing rain. Lying in bed in the faint glimmer from the grate he could hear the waves on the beach. . . .
>
> For a while he floated helplessly on the tide of this feeling, watching his big red curtains slowly inflate themselves and bulge forward, only to be sucked back, with the retreat of the wind, into hollow answering concavities. Then something in him gathered itself together, as it always did, to resist this hopelessness. And as he felt so preternaturally self-conscious tonight he began once more trying to analyse the precise nature of this power in him upon which at a pinch he seemed always able to call. (39)

In this scene warmth mingles with coldness, inside with outside, land with sea, father with son, hopelessness with determination, subjectivity with objectivity; and all these junctures occur at a further border: the moment of lapse between waking and sleep. The red curtains, which form the evanescent boundary between one world and another, move to the same rhythms as the waves and the tide, as well as the silent observer's heart and breath: they "slowly inflate themselves and bulge forward, only to be sucked back."

The impatient skeptic in us may protest that all of this intricate patterning, arranged by the author, expresses little more than the illusions of a sleepy character who is unwilling to face life squarely.

Yet surely much of modern literature and modern psychology has taught us to look for the center at such margins. Between light and darkness, sleep and waking, new realizations rise up from unconscious depths that broad daylight, full consciousness, and social constraints would never allow. Two things about this scene are noteworthy. First, however illusory we may think it is, Magnus's experience still gives him new strength to go on living. Unlike his Victorian father, who seemingly needed only to rest in his comfortable certainties to remain sane and whole, Magnus must again and again achieve a difficult personal integration precisely through such subtle and mysterious conjoinings of normally separate states. His is a receptiveness, a way of seeing, that his father's sturdier, premodern imagination did not require and could not have grasped.

Second, this experience, which seems to take place in ultimate privacy—at night, behind closed bedroom doors, largely within Magnus's own consciousness—nevertheless is duplicated in several other characters. Night and sleep break down the rhythms and the order of daytime society and replace them with a form of night-time community. One might apply to this sleep community such available terms as "collective unconscious" or "mystical communion of souls"; or one might rather argue that, when the masks and the role-playing that characterize social intercourse are dropped, and we sink deep into our private idiosyncrasies—for example, into the "family romances" and obsessive peculiarities that Powys is so adept at portraying—we are behaving most naturally, and therefore we most resemble one another and impose least barriers to a deeper community of mind.

Powys portrays many of his characters drifting into sleep to the sounds and smells that enter their rooms through open windows. To take only two instances: Perdita Wane, "With the approach of sleep" during her first night at Sark house, experiences the illusion of the Jobber's presence, begins to fall in love with him, and recalls her unhappy childhood as she "listen[s] to the sea" (60–61) outside her room; Daisy Lily through a small opening at the top of her bedroom window hears "the subsiding wind utter faint expostulating murmurs" (88) and imagines that she hears waves, as she recalls Peg Frampton and begins to reorder her life. Both women, like Magnus, enter borderline states of consciousness and, within that mysterious threshold or ante-room, undergo mental transformations.

Similarly, in *A Glastonbury Romance*, the night wind blowing through the open windows of the town causes a breakdown of social constraints, of class- and custom-bound fragmentation, thus forming a shadow community between sleeping minds that is even closer and more radical than the daytime "commune" set up by Johnny Geard, Dave Spear, and Red Robinson.[10] Can this dream community be no more than "mystical" in some unreal or old-fashioned sense that trickles down from romantic "spilt religion"? In both works, Powys experiments with a new form for the novel that we might appropriately call "postmodern" if that term had not already been preempted to describe, for the most part, the last ingrown dwindlings of decaying modernism.[11] In a highly significant article, Charles Lock argues that *A Glastonbury Romance* is a "polyphonic" novel, reflecting the Powysian "multiverse" (a term Powys borrowed from Henry James's brother William) and based on Dostoevskian or Bakhtinian "dialogic" instead of on the Jamesian single-character viewpoint and deepening subjectivity that characterize high modernism.[12] *Wolf Solent* has often been called Powys's venture into the Jamesian or the Joycean Bildungsroman, and *A Glastonbury Romance* his retreat back to a technically more primitive form—in fact, back to *Middlemarch* and the nineteenth-century panoramic novel of village life, which examines complex social interrelationships on a broad, objective canvas. We can argue more persuasively, however, as Lock has done, that *A Glastonbury Romance* is a step forward rather than a step back; that in it Powys has found the way out of the modernist trap of monocular subjectivity.

Weymouth Sands, too, is remarkably innovative both technically and conceptually in this respect. A whole range of characters, far from being reduced to objects externally observed, are allowed to express competing subjectivities. Often one character has the stage alone, but seldom for long. Sometimes Powys presents a whole group of characters projecting their separate visions all at once, to considerable comic effect, as when the Jobber, Daisy, and Hortense Lily crowd into Mrs. Lily's two-seater car and ride off together to the rescue of Captain Poxwell. They are all squeezed together physically, yet they are mentally at cross-purposes, as if the little car were crowded not only by three people but, even more, by their three incompatible subjective perception systems.

As Daisy sits on his knee, thinking her own private thoughts, the Jobber combines this pleasant contact with recollections of Perdita in his mind; meanwhile Hortense admires the passing villas, and the conversation moves at cross-purposes. At the same time, their sharply opposing attitudes toward the absent Dog Cattistock (one wants to marry him, one fears him as a prospective step-father, and one wants to kill him) provide an unspoken subtext to the conversation, embodied not only in silence and avoidances, but also in glances, turns of the neck, and the pressure of the stone with which the Jobber intends to murder Cattistock in his pocket pressed against his leg by Daisy's pleasant weight. Then, mischievously, Powys finishes exploding the post-Jamesian conventions by adding to this ill-assorted crowd of characters and their imaginings still another, purely author-invented point of view: "Had the painter Correggio been driving by Mrs. Lily's side, instead of the Jobber, he would have been forever afterwards trying to catch the Ariel-like equivocation of this ambiguous glance" (77–78).

Glen Cavaliero has already remarked on the clash of subjective cross purposes, at once comic and tragic, in another scene in which Magnus and Curly Wix embrace each other on the hill near Maiden Castle, yet "all the while he is thinking of his father and she is listening fascinated to the sound of her other lover's motor horn on the road below."[13] The scene is emblematic of how little intimate conversation, or even an embrace, can connect two people whose inner beings represent conflicting visions of life as well as disparate Jamesian "points of view."

That Powys was conscious of these sorts of technical considerations and of the place his novel occupies in the tradition is suggested by his references to the two key predecessors and exemplars: Henry James and George Eliot. Perdita Wane, despairing that the Jobber will notice her, imagines growing old without ever having truly lived or loved:

> I shall find some appalling drudgery; . . . and then, old before my time, with a passion for Persian Cats and the Works of Henry James, they'll come one day and find me stiff and stark—old Miss Wane of the Back-Attic!—and give me a pauper's funeral and chloroform my cats and sell my Henry Jameses—and that will be my story's end! (171)

Meanwhile, we have already the Jobber reading George Eliot as he sits at his lonely bachelor supper: "He ate slowly, turning over the pages of "Middlemarch" with patient resolution—one page to about ten mouthfuls" (73). It is a witty juxtaposition: simultaneous nourishment of body and mind.

Not that the Jobber much likes George Eliot. Actually, "Old Miss Burt," the rental librarian, has recommended the book to him, and her tastes run far from what she disparagingly refers to as "this modern realism." Because of her questionable advice, the Jobber's reading has not gotten past "the middle of the nineteenth century." Thus, although he likes the idea of reading, he does not much enjoy what he reads. "George Eliot must have been rather like Miss Burt," he concludes to himself, and Powys arranges a last comical juxtaposition between this proper Victorian forerunner and the obtrusive realities of life. At this point, the unceremonious supper is interrupted by a caller at the door: "The Jobber, while this unbolting went on, mechanically closed "Middlemarch" and placed the mustard-pot on the top of it" (73–74). That is the last we see of *Middlemarch*.

These two scenes are clear signals, I think, that Powys wants to call the attention to his more technically minded readers to the relationship between *Weymouth Sands* and the work of his two most influential predecessors, yet at the same time that he considers their techniques old-fashioned and unsuited to the story he has to tell. If Powys is unfair to his two parents in art, such is the way of the creative writer, who chooses to appropriate various parts of his predecessors' work yet to swerve, Bloomian fashion, in a new direction. As I have suggested, what Powys did was essentially to force a marriage between George Eliot and Henry James (a daunting thought), and thus construct his novel in the liminal regions between the objective village-society novel, of which *Middlemarch* is the finest exemplar, and the subjective psychological novel, of which *Portrait of a Lady* and its great successor, *A Portrait of the Artist*, are appropriate examples. In *Weymouth Sands*, even more than in *Ulysses*, the distinction between the "objective" novel, so sharply criticized by Virginia Woolf in her modernist manifesto, "Mr. Bennett and Mrs. Brown," and the newly dominant "subjective" novel, is broken down. Thus, the long degeneration of the Cartesian mind-body split in western culture—of which one aesthetic reflection is the tendency of twentieth-century novels to break up into wholesale solipsism and reification—begins to reverse itself.

Still other characters respond to variations on the theme of the open window. As Rodney Loder and Daisy Lily, who had previously known each other only as adult and child, accidentally meet and fall in love, their polite conversation over tea in an overheated room is merely trivial; it says nothing about what either of them is really thinking or feeling. But below that conversation a profound reordering of both their subjectivities takes place, a complete realignment that will bring the two of them closer together and harmonize their viewpoints. Powys represents this subterranean process of falling in love—precisely the mirror-image of the encounter between Magnus Muir and Curly Wix, which is intimate on its surface but conflicted in its depths—by a penetration of outdoor nature into the room. Ironically, the two characters are so intent on each other that they fail consciously to notice this crucial invasion of their psychic space:

Perhaps it was the fact that as they sat talking in that over-heated room there came through the open chink of the window a sudden harsh crying of sea-gulls that that particular essence, caught and lost, lost and caught again, so many times since that summer day, came back to him now, connected so vividly with this girlish shape under the purple wool. But the sea-gulls of the actual moment he did not hear, so absorbed was he in this new feeling—this feeling that had suddenly swept in upon him from some open window-chink of pure chance—that a woman's heart had taken pity on him as none had ever done before. . . .

Neither did Daisy. . . . The girl actually felt as if from depths within her that were boundless—depths that began at her breasts, but sank away into a solidity of such strong, calm, competent, pitying flesh and blood as would have needed the stature of some full-bosomed earth-titaness to supply—there rose arms, there rose hands, there rose a mounting up of irresistible protection, into which that forlorn forehead and pale unhappy eyelids might sink and be safe!

Thus while the seagulls, outside that over-heated room, kept on crying: "Ei-ar! Ar-ei! Ei-ar! Ar-ei!" those two pairs of human ears remained completely oblivious. (188–89)

The immediate result of their inattention to nature, Powys suggests, is a conversational blunder on Rodney's part that nearly puts an end to their growing affinity (190). In the condescending tone of an adult addressing a child, Rodney asks Daisy how her doll Quin-quetta is, and thus, unaware of what he has done, almost turns the newborn man-woman relationship back into its old form as a fruitless adult-child relationship.

Still, somewhere below the conscious level, invading nature, repre-sented by the crying of the gulls entering through the small chink of the window, has an effect on the apparently oblivious listeners. Even Rodney's blunder works out for the best. For Daisy goes home, takes out Quinquetta, whom she had put away as a childish indul-gence, and makes up with her. Like other characters in the novel, she grows up partly by allowing herself to persist in the right sort of childishness.

The episode with Quinquetta introduces still another kind of threshold: a phenomenon that, the author remarks, would go unrec-ognized by "the Holy Office of Exact Sciences," which governs our thinking in this modern age. This is the subtle threshold between the inanimate and the animate, between the material object and the "invisible eidolon" that an observer projects upon it, here represented by Quinquetta but also common to any similar "object adored by a fetish-worshipper." There is, Powys argues, a "something more" than the merely material to any beloved object, something that "would have been instantaneously recognized by any savage who had entered Daisy's room; but the scientific instrument to register it has yet

to be invented" (198–99). Implicit in the scene is Powys's consciousness of another boundary: the delicate line between "reason" and
"superstition" that marks the right balance between sensibleness and
sensitivity, and that is close (I have suggested) to the problematic
root of the modernist style and the modern mentality: a balance
between romanticism and skepticism, or what might be defined as
a constant desire for—yet constant fear and suspicion of—transcendence of the ordinary material object.

Many small objects in *Weymouth Sands* raise the question of liminality: for example, the stone with seaweed growing on it, which the
Jobber picks up off the beach and throws into the dark sea, producing
a mental image of great significance to Perdita. Seaweed only grows
on stones at the boundary of sea and land, or of sea and air. The
weed and the stone form a symbiotic pair, inanimate and animate.
They also represent the Jobber and Perdita, one a tough, amphibian
working-man, first glimpsed in his boat among the pilings; the other
a lost lady in distressed circumstances, an exile from the sea-girt
channel islands. A similar emblem is finally produced by the round
stone from Chesil Beach, with which the Jobber has intended to
kill Cattistock. In the end, Perdita gives it to Magnus Muir to give
to Richard Gaul to use as a paperweight to keep his "Philosophy
of Representation from blowing away" (567). The stone is more
than just a refutation of that philosophy (which, as Powys remarks
elsewhere, resembles his own).[14] Rather, like the mustard jar perched
irreverently atop *Middlemarch*, the stone pairs off with the written
word to represent a juxtapositon of fact with theory, subjective interpretation with stubborn object, the full meaning of which may be
said to emerge at the area of contact with the written sheets of
paper, where it forms a tiny margin or threshold.

The most marginal characters in *Weymouth Sands* are Gipsy May
and her adopted son Larry Zed; appropriately, they live on the
edges of that most marginal and liminal of places, Lodmoor, a marsh
that tourists are said to overlook until it returns to their minds
"with what Thomas Hardy would call a taciturn congruity." Midway
between the "last houses of the town" and the Coast-Guard Station,
"nestled between the cliff path and the rocky shore," "on the edge
of the highway and on the edge of Lodmoor," is their "singular
little hovel" (132). Could a dwelling or a way of life be more marginal
than this? Juxtaposed to this marginality is an equally insistent
liminality. We first see Larry Zed at the threshold moment of dawn,

> while the marshes were still wrapt in a wet and ghostly mist . . . standing
> in a tumble-down wood-shed that served as a receptacle for hay . . .

peering forth from this, through a crack in the time-worn boards, into a larger and better-preserved barn, where Blotchy the cow was staring back at him, alert in her clean straw-bed.

"Ye be always awake when I do come, Blotchy," murmured Larry Zed. "Don't 'ee *ever* lay head to straw and sleep dead-sweet, and let the Nothing-Girl take 'ee on lap and give 'ee her titties to suck? . . ."

The cow knew perfectly well that Larry was bound ere long to bring her the accustomed armful of hay; so she gave her head a few careless tosses and turning her rump to the crack in the wall set herself to observe the door.

"Voices," she thought, "may come from cracks. Hay comes from doors." (133)

Comically, the cow is allowed to represent the voice of modern skepticism and demystification. There are two kinds of openings here: the crack, like a primitive window-chink, through which a human being and an animal may confront one another and may seem—almost—about to have a meeting of minds; and the door, through which ordinary business is conducted and the normal differentiation and ranking among men and animals is maintained.

Yet, even through the door, Larry Zed brings with him an aura of margins and liminality:

With his entrance a breath of the wet dawn came into the shed, together with a strange, almost mystical fragrance from the wide-stretching salt-marsh mud, as if in the night the silent daughters of the Old Man of the Sea had been sleeping upon it. It was not permitted by Nature that Blotchy should derive more than a very vague and very diffused aesthetic pleasure from the sight of that bare-headed human figure standing in the doorway. And yet with the cold, whitish light about him, with the curious dawn-smell entering with him, with the unique chilliness amid the vapours which suggested the slippery motions of great cold-bodied eels in the wet mud, with the sense in every direction of thousands of inert wintry marsh-plants invisible in the mist, Larry's figure had an almost mythical remoteness. Larry himself certainly derived a vivid sensual pleasure from entering the shed. He drew into his nostrils a delicious fragrance of trodden straw, mingled with a cow's sweet breath and a cow's wholesome dung; and mingled too with emanations of a more bitter savour that proceeded from a small heap of turnips piled up behind some rails and covered with a hurdle. (134)

Once again the place where opposites meet—outside and inside, cold and warmth, wet and dry, marsh smell and cow smell, human observer and animal observer—becomes an ante-room in which the lingering consciousness encounters conflicting states, and through which the strange and the transcendent enter the everyday world. Neither Blotchy nor Larry Zed is a fully competent observer; but, over the shoulders of these characters, there are always further shadowy observers looking, and eavesdroppers listening: whether it might be Homer, Watteau, Correggio, Thomas Hardy, or "any savage," or just John Cowper Powys guiding his privileged readers along those borderlands where varieties of normality encounter strangeness and create newly invented ante-rooms, newly discovered centers of experience.

In "Tup's Fold," a last lovers' meeting takes place between Marret and Sylvanus, who has temporarily escaped from "Hell's Museum," to which his family has confined him as a madman. Like all such delimiting borders in the novel, the line between madness and sanity is impossible to draw with any conviction or distinctness. It is scarcely clear, for example, that Jerry and Hortensia Cobbold are saner than Sylvanus, or that they have found healthier adjustments to their inward difficulties. Indeed, one of the chief liminal territories that *Weymouth Sands* explores is the ambiguous yet fruitful region between the so-called normal and the so-called mad.

The meeting and embrace of the two lovers takes place at earliest dawn:

> Minutes and minutes flowed over them, and the link between them became like another dawn, whiter, ghostlier, more inscrutable still, mounting up through a yet deeper dark. Then came a time when the whole wide stretch of waters threw open its tremulous dawn-porches to their intense gaze. Grey, and yet not grey, metal-livid rather, like the dumb glimmer of ten thousand sword-blades, the sea unrolled its leagues of shivering expanse. It grew whiter and ever whiter, and its whiteness was not the whiteness of death, nor yet the whiteness of light or of life. It was the whiteness of the spirit. It was the whiteness of that mysterious act of creation that came even before the word. Nor did this whiteness last for long. It lasted long enough to add something of its own immortal nature to the mortal weakness of their human feeling. But then, soon, too soon, it began to fade, and its place to be taken by something else. And what now took its place was the natural, the secular diffusion of ordinary daylight, of the accustomed, the familiar, the common day, one more day, just one more, among all the other days that had spread themselves out over two human lives. (516)

What does the whiteness signify? It would be useless, I think to attempt any simple paraphrase. Something transcendent, something to do with spirit and creation, something momentarily beyond the Wordsworthian light of "common day" into which it fades. The transcendence of this predawn whiteness may owe as much to the embrace, the lovers' psychic history, and the present state of their consciousness and perceptions as to the approaching sun. Yet—ironically reversing all of those earlier experiences, when outdoor sounds and smells penetrated confining rooms, bringing with them opportunities for psychic growth and freedom—this expansive, outdoor love scene is penetrated by a reminder from indoors of inescapable confinement. As Marret embraces Sylvanus, "the sickly-sweet Hell's Museum smell of the garments they had put on him" (517) confirms to her the inevitability of future loss. Still, at this moment, she feels "happier than she had ever felt in all the days she could remember."

Not long after their embrace comes their parting. It would be hard to accuse Powys of facile optimism, in view of passages like the one in which he describes Sylvanus's state at this later moment:

> In every man's life there are moments when a desolation takes possession of him which resembles the terrible look which a dead planet might turn upon a lonely voyager travelling through space. At such a moment the heart feels as if an abyss of hopelessness had suddenly been revealed to it through some ghastly crack or crevasse in the buoyant etheric expanse. . . . Nature has piled up all her resources to hide the yawning void through which this frozen look bids us despair. Viaduct after rainbow-viaduct have our own hearts thrown across this fissure in the familiar landscape, but perhaps it will only be when the Original Jester himself repents Him of His Joke and ceases to cry "Judy! Judy! Judy!" across our shining sands that that look out of the void will melt away. Or perhaps— (519)

This anti-transcendence, coming to the observer "out of the void" "through some ghastly crack or crevasse," "across our shining sands" like the voice of the murderous Punch-and-Judy man, is as much as any deconstructionist, probing for *différance* or the void, could wish for; but it is not, of course, the novel's last word. *Weymouth Sands* ends on a variety of notes, sad and joyful; the reconciliation of the Jobber and Perdita, whose suffering has reduced them to the appearance of two skeletons; the desolate loneliness of Magnus Muir, abandoned by Curly Wix; Sue Gadget's sudden awakening to womanhood as she hears the break in Magnus's voice when he recites an old love ballad—an awakening to a sense of the "pity and trouble and pain and weariness of being alive in this world"; and, finally, Perdita's gift of the Jobber's stone, to keep the Philosophy of Representation from blowing away. Thus Sylvanus's despairing vision is simply one of several powerful extremities between which actions, confrontations, new experiences, and mental transformations take place: another margin, another threshold.

As a whole, *Weymouth Sands* is like a threshold among thresholds, a threshold so expansive that only the images of wide-stretching sands or of the horizon line are large enough to characterize it. Critics have occasionally argued that its characters are less fully developed than its landscape. Such judgments are hard to argue with; no doubt one reader's "life-like character" is another's "bundle of conventions" or "space in the text." Still, John A. Brebner is closer to the mark when he complains that the novel contains "too many characters introduced far too forcibly."[15] If we view the characterizations in E. M. Forster's terms, then this alleged over-richness in *Weymouth Sands* amounts to an achievement that violates the major convention, well-developed in the English novel, that only a few principal characters should be "round," and the rest "flat."[16] As Forster notes, there are exceptions to this rule, most notably in the Russian novel. But if readers weaned on the English novel have trouble with all the names and characters in *War and Peace* and *The Brothers Karamazov*, that is surely their weakness, not Tolstoy's nor Dostoevsky's. The kind of novel that transcends the Jamesian single point of view but refuses to give up its focus on the rich interplay of subject and object requires many complex characters of this sort. Indeed, Powys revealed that he would have laid *Weymouth Sands* on still larger foundations—meaning, presumably, that he would have introduced and developed more major characters—if the economics of publishing and the constraints resulting from the libel suit against *A Glastonbury Romance* had not forced him to moderate his ambitions.[17]

Brebner has also faulted the novel for having too many characters who remain unchanging, without development, while other characters change too quickly, with "facile resolution" (136–37). Again, I think these are acute insights but not necessarily grounds for complaint. Many of Powys's characters (like many of Trollope's) remain the same, do not "develop," because such is human nature. Many of our "character flaws" are, after all, too deep to be changed; at least, that is the gist of Freudian pessimism. Other characters may change, not because of any external or logical "motivation," but in response to a whole field of subterranean interactions in and among subjective world views, played out against the expanse of nature and landscape. Who is to say that people are less likely to fall in love because they hear, unconsciously, the crying of gulls through a window—which in turn recalls to them by association memories of intense youthful happiness—than because they have good logical reasons for doing so?

I have suggested, in the course of this discussion of *Weymouth Sands*, that Powys's powerful use of margins and thresholds qualifies him to be placed squarely in the mainstream—the "great tradition"— of the modern novel. In spite of the strong advocacy of such major and disparate critics and artists as George Steiner, G. Wilson Knight, Robertson Davies, Angus Wilson, J. B. Priestley, James Purdy, and Theodore Dreiser, Powys still remains on the margins of canonicity. No rational argument will move him to the center, which is one reason why I have been content to suggest rather than to argue. Yet there is (as I hope is sufficiently evident by now) potency at the margins.

> Ma nel mondo sensible si puote
> veder le volte tanto più divine,
> quant' elle son dal centro più remote.[18]

In the natural evolution of literature, margins are also places of origin. The history of modernism is also a history of marginal figures and of outsiders who have become insiders. It is something of a truism that the best fiction and poetry since 1890 or thereabouts has been centripital and, in important ways, culturally marginal. As George Stade writes:

> The great English literature of the modernist era, from about the nineties until World War II, was written by Irishmen, Americans, a Welshman, and a Pole. . . . If the writers were not American or Polish or from one of John Bull's other islands, they were Catholics (usually by choice rather than by birth) like Ford, Waugh, and Greene, or from the working class, like D. H. Lawrence, or women, like Virginia Woolf, or homosexual, like Forster and Auden.[19]

To speak only of the foreigners who came into England to remake its literature, where would poetry or the novel be without Yeats, Eliot, and Pound, or without James, Conrad, and Joyce? As renewal has come increasingly from the margins of the old empire, so it might be argued today that the best British novels are being written by writers like V. S. Naipaul, who arrived from the West Indies to write in England like Pound and Conrad before him, or by Robertson Davies, who is remolding British traditions from Canada as Yeats did mainly from Ireland and Joyce from Trieste.

Native English writers of an earlier generation, like Galsworthy and Bennett, served mainly as cautionary examples for greater writers to avoid. More recently, the emergence of writers such as Wain and Amis, Braine and Sillitoe, and Donleavy and O'Brien convincingly shows that working-class, provincial, and minority religious and sexual origins no longer stimulate much more than a few momentary explosions of energy beyond the disappointingly workmanlike level of competence that has characterized British fiction since the Second World War. More hopeful, though still far from unquestionable greatness, are those writers who have preserved their "difference" from the old imperial center of English language and culture while avoiding the traps of experimentalism or mere spluttering opposition: Naipaul again, or the early Doris Lessing. Iris Murdoch, Brian Aldiss, and J. G. Ballard have all put the energies of officially despised "genres" to powerful use in such notable works as *The Unicorn,* the *Heliconia* trilogy, and *Empire of the Sun.* Ballard, who has been working on the outskirts of literature for his entire career, generally unreviewed and only supported by the sale of his brilliant fiction from genre paperback racks, was at last nominated for the Booker Prize for *Empire of the Sun,* which has, I think rightly, been called the best novel yet on the Second World War. Unhappily, in what I call a failure of nerve, the jury gave the prize to a run-of-the-mill alternative.

How do Naipaul, Murdoch, and Ballard succeed in writing first-rate novels at a time of wholesale diminishment in the genre? In a word, by marginalization. There is good precedent. Conrad found a way of representing the essence of modernism in the Congo, in "Costaguana," and at last in subterranean London in *The Secret Agent. Heart of Darkness* not only probes the depths of the human psyche; it also bares the heart of the English Victorian empire indirectly by traveling up the Congo, visiting Brussels, and evoking the conquest of Roman Britain. Based on the use of marginality and liminality, it would not be hard to make a similar case for *Owen Glendower* and *Porius,* novels in which, among other things, Powys probes the essence of modern Britain or its English center by way of an invaded Renaissance Wales or through the conflicts of religions and tribes in ancient Prydein. T. S. Eliot produced a classic of modernism out of personal and marital breakdown, which he objectified in *The Waste Land;* Joyce did the same out of the perambulations of the undistinguished outsider Leopold Bloom around the gray, provincial city from which his author had exiled himself. Yeats—arguably not even a proper Irishman—invented his own space and filled it with odd and disparate subjects: Cuchulain, Byzantium, Coole Park, Lady

Kyteler, Madame Blavatsky. Perhaps the greatest of postwar English novelists, Samuel Beckett, has taken the contemporary novel to new extremes of triumphant minimalism and exhaustion.

The fascination of modernist and postmodernist novels alike is with human loss and diminishment; the familiar themes are isolation, injustice, alienation, estrangement, madness, human and economic failure, internal exile, and, at last, the void. Yet in the greatest modernist works, this bleak vision is balanced by affirmation of one kind or another: Bloom's warmth; flashes of music, remembered vision, and longed-for sympathy in *The Waste Land;* the terrible power of Yeats's poetry. Central to modernism, I would argue, is the Joycean theory of epiphany or of ambiguously transcendent revelation emerging from patient examination of the ordinary and the marginal. Great literature has always been concerned with great issues: God, man, woman, society, nature, the interrelationships among all these. Great modern literature, however, has had to deal with such issues obliquely, from a position of deprivation, using tools of irony and indirection. At its best, modernism has used and transformed irony and marginality; at its worst, it has succumbed to them.

John Cowper Powys knew all this. His early life through his graduation from university could hardly, in appearance at least, have been more English, or better suited to integrate him into the majority culture. Born into a quintessentially English family, son of a vicar of the Established Church, member of a large and loving family, he grew up in a succession of fine houses, was in close contact with the south English countryside at its loveliest, attended a good public school where he suffered only a modicum of the usual tortures, attended Corpus Christi College, and emerged the possessor of a Cambridge degree: all of which should have fitted him for integration into society and conventional success.

Of course, it did not. Not unlike Ford Maddox Ford and Evelyn Waugh, he systematically threw all his advantages away. He saw to it that he would become a failed conventional novelist and poet, a small-time schoolteacher, a university extension lecturer, a voyeur of girls on the beach, a connoisseur of burlesque, an offender of academics and of women's clubs in New Jersey and the Middle West, a "charlatan" lecturer to Jewish, Catholic, and Communist audiences in Greenwich Village. There is ample testimony that he was a powerful public speaker and that he made many friends[20]; still, by conventional standards, what a waste it all seemed to be.

Having thus parted himself thoroughly from the whole culture in which he was brought up, he finally reached the stage at which he could become a great writer. He was then about fifty-five years old and apparently past salvaging. Who could have predicted that he would settle down at this point in his disjointed life to write many of his best works at Phudd Bottom, in upstate New York? His final gesture of estrangement (about which he spoke in terms of seeking his roots but which, practically speaking, amounted to the opposite) was to transform himself into a Welshman and retire to Blaenau Ffestiniog, about as severe and unfashionable a place as one could hope to find anywhere in Britain.

In life as in art, Powys deliberately sought out the marginal, the uncanonical, and the rejected. His "inevitable cronies" and "natural camerados," whom he found in places like bohemian Chicago, were "oddities" and "half-mad ones." "Dwarfs, morons, idiots, imbeciles, hunchbacks, degenerates, perverts, paranoiacs, neurasthenics, every type of individual upon whom the world looked down, I loved, respected, admired, reverenced, *and imitated.*"[21] In this admiration and imitation, Powys found a new air to breathe, a new culture to inhabit, a new country of the mind, and finally a new way to write. Unexpectedly, but in a manner familiar enough in the lives of other modern writers, his self-imposed exile, both in America and within the barriers of his calculatedly eccentric and off-putting behavior, put him back in touch with the England of his childhood. One of the results was *Weymouth Sands,* a novel in which the self-marginalization of the writer allowed him to see and tell about things that more "ordinary" English writers were unable to see.[22]

Such eruptions into the literary scene are always unexpected; sometimes they take generations to accept and digest. Conrad and Lawrence took at least a full generation. Only now, after nearly a century, are we beginning to see Hardy as central to the modernist tradition. But, as lesser, more conventional writers—including those who merely claim to be revolutionaries and iconoclasts—dwindle away, more space is left for the greater ones to fill their places. As we have seen, marginality is not always a stable or permanent condition: what from one point of view seems marginal may, through a powerfully innovative shift in perspective, suddenly appear at the center. Thus margins become origins. Since the days of *Nostromo* and *Ulysses* and *Women in Love,* how many really major novels can we now confidently name? How many can we name as representing an evolution or an advance on those seminal works? Considering both its scope and the brilliance of its execution, *Weymouth Sands* belongs to that very small company of elect works that might come reasonably to mind.

Notes

1. John Cowper Powys, *Autobiography* (1934; reprint ed., London: Macdonald, 1967). For the sequence of composition, see extracts from Powys's correspondence in *Essays on John Cowper Powys*, ed. Belinda Humfrey (Cardiff: University of Wales Press, 1972), pp. 329–42.

2. Powys, *Autobiography*, p. 18.

3. Of course Powys returned many times to Weymouth; see *Autobiography*, passim, and the brief note "'Remembrances': *Weymouth Sands*" (1933), reprinted in *The Powys Review* 3.3 (1982–83):16–17. Among valuable articles, this special *Weymouth Sands* issue reprints an evocative late-nineteenth-century photograph of the beach (cover and p. 21). For details of the landscape, see Ordnance Survey map no. 194, "Dorchester & Weymouth," 1:50,000 series.

4. Powys, *Autobiography*, p. 19.

5. Glen Cavaliero, *John Cowper Powys: Novelist* (Oxford: Clarendon Press, 1973), p. 91.

6. John Cowper Powys, *Weymouth Sands* (1934: reprint ed., New York: Harper & Row, 1984). Subsequent references refer to this edition and are cited parenthetically by page number. (Except for new introductory matter, pagination and text are the same as the 1963 Macdonald edition.)

7. The standard study of play is Johan Huizinga, *Homo Ludens: A Study of the Play-Element in Culture* (Boston: Beacon Press, 1955); among more recent works see Victor Turner, ed., *Celebration: Studies in Festivity in Ritual* (Washington: Smithsonian Institute Press, 1982). On festivity and carnival, a seminal work is Mikhail Bakhtin, *Rabelais and His World*, trans. Helene Iswolsky (Cambridge: M.I.T. Press, 1968); on the polyphonic novel and multiple viewpoints, see also Bakhtin's *Problems of Dostoevsky's Poetics*, trans. R. W. Rotsel (Ann Arbor, Mich.: Ardis, 1973) and his *The Dialogic Imagination*, trans. Caryl Emerson and Michael Holquist (Austin: University of Texas Press, 1981). Other works on festivity include Wayne A. Rebhorn, *Courtly Performances: Masking and Festivity in Castiglione's Book of the Courtier* (Detroit: Wayne State University Press, 1978) and Terry Castle, "The Carnivalization of Eighteenth-Century English Narrative," *PMLA* 99 (1984):903–16. On marginality, see Barbara Herrnstein Smith, *On the Margins of Discourse* (Chicago: Chicago University Press, 1978); on play and liminality, see Victor Turner, *The Ritual Process: Structure and Anti-Structure* (Chicago: Aldine Publishing, 1969).

8. On the evolution of romanticism into modernism, see esp. Frank Kermode, *The Romantic Image* (1957; reprint ed. New York: Vintage, 1964); and on modernist and postmodernist deformations of romanticism, see Alvin B. Kernan, *The Imaginary Library* (Princeton: Princeton University Press, 1982).

9. James Joyce, *Ulysses* (1918; reprint ed., New York: Random House, 1961), p. 37.

10. John Cowper Powys, *A Glastonbury Romance* (1933; reprint ed., London: Macdonald, 1955), pp. 755–60.

11. For prophetic fulminations on this theme, see Harry Levin, "What Was Modernism?" (1960), reprinted in *Refractions* (London: Oxford University Press, 1966), pp. 271–95.

12. Charles Lock, "Polyphonic Powys: Dostoevsky, Bakhtin, and *A Glastonbury Romance*," *University of Tornoto Quarterly* 55 (1986):261–81.

Of course, not all the major English modernist novels are limited to a single viewpoint; yet the Jamesian method—and the Arnoldian isolation—have been hard to escape. In *Mrs. Dalloway*, for instance, Virginia Woolf brings off the tour de force of a novel told from two viewpoints, which, however, never meet. *The Waves* has always seemed to me a powerful failure. *Ulysses* has several viewpoint characters but no real encounter (either communal or antipathetic) among them; so too *Nostromo*.

13. Cavaliero, *Novelist*, p. 86.

14. Powys, "'Remembrances': *Weymouth Sands*," p. 17.

15. John Brebner, *The Demon Within: A Study of John Cowper Powys's Novels* (London: Macdonald, 1973), p. 136.

16. E. M. Forster, *Aspects of the Novel* (New York: Harcourt, Brace, 1927).

17. John Cowper Powys, letter to Theodore Powys (15 November 1932), reprinted in *Essays on John Cowper Powys*, p. 335; also see the similar remark, putting a more positive face on these cuts, in the letter dated 21 November 1932 in John Cowper Powys, *Letters to His Brother Llewelyn*, 2 vols. (London: Village Press, 1975), pp. 150–51.

18. Dante, *Paradiso* (28.49–51): "But in the world of sense the revolutions may be seen so much the more divine as they are more remote from the center" (trans. Charles S. Singleton, 3 vols. [Princeton: Princeton University Press, 1975], 1:314–15).

19. George Stade, "Introduction," *Six Modern British Novelists*, ed. Stade (New York: Columbia University Press, 1974), p. vii.

20. See, e.g., *Recollections of the Powys Brothers*, ed. Belinda Humfrey (London: Peter Owen, 1980), pp. 174–265.

21. Powys, *Autobiography*, pp. 515–16.

22. For a perfect illustration of the "normal" English reaction to such "marginal" or "coastal" explorations, even on the fiftieth anniversary of *Weymouth Sands*, see Auberon Waugh's curmudgeonly review of Paul Theroux's *The Kingdom By the Sea* (Boston: Houghton Mifflin, 1983) in *New York Times Book Review* (23 October 1983), p. 9: "Nobody of intelligence or discrimination in England goes anywhere near the coast, which is a wilderness of retirement bungalows, rotting caravan sites, deserted bathing huts, holiday camps and litter-strewn amusement parks. . . . Other coastal resorts have been requisitioned for the rehabilitation of long-term mental patients. . . . [D]esolate, ruined landscapes. . . . It never seems to have occurred to him [Theroux] that England was elsewhere, that by going round the coast he was missing the whole country."

This reaction is more suggestive, in some ways, than the book it attacks. Exploring the margins may reveal too much for our immediate comfort.

The Battered Center: John Cowper Powys and Nonbeing

H. W. Fawkner

> Neither snow nor rain nor heat nor gloom of night stays these couriers from the swift completion of their appointed rounds.
>
> —Motto of the United States Postal Service

1

As I have suggested in my recent survey of John Cowper's literary achievement,[1] the metaphysical horizon of the great Powys novels can be conceived in a Hegelian as well as Derridean fashion. On the one hand, all outward-bound psychocosmic forces can be viewed as also home-bound and inward-bound movements. The spirit leaps out into the unknown, only to use this transit through negativity to return to its point of central origin. This is the Hegelian model. On the other hand, all outward-bound forces can be viewed as precisely that: outward-bound. Far from really turning back to the center and origin, they explode violently into the margin.

The conflict between these two models of the universe is not only crucial inasmuch as it amounts to one of the strongest sources of metaphysical contradiction in Western culture; it is, of course, also crucial inasmuch as it forms the intellectual scenario of the current phase of critical theory and critical debate: poststructuralism.

It is fashionable, in the wake of Jacques Derrida, to simplify the metaphysical conflict by positing Hegel as a centralist and Derrida as a decentralist. In this way, the two philosophers establish a mechanical opposition: Hegel calls all psychocosmic forces back to the center; Derrida sets them free into the margin. Hegel calls all forces back to God, Being, and Truth; Derrida acknowledges a zone of Nietzschean becoming, where God, Being, and Truth no longer are fully operative, no longer master the violent cutting-edge of the explosively creative spirit.

As I have tried to suggest in the introduction to my monograph, however, the hesitation between the two alternatives in a sense *is* Hegel, in a sense *is* Derrida. When the two philosophies are read as texts rather than systems, the two different bodies of thought no longer oppose one another in a dead and mechanical fashion: we can see the "Derridean" moves secretly at work in Hegel, just as we can see the Hegelian moves secretly at work in Derrida.

I introduce this subversion of the naive Hegel-versus-Derrida model to call attention to a complex metaphysical tension in John Cowper Powys that follows exactly these lines of movement. On the one hand, we can perceive a very obvious conflict between a centripetal "Hegelian" Powys and a centrifugal "Derridean" Powys; on the other hand, it is not possible in the final analysis to posit these two Powyses as mechanical opposites, pure negations of one another.

It follows logically from what I have so far clarified that three Powyses need to be identified as metaphysical options: (1) a centripetal Powys, (2) a centrifugal Powys, and (3) a Powys that dismantles this opposition between the centrifugal and the centripetal. Because my monograph constantly returns to the idea of a centered and centripetal Powys, I use this essay to suggest the centrifugal alternative to that centered conception. Finally, I forward notions of how the centripetal/centrifugal opposition can be viewed as something dismantled by the texts themselves—or at least by certain fascinating passages in them.

2

If we turn very briefly from Hegel and Derrida to the father of modern phenomenology, Edmund Husserl, we can open a problematic that may clarify the significance of the "second" John Cowper schematized a moment ago—the "centrifugal," Derridean John Cowper. Husserl's phenomenology, which has been displaced recently by Derrida's postphenomenology, promotes the necessity of a "phenomenological *reduction*." The phenomenologist *reduces* the phenomenal world to certain "essences." These essences are not Platonic, because they belong to the realm of the visible and phenomenal rather than to the realm of the invisible and supraphenomenal. At the same time, however, the phenomenological essences are transcendental rather than empirical—the function of an act of the will rather than a function of passive observation. Whereas the empiricist or ordinary laboratory scientist merely records what he sees and identifies certain optical givens, the phenomenologist penetrates seeing itself. He sees, but he sees inside seeing; he observes, but he pushes the intensity of his vision to the point where what is viewed is the visible essence of the thing rather than the thing as optical intuition. *After* the "reduction," the visible thing emerges in its transcendental purity; it is perceived in its "first idea," as Wallace Stevens put it.

Now if we look at the *theory of vision* that John Cowper Powys forwards, we can see (1) that it is astonishingly similar to Husserl's ideal vision, and (2) that it nevertheless is ontologically quite different from Husserl's ideal vision. Moreover, the difference between phenomenological seeing and Cowperist seeing is precisely the kind of difference that exists between Husserl's phenomenology and Derrida's postphenomenology. I return to this point presently; to begin with, however, let us consider the similarity between Husserl's "reduction" and John Cowper's "reduction."

What evidence have we that Powys in any way interested himself in an optical-metaphysical reduction? If we look at the novels, we can quickly see that the idea of a reduction is absolutely vital. *Weymouth Sands* promotes this notion not only through the thought of the philosopher Richard Gaul, but also through the peculiar self-consciousness of several other important characters. The tendency of these various individual attitudes to resemble and overlap each other creates the impression that the novel as a whole is promoting a coherent—although variegated—optical and metaphysical doctrine. Since a number of these characters, like Magnus Muir and Sylvanus Cobbold, have psychological and philosophical features that are unmistakable properties of John Cowper himself, it is very difficult to differentiate clearly between the general philosophy of the novel and the philosophy of Powys himself. Indeed, I am prepared to say that there is no such thing as a Powysian philosophy existing "outside" the sphere of Powys's texts, whether fictional or nonfictional. I refuse even to accept a mechanical division between the fictional and nonfictional texts. There is not one Powys in the fictions, another Powys in the philosophical works, and a third Powys in "life." Nor is there any absolute distinction between Powys and the Powys heroes. I am not suggesting that all the characters merge into a single homogeneous unit of metaphysical thought; I am arguing that Powys and the Powys heroes have certain things in common, and the idea of an optical-metaphysical reduction is one such important common denominator.

Let us examine how the various individual notions of reduction float into one another in *Weymouth Sands*, giving the novel a general ideology of phenomenological reduction. At the beginning of the novel, Magnus Muir discusses a "power" that he can use at any moment (*WeS* 39).[2] This power, like Wolf Solent's "mythology," is associated with the father.

> It had something to do with seizing upon some dominant or poetical aspect of the physical present, such as this sea-wind now blowing into his room, such as these dying coals, such as that bulge of the red curtains, and drawing from it a fresh, a simple, a childish enchantment—the mystery of life *reduced to the most primitive terms*—that was able to push back as it were by several mysterious degrees all the emotional and mental troubles of life. (39, emphasis mine)

As Husserl wished for a "reduction" that would rid the seeing mind of its subjective prejudice and intellectual bias, so Magnus Muir here implements a reduction that could "push back" the "emotional" and the "mental." Sylvanus Cobbold—who lives in a "borderland" rather than a "real home," in a margin rather than in a center—also forwards a psychocosmic reduction: "By *reducing* the sensations of consciousness to the most primitive elements he had at last arrived at the point of establishing a certain rapport between himself and the cosmos" (271, emphasis mine). The transcendental reduction spills over into the erotic dimension of his existence: "He had long ago acquired that precious power . . . of *reducing* the intensity of his physical desire to a level that lent itself to the prolongation rather than to the culmination of the erotic ecstasy" (380, emphasis mine). Turning to a third character in *Weymouth Sands*, Richard Gaul, we see that he theorizes a similar strategy: "The great thing is to put our basic human cravings into a rigorous mental crucible, until we extract their purest essence" (159).

As in modern phenomenology, then, the idea is to "extract" the "purest essence" from phenomena; but this essence also is the visible itself—the visible made *more* visible than it was a moment ago. The "idealism" that emerges is not traditional idealism, because the "idea," far from being a Platonic "Idea," is the thing itself—its manifest optical actuality. Wolf Solent is absolutely lucid on this point: "It's absurd to talk of souls being inside things! They're *always* on the outside! They're the glamour of things . . . the magic . . . the bloom . . . the breath. They're the *intention* of things!" (*WoS* 441).[3] (Husserl's concept of "intentionality," of course, is immensely cogent in this context.)

In Husserlian fashion, then, an "idealism" is introduced that really is a negation of idealism. The poignant *idea* of something, its essence, is the thing itself. Yet just as the new idealism deviates from orthodox idealism, it also deviates from empiricism and positivism; because the "thing itself," rather than being a passive fact (of science or intuition), is something *created*—something that the truth-yearning mind or visionary imagination has actively "extracted" by an act of will and desire. In a state of immense and almost abnormal concentration, the phenomenological mind *sees* the object as Absolute, as the perfect illumination of its own planetary possibility. The point is established with great force in *Weymouth Sands:* "Sylvanus received a final revelation then of what he had often suspected, namely that the Absolute was to be found in the concrete and not in the abstract, in thought dipped in the life-juice, and not in thought gasping in vacuo. But it was in thought, none the less, *in thought first and last*" (*WeS* 402).

The strange idealism (*"thought first and last"*) that is forwarded through Sylvanus is related in significant ways to Richard Gaul's "Philosophy of Representation." This theory, far from being an orthodox, Platonic "correspondence theory," is a philosophy that disrupts idealism's notion of a metaphysical overworld (158). As narrator, Powys assists this disruption of orthodox idealism by observing that Weymouth, if it is somehow held together by a vast semiconscious sense of coherence, is not necessarily dominated by "any overconsciousness." Because a quasi-spiritual "omnipresence need not imply superiority" (a Platonic overworld), the "overconsciousness" might just as well be identified as a "subconsciousness," although obviously not in the Freudian sense (197). We can best move away from confusion by eliminating the entire vertical structure of the orthodox dualism utilized by classical idealism: above-versus-below. Instead, we should begin to conceive the dualism—which is not quite a dualism—in terms of a lateral cleavage. The world falls apart, into two halves: but *both* sides of the cleavage are still present and actual in the concrete reality of the thing. (Of course, this central self-reduplication in the final analysis unsettles presence and presentness.)

It is this subtle artistic and metaphysical apprehension of dualism (and idealism) that accounts for the dynamic activity of a kind of irresolvable contradiction at the heart of the Cowperverse—a contradiction that helps the writer continue to produce increasingly complex slidings of thought, but which also frustrates any critic who wishes to impose some crude procrustean philosophy on John Cowper's literary vision.[4] On the one hand, Powys's cosmos affirms an absolute divorce between two alien spheres; on the other hand, that same cosmos contains things, especially concrete objects, that function as points of absolute truth where these two alien dimensions amount to a single reality or essence. Again, the viewpoint of Husserl's phenomenology is relevant: the object is at once the site of its pure essence and the locus where that absolute essence is normally concealed.

3

As I pointed out initially, the Powysian reduction is not reducible to Husserl's phenomenological reduction—because John Cowper's reduction, as something more complex and suggestive, acknowledges the kind of reality that Husserl had to murder to achieve the artificial and mathematical purity of his truth. What Husserl murdered in the name of philosophy (and much has been murdered in this name) was space and spacing—the kind of nonpointlike reality that Derrida recently has discussed by developing the notion of "différance."

As we begin to map the exact movement of the Powysian "reduction," the Derridean revision of phenomenology is more interesting than Heidegger's, because like Nietzsche and Derrida, John Cowper suggested dimensions of reality that exist outside and beyond Being/God, whereas Heidegger's ontotheology mainly probes into the being of a Being/God.

To quickly see how far Powys is from the ontotheological affirmation of Being and how close he is to the Derridean disruption of philosophy and ontotheology, consider the following arrogantly perverse account of Richard Gaul's ideology:

> [I]f some student at Jena or Heidelberg were to ask the famous expounder of the Philosophy of Representation what object or group of objects would most vividly "represent" the seacoast of his native land, he might very well reply: "A couple of pairs of girls' stockings carefully kept in their place by pebble-stones, and sprinkled by drifting sand!" (*WeS* 336).

Clearly, that kind of notion fails altogether to conform to any paradigm of representation or idealization known to the sober and reassuring world of classical philosophy. Indeed, the use of erotic levels of general suggestion exactly parallels Derrida's consistent use of such erotic force for the displacement of philosophic meaning—a strategy inspired by Nietzsche's rejection of philosophy as ascetic thought. The paradigmatic foregrounding of Sylvanus Cobbold as an erotically obsessed thinker creates a situation in which the erotic, or generally ecstatic, becomes a lever for the upsetting of orthodox metaphysics. Love, far from being a synthesizing factor in Hegelian fashion, becomes something so eccentric and evasive that it displaces philosophical thought rather than confirming it. As voyeur or erotic experimentalist, the Powys hero peeps through a hole or slides along a sensual margin. Such a hole or margin suggests a wall between Being and Nonbeing—so that the hero, rather than being master of either of these worlds, is the magician who negotiates the action between the two. In this liminal capacity, the erotic hero is caught in dualism as well as monism, in contradiction as well as in the lubrication that smoothes the differences of that contradiction.

Having said that much, I need at once to clarify what I mean by "Nonbeing." "Nonbeing" can, of course, be conceived in lower-order fashion so that it in existentialist fashion simply is "death." John Cowper's cosmic conception is altogether different from existentialism, but we may nevertheless comprehend his crucial conception of Nonbeing by first considering how death can engage existentially with the kind of phenomenological reduction that we have discussed in *Weymouth Sands*. If we turn back from the luminous world of that novel to the more sinister territory of *Wolf Solent*, we can see how the quasi-phenomenological *reduction* can be apprehended as a function of death and negativity. Mr. Urquhart forwards the idea that man's vision would be heightened and purified to an absolute degree only in the interval between a decision to die and death itself:

> "Perhaps the only completely happy moments of a man's life are when he's decided on it. Things must look different then—different and much nicer, eh, Solent? But different anyway; very different. Don't 'ee think so, Solent? Quite different. . . . Little things, I mean. Things like the handles of doors, and bits of soap in soap-dishes, and sponges on washing-stands! Wouldn't you want to squeeze out your sponge, Solent, and pick up the matches off the floor, when you'd decided on it?" (*WoS* 293)

I highlight this remarkable and important section of *Wolf Solent* not to foreground the importance of death, but to suggest the general tension between Being and Nonbeing. This general tension is hyper-ontological rather than existential, philosophical rather than psycho-empirical. What Powys is saying, through Urquhart, is that objects would be heightened in visual significance if their reality was apprehended inside the hyperontological sphere of Nonbeing rather than inside the ontological sphere of Being—as units of (potential) absence rather than as units of presence. If the various items are merely a function of life/existence/Being/presence, their reality is only the uniform and simple self-performance of that life/existence/Being/presence; but if the items already also belong to the sphere of death/nonexistence/Nonbeing/absence, then their *presence* is curiously dramatic and unstable. Their physical reality, although remaining equally or indeed more physical, is energized from within by a negativity that cannot be mastered—truly grasped, limited, comprehended, measured, or thought.

What is at stake here is no representation in the sense of emblematic signification: the objects, as markers of death, do not just symbolize something beyond their empirical presence; rather, that presence itself is intuited as something that is miraculously enigmatic from the outset. The ability of an object to at all *be* is conceived as force rather than presence, movement rather than stasis, desire rather than being, uncanny violence rather than stable positivity.

As we follow the extension of Urquhart's thought, we perceive that the sliding of the objects from Being/life into Nonbeing/death is identified precisely as a *reduction:*

> "You'd see 'em in a sort of fairy-story light, I fancy," he went on, "much as infants see 'em, when they're so damned well pleased with themselves that they chirp like grasshoppers. It would be nice to see things like that, Solent, don't you think so? *Stripped* clear of the mischief of custom?" (295; emphasis mine)

To see things stripped clear of the mischief of custom was precisely the aim of Husserl's phenomenology; but what that phenomenology entirely lacked was the sense that aboriginal Nonbeing is a centermost constitutive dimension of Being. Put differently: that difference and spacing—the void between one thing and another—far from being a secondary thing that arrives as latecomer, is the gap, negativity, and violence that makes the thing possible from the beginning. If otherness does not "precede" the object, the object cannot *be*. As I shall now try to show, John Cowper Powys shapes the genius and difference of his literary vision precisely by foregrounding this Nonbeing and absence as the centermost constructional force of the universe.

4

In what way is Nonbeing important in the Powys world? Look at novels like *Maiden Castle, Weymouth Sands,* and *Wolf Solent. Maiden Castle* discusses the "yawning gulfs of Not-Being under every particular manifestation of Being" (84).[5] As "corpse-god," or "*rex semimor-tuus*," Uryen seems to carry the presence of Nonbeing in his very face (166). "Uryen's massive features composed themselves like a dark stream on the surface of which an unknown animal has been swimming, leaving curious ripples" (167). It is, we are told later, "as if the man's lineaments were decomposing, as if the ghastly ripples of some actual commencement of physical death were passing and repassing across his face." Dud almost feels that "an actual smell of death" is produced by "the man's death-thoughts" (253). Dud observes a similar facial decomposition in Nance; the dark water imagery is foregrounded once more. When the features are deformed by negativity, they return in the form of a negative presence or an absence presencing itself—"as shapes in a flooded landscape when the waters have subsided. But such shapes, returned though they are to light and air, carry upon them an indescribable film, the ashen-grey deposit of their long submersion" (274). John Cowper also uses the idea of sleep to suggest Nonbeing as a complete evasion of Being. Here, sleep must be dreamless to lose all suggestion of Being. In dream-sleep, the mind obviously still belongs to consciousness, is still partly illuminated by items of Being. But Powys wants to depict sleep as the sphere of Nonbeing rather than Being and stresses the "loathing and contempt for dreams" that Wizzie Ravelston and Dud No-man share. "It was an element *sui generis*, an unfathomable dimension peculiar to itself, the everlasting *other side* of the turmoil of life" (475).

In his nocturnal dreams, man is still remembering Being and consciousness. The phenomena of dreams recall and retain the phenomenology of Being. But when man's sleep is dreamless he inhabits Nonbeing utterly. He still *is*, but that being of his is provisionally severed from the entire mastery of Being: consciousness as self-presence. In dreamless sleep, man forgets Being. Absolutely. This idea of the forgetting of Being is quite crucial in the Cowperverse; it dominates the entire conclusion of *Wolf Solent* (569, 595, 599, 617, 631). Indeed, chapter 24 is called "Forget." In *Weymouth Sands*, there is a parallel use of forgetting as an ontological marker. This imaginative feature of the artifact subverts phenomenology and a phenomenological closure of the novel by positing what I like to call a *negative phenomenology*. John Cowper stresses that certain items of Being slip past the appropriating and self-presencing circle of conscious Being—past the individual center of consciousness but also, in the final analysis, past Being. Certain units of Being drift erratically or recklessly into a margin of reality where the identity of their activity is lost. The writer/narrator does not even himself bother to center and appropriate these drifting and self-dispersing units: he merely records the negative, decentering, absencing force of their vanishing actuality. In chapter 6, it is emphasized that Rodney Loder "heard nothing" of the crying seagulls "of the actual moment" (*WeS* 189). As presence, as absolutely self-present now, the sound is perfectly cancelled, because Rodney simply is not aware of it. This absolute obliviousness, far from being a casual and structurally contingent event in the novel, belongs to an entire constellation of units that all point toward forgetting as a hyperontological macro-structure—to forgetting as the forgetting of Being. "And the *obliviousness* of Rodney and Daisy to that crying of the gulls above Spy Croft *added* a new burden, a new weight, a new *quota of insensibility* to the age-old indifference of so many human souls of the two Boroughs to the objects and to the sounds that had become the tutelary background of the place" (189–90; emphasis mine). The units of absence and oblivion, then, add up. Because the inanimate objects of Weymouth—eg, St. John's Spire, the Statue of Queen Victoria— also are centers of *un*consciousness (in the full human sense), all the units of reality in Weymouth that are not phenomenological units of human self-consciousness accumulate into a dimension of reality that seems to run parallel to Being—outside and beyond it. It is this cumulative movement of the units of Nonbeing (or nonself-presence) that accounts most of all for the strong anti-anthropocentric energy of the Powys novel. The decentering of Being, consciousness, and memory also is the decentering of man.

As in *Maiden Castle*, in which we glimpsed Dud and Wizzie in nondreaming oblivion, there is in *Weymouth Sands* an emphasis on sleep as the other of Being. Various units of reality fail to make contact with consciousness, and this noncontact, instead of being an unimportant event, helps to forward a general impression of what I have called negative phenomenology: the furtive and mysterious actuality of a reality moving its forces outside and beyond Being. As Perdita Wane sleeps with the Jobber in that odd inn called the Sea-Serpent's Head, certain movements of the cosmos, beautifully symmetrical in their dispassionate tracings, outline the geometry of Nonbeing, the nonphenomenology of oblivion, the structure of absence itself—Absolute Unknowledge:

And meanwhile *totally unknown* to this girl in the bed and to this man . . ., the measureless starlit heavens above the silent stone roof of the Sea-Serpent's Head were slowly crossed, several hours before dawn, by a long procession of small white clouds. And as if in occult confederacy with these clouds, by flying in the opposite direction, three large migratory birds, such as few Portland dwellers *could have identified*, passed swiftly, one behind another, with flapping soundless wings, over the Head's chimney. At all spots on the earth's surface, in these hours when the life-pulse is lowest, every slightest material movement is accentuated to an impressive degree, and rendered fatal and significant, like a solitary football in some vast empty universe. (364–65; emphasis mine)

I am arguing, then, that the promotion of Nonbeing at the expense of Being shapes itself chiefly in terms of forgetting and absence. Being, as self-presence and memory, its knowledge and ongoing recollection of itself, gives way—at certain crucial junctures—to the forgetting of Being. Sylvanus, we are told, "*had* to forget himself." Even the sight of his own shadow disgusts him (381); he does not wish to have a fixed identity, to *be*. His ecstasies, precisely, help him to evade Being, to move outside and beyond it. The sight of a large piece of cork in the sand causes him to lose and forget himself, to become "as one transported out of himself" (478). Other characters, most of them in the margin of society, eccentrics deficient in the qualities that normally center man as the midpoint of Being, also promote forgetting and absence. Caddie is not even fully present in language:

> "'Does . . . Marret . . . live . . . *with* Mr Cobbold?'
> Caddie articulated these words as if they were not her own language, . . . as if she had learnt the language and ways of men very carefully and thoroughly but was in constant danger of *forgetting* them, being in her heart, as far as the human race was concerned, as *remote* as if she had been a sick seamew." (374–75; emphasis mine)

Caddie's consciousness is not fully and really conscious—is not fully and really consciousness. The locus of her presence, if it still is a presence, situates itself on the outskirts of consciousness, and therefore also on the exterior margin of Being. It hovers undecidedly between Being and Nonbeing, consciousness and oblivion, self-memory and self-forgetting. Similarly, the thoughts of Gipsy May hover between the human and nonhuman. With a "gaiety" that is Nietzschean and Derridean because it marks a readiness to joyfully lose Being at any moment, Gipsy May altogether fails to manifest the continuity of consciousness that defines human self-consciousness as something entirely different from other forms of consciousness:

> The truth perhaps was, as we might surmise of the thoughts of a raven or a magpie, that this singular woman jumped from one entirely concrete matter to another, pouncing upon it, snatching at it, picking

it to bits, wrapping it up and hiding it and all the while thinking of it with a whimsical interest that was far *removed* from covetousness, an interest that was prepared to *relinquish* it at any moment with a complete *gaiety* of temper! (379, emphasis mine)

Sylvanus's interest in an unframed oil painting that is completely "worthless" (392) signals a parallel possessiveness. As in the case of Gipsy May or a magpie, possession here in no way signifies private property as a function of Being and self-conscious retention. The act of appropriation is instinctive, spontaneously immediate and natural; therefore it can transform itself at once into its opposite—absolute spending and absolute relinquishment. Cattistock, as a centered human entirely lacking this ability to "spend," opposes this sovereign impetus in the eccentric characters by representing a philosophy of "secret possession," possession "without scattering" (441).

Generally speaking, then, I am arguing that *Weymouth Sands* projects items of Nonbeing through the concept of the forgetting of Being. In the cumulative buildup of these units of Nonbeing, there is created a sense of a dimension of reality that exists outside Being—and therefore also outside man (who is the thinker of Being). Two main structures support this notion of a reality outside Being. On the one hand, there is the emphasis on inanimate, nonhuman units—giving the novel its vaguely pantheistic or polytheistic horizon of occult suggestion. On the other hand, there is the tendency of the narrator, or of someone serving as his mouthpiece, to explicitly forward a philosophy of Nonbeing. Richard Gaul declares that we can all feel a point of contact with "something that is beyond and outside the astronomical world" (161). There "is something in the deep places of life—though doubtless outside the material world—" that monitors reality (158). The narrator enhances this sense of a cosmic dualism by discussing moments of heightened awareness. Such moments create the sensation of a "spiritual screen, made of a material far more impenetrable than adamant, between our existing world of forms and impressions and *some other world*" (49). As I have emphasized, this "*other world*" is emphatically not a Platonic overworld of divine Ideas or invisible cosmic concepts. *Wolf Solent* advances exactly the same dualism. Wolf tells Christie Malakite about a feeling that his soul sometimes seems to belong "to a world altogether different from this world" (253). When Christie refines the description of such an intuition, she enhances the sense of Nonbeing that I have called attention to: the other dimension takes the shape of "an enormous emptiness" round her, a halo of negativity, a circle of cosmic absence (253).

5

As I pointed out in my introductory remarks, the Cowperist reduction differs from Husserl's phenomenological reduction by affirming spacing and difference. The pure "idea" or "essence" pinpointed by phenomenology is like a mathematical figure or a classical metaphysical concept—its ideality freezes it, fixes it, removes all movement, time, contradiction, desire, and indecision from it. It becomes determinate. It *is*.

John Cowper's "ideas" or "essences" differ from this classical philosophical paradigm. They have to, otherwise they could not affirm Nonbeing, only be passive supports for Being. The Cowperist reduction thus does not only deviate from phenomenology by forwarding the kind of negative phenomenology I have reviewed—the foregrounding of items of reality absent from consciousness. In addition, ordinary phenomenology is displaced by the fact that John Cowper Powys builds restlessness and change into the center of the phenomenologically interesting unit of observation. The process of decentering created by this inclusion of ongoing metamorphosis is reflected in the words and terms that philosophical thought uses to fix its objects of inquiry. Normally, the act of naming is one of identification; but because Powys believes that the center lacks absolute determinate being, naming cannot simply take the form of strict identification. Wolf Solent distrusts the "stripping" (349) known to Jason, because that process of reduction leads to "reality," and Wolf, following a paradigmatic line of thought in John Cowper himself, does not believe in "reality" (349–50). "The 'thing in itself' is . . . fluid and malleable" (350). But if the irreducible indeterminacy of reality prevents a classical act of metaphysical naming, the metaphysical names that already exist also are prevented from simply meaning—from simply corresponding to exact points of pure identity in a stable reality. Philosophical terms are no longer fixed centers of abstract thought that refer reassuringly to fixed centers of concrete reality. Instead, such terms are energized from within by the things they normally come to deny: indeterminacy, change, metamorphosis, metonymic displacement, errancy. At the beginning of *Wolf Solent*, Christie Malakite obviously comes to speak for John Cowper: "[A]ll these queer non-human abstractions, like Spinoza's 'substance' and Leibnitz's 'monads' and Hegel's 'idea,' don't stay hard and logical to me. They seem to melt" (90). Wolf joins this line of thought when he eventually comes to discuss his love of philosophical phrases. It is not "the word itself" that fascinates, "its immediate meaning," but the "trailing margin" of its general power of overall suggestion (354). This "margin," rather than calling forth a center of meaning, presents what is absent: the provisional actuality that such a philosophical concept has had for various "faroff" sets of human nerves that took intellectual delight in its force (355). Powys thinks of an entire history of intellectual pilgrims, each affected in a slightly different way by the power of the philosophical clue-word.

Because, in this way, the intellectual intensity of a metaphysical clue-word is operative in its partly absent and concealed margins rather than in its platonic center of divine meaning, the clue-word itself emerges as a mobile, restless, self-changing thing. I suggest that such a Cowperist clue-word is a *nomad* rather than a *monad:* something that challenges the static and abstract quality of the orthodox metaphysical concept by including a nomadic, migratory energy in its condition of intellectual possibility. Wolf promotes this idea when he considers the peculiar effect on his nerves of the expression "immortal souls." Through a paradigmatic process of "transformation," the sounds of that phrase go astray: they "went wavering away over the fields like a thin spiral cloud," they "slipped like a boat from its moorings" (306).

This intellectual tendency of the metaphysical clue-word to assert itself in terms of a migration from absolutely centered meaning devalues certain automatically rigid concepts. Christie fails to acknowledge the word "truth" (90–91) because there are so "many truths" (91); Wolf fails to recognize the absolute worth of the term "God" because, in his "essentially polytheistic" cosmology, there are so many gods (307).

A *nomad*, then, is a philosophical notion that goes astray: not to lose its identity, but to attain it. John Cowper was nomadic: "I wrote *Wolf Solent*," he says, "travelling through all the states of the United States except two" (11). But this nomadic inclination, to always "go about," is also integral to philosophy and its magnificent concepts. "I regard each philosophy," says Christie, "not as the 'truth,' but just as a particular country, in which I can go about—countries with their own peculiar light, their Gothic buildings, their pointed roofs, their avenues of trees" (91). This conception of philosophy, far from being naive and primitive, is exactly the conception that Derrida, following Nietzsche, has clarified recently. When Derrida reads Hegel, as he does in *Glas*, he reads him precisely as a landscape in which he can "go about" nomadically. A philosophy emerges as a text rather than as a collection of rigid propositions without contextual or rhetorical qualifications; thus the modern interpreter of philosophy needs the talents that great literary critics are endowed with rather than just the ability to perform cognitive operations of deduction, induction, and analysis. In *Weymouth Sands*, John Cowper uses the odd philosopher Richard Gaul to drive home this point:

> Unlike most philosophers who are content to use their one grand, basic inspiration about life and then bolster it up with infinite logical and rationalistic devices, Mr. Gaul by a bold original method of his own kept his argument fluid, flexible and porous; subject in fact to the various *daily* inspirations that came to him as he lived in Brunswick Terrace. What he would argue was that the rigidly *monumental* method of exposition adopted by most philosophers was an unnatural method and was a method, moreover, that sacrificed a great deal of organic flexibility to the dead hand of logical abstraction. (99)

The smallest units that phenomenology works with, after its processes of "reduction," are pure perceptions. But the smallest units that the Cowperverse is broken down into are not perceptions but states. Unlike a perception, which can be pointlike and windowless like Leibnitz's windowless monads, a state always includes absence, difference, and spacing in its field of vision and thought. Therefore, the contraphenomenological process of reduction in the Powys world never gets bogged down in the logical miasmas that eventually trouble phenomenology. Far from being windowless, the philosophical vantage point in the Powys world is itself a window, or its sill. "Philosophy," says Wolf, is "life *framed* . . . framed in room-windows . . . in carriage windows [that is, *moving* windows] . . . in mirrors . . . in our 'brown studies,' when we look up from absorbing books . . . in waking dreams" (*WoS* 91).

6

Working toward the conclusion of this inquiry, I wish to draw attention to a figure that not only brings the question of Nonbeing to its most poignant crisis but that also adumbrates the vision of a possible ultimate coalescence of Being and Nonbeing. This figure is woman.

The erotic dimension, as I have said, disrupts philosophy and its equanimity of thought, because the erotic force of life is erratic and unpredictable enough to throw metaphysics and its ascetic world off balance. In the traditional philosopher's role of an ascetic recluse, Sylvanus Cobbold has failed to attain "the Absolute"; therefore he has turned to women and their margins of erotic suggestion to reach the secret clues to the cosmos "which as a hermit and as a solitary he ha[s] been unable to reach for himself" (*WeS*, 272). Woman becomes a medium mainly as a figure who triggers ecstatic modes of awareness—someone who facilitates contact with the deep structure of the universe. Why does she become a crucial instrument of deeper knowledge? Because she brings Nonbeing to the forefront. Mere meditation and familiarity with the philosophical classics only brings the contemplative mind in contact with Being—or with God, if you will. But woman, by somehow being a supplement to God, adds a dimension of thought that "masculine reason" alone cannot provide (272). Woman intervenes in Being, opening up a slit or hole in its body, as we can see from Sylvanus's account of his fascination with Marret:

> "It's funny," he said to himself. "She's helped me to get hold of God; and yet there's a sweetness in her that I can't mix with God."
> He tried in vain to analyse what he felt, but it was as if his great Being, whose Centre was everywhere and his Circumference nowhere, had an infinitesimal fragment of his rounded completeness *chipped off*, leaving a tiny gap, a gap of too-sweet, too-dear Time in the bosom of the Eternal! (503)

Woman, in fact, paradigmatically implements a central absence in the Cowperverse. Because she creates the most reckless forms of infatuation in the Powys hero, she works through absence rather than presence, mystery rather than identity. There is a "faraway" expression in the eyes of Curly Wix, a "far-off trance of luminous wistfulness" (370), and it is the distance, or absence, created by this "far-off gaze" that unleashes Magnus Muir's adoration (371). What is attractive in women, then, is not her identity or human personality, but a certain enchanting aesthetic quality in her physical appearance. What agitates Dud's erotic nerve in *Maiden Castle* is not the full character of Wizzie Ravelston (which he finds disconcertingly banal), but things like "the way the shining strands of her hair were caught up, tight and smooth, above the nape of her neck" (150). Such fascination with the more or less irrational aspects of erotic attraction is commonplace, in literature as well as life; yet in Powys's creative imagination, this common emphasis on the marginal and irrational is pushed to eccentric levels of signification. The male often seems to prefer the perfectly contingent supplements of the woman to her center and flesh; thus we find Dud No-man worshipping Wizzie's lavender-colored tights more than Wizzie herself (318), Wolf Solent caressing the minutely indented surface of an ash rather than the woman he has drawn up against its trunk (*WoS* 370). The fetish, as a supplement to the woman that seems to embody her appeal as Nonbeing, comes to play a major role in the erotic scenario, and the woman's function sometimes seems to be that of producing such items of fascination in the margin of her presence rather than that of producing her presence as such—her being. Because the erotic woman is foregrounded as margin rather than center, absence rather than presence, physical consummation—although still a magnificent thing—is not absolutely essential as a culminating erotic event. Instead, the erotic culminates outside its own culmination. It finds its true center outside its true center. In fact, erotic woman has no center that can be found or identified; that center is the "evasive point" that frustrates Sylvanus's reason but that also maintains the lasting energy of his erotic yearning (*WeS* 271).

The relevance of the current problematic may be appreciated by considering certain erotic moves in John Cowper's own private life. In a recent essay in *The Powys Review*, Oliver Marlow Wilkinson enlarges our knowledge of the remarkable relationship between his mother, Frances Gregg, and John Cowper Powys.[7] Powys, who had fallen greatly in love with Frances, married her off to his friend Louis Wilkinson, and even went on the honeymoon trip to England. The general significance that emerges from that essay, I think, is not that John Cowper promotes nonpossessive love at the expense of possessive love, but that his special mode of erotic propulsion dismantles the dialectical opposition possessive/nonpossessive: he possesses in *terms* of nonpossession. There is no question of giving up possession. But it operates through absence and distance rather than through presence and closure—in the final analysis, through Nonbeing rather than Being. To possess the loved one only as presence would be to claim her only insofar as ongoing reality moved through its phases of presence; that kind of loving would have to forsake the entire drama of Nonbeing and vertiginous negativity that John Cowper apprehended as the most magical and intense aspect of the universe. Frances and John Cowper tried for a short time to live together, in 1919, but failed. Later, Frances innocently explains the failure in terms of Being rather than Nonbeing: "There have to be lovers, but it is dangerous not to understand a woman and not to know her as she really *is*."[8] The crux of the matter, of course, is that Powys never believed in "is"—in the idea that things of people simply are. His refusal to accept this centered, logical, and prosaic intuition of reality can be rashly dismissed in terms of romance and poetry: he was simply a romantic escapist; but as I have tried to suggest here, different and altogether more subtle reasons can be found for such an attitude.

Oliver Wilkinson ends his moving account not only by presenting evidence of an ultimate reconciliation between the lovers, but also by recording John Cowper's remarkable reaction to the news of Frances's death after enemy bombing on 21 April 1941. Powys's reaction to this news is interesting because he sums up the force of its presence in terms of absence. Indeed, the entire movement of this dreadful information is a movement through spacing, difference, and absence. The news only becomes fully operative after a detour through negativity and Nonbeing, and for John Cowper this detour is more significant, emblematic, and impressive than the death itself.

When Powys begins to read the news of the death of "my mother," he at first lives in the illusion that the letter is written by Frances herself. He was *"certain"* that it was from her.[9] Gradually, however, this potent misreading fails to make sense until finally the terrible words "death of my mother" shine forth in their true light. Yet when John Cowper answers Oliver's letter, these words are turned into the quasi-metaphysical clue-word that I have called a "nomad." Like that haunting phrase "immortal souls," the words "death of my mother" form a cognitive cluster that begins to move. It moves like that other magic phrase, into a certain orbit of unknowledge: into a horizon of absence and loss rather than of presence and identity. He writes:

> I was up the mountain here this morn very early before breakfast at sunrise and in the larch-wood where I get kindling for the fires every day. I thought of her in that way we do when a letter from a person is awaiting our return—I always have been of late every day thinking of her & praying for her up in that larch-wood but this morning it was more like when you have the feeling that there's a letter & when I saw yours I was *certain* it was from her . . . And so now, just as you have that feeling about the telegram *you* received, so the words 'death of my mother' (which I thought was Frances speaking [of *her* mother]) will always be written *on the air* or on a particular segment of the air that will come round & round & round again, as the earth turns on its pivot & day follows night.[10]

Apart from *"certain,"* three words are deliberately emphasized: *on the air*. Here it seems rather clear to me that this idea of an inscription in air, a permanent inscription in air ("always be written"),

only reaches the fullness of its reverbatory power when it is comprehended as a function of the negativity that I have been mapping:
negativity as absence and Nonbeing. It does not seem mysterious
to me that this Nonbeing can come back again, with the turning
of the planet, because the entire notion of writing as recurring absence, or absent recurrence, is inscribed already in Powys's introductory comments: that he was in that mood when we expect a letter
to be present at our *return*, when we expect, without ever being
certain, that the presence of the other one will be presenced in
terms of an absence-in-presence or presence-in-absence: a letter, a
postcard, certain marks on paper.[11]

This, then, is where I leave you: in the site of an inscription.
In Powys, inscription is not writing as logocentric "expression," but
instead the curious alphabet of difference itself, what marks yellow-
hammers' eggs with "mischievous crooked scrawls" (*WoS* 325)—to
distinguish them from other eggs—and what here inscribes the name
"Frances" "on the casualty list in the very centre of battered Ply-
mouth."[12] That this "centre" should be "battered" should not surprise
us by now—for as I have tried to suggest, that kind of battering
of the center is paradigmatic in Powys's writing. What saves and
redeems that sense of battering and central loss is perhaps what
John Cowper and Frances in different ways themselves projected
into the world: beauty. Beauty, however, is much like "truth," "reality," and a host of other human concepts, something that is problematic rather than reassuring for John Cowper. Curly Wix is taken
"beyond the margin of her reason" by beauty, so that this "*beauty
itself*" decenters intelligence and tranquil Being, overspilling its circumference (*WeS* 371). Similarly, the attention given to ugliness and
monstrosity, partly through the "anus" that terminates the name
and identity of Sylvanus (381–82), destabilizes orthodox aesthetics—
suggesting to us that there are impressive forces in the universe
that operate alongside beauty, or even contrary to its nature. If beauty
is the aesthetic currency of Being, perhaps the disturbing ugliness
presenced by characters like Uryen suggests an inverted beauty as
the aesthetic currency of Nonbeing.

In the final analysis, then, the Absolute in the Cowperverse is
a unit of unknowledge rather than knowledge: the Absolute, as a
truly unknown Other, cannot be known, identified, or appropriated.[13]
Uryen consistently forwards this notion of the irreducible alterity
of the other, of the *Not* of Notbeing, by idealizing a miraculous
gesture that will permit man to "break through" (*MC* 467–68). But
in the distraught gulfs of pessimism created by this sense of the
permanent absence of the other side of things, it is possible, with

Dud No-man, to employ the shrewd logic that Hegel employed to refute Kant. "We couldn't think of a barrier if there weren't something in us *already outside it*" (493). To say that there is an ungraspable unknown entirely beyond and outside our cognition is to advance a logical absurdity, because it we can identify that unknowable *as* unknowable with great philosophical equanimity, do we not already know something essential about it? Do we not know precisely that aspect of the other that causes it to be what it is: an other?

Because, in this way, all the various states of the Cowperverse, however nomadic, can be *thought* in their possibility of endlessness by their creator, these states do indeed coalesce into a coherent union: a union of states, a United States.[14] This unity, however precarious its foundation may be, is what I have discussed here in the light of Nonbeing.

Notes

1. *The Ecstatic World of John Cowper Powys* (Rutherford, N.J.: Fairleigh Dickinson University Press, 1986), pp. 16–20.

2. John Cowper Powys, *Weymouth Sands* (London: Picador, reprint ed., 1980). Abbreviated *WeS* in text where clarification is needed.

3. John Cowper Powys, *Wolf Solent* (Harmondsworth, Middlesex: Penguin, reprint ed., 1978). Abbreviated *WoS* in text where clarification is needed.

4. The "Cowperverse" is the universe/multiverse that forms John Cowper's imaginative world. See Fawkner, *The Ecstatic World,* chapter 1.

5. John Cowper Powys, *Maiden Castle* (London: Picador, reprint ed., 1979). Abbreviated *MC* in text where clarification is needed.

6. Translated by John P. Leavey, Jr. and Richard Rand (Lincoln and London: University of Nebraska Press, 1986; French original, 1974).

7. Wilkinson, "The Letters of Frances and Jack," *The Powys Review* 19 (1986): 43–57.

8. Ibid., p. 55. Emphasis mine.

9. Ibid., p. 57.

10. Ibid.

11. In *La Carte postale* (Paris: Flammarion, 1980), Derrida argues that the fabric of the universe can be conceived in terms of an eternity of relays: relays that are joined, but also severed by the postmen and postcards that maintain the process of general circulation and information (205–6). In this crisscross reality in which everything is somehow mediate and nothing perfectly immediate (209), the eternal structural possibility of the letter to *fail to properly arrive* causes a lack of exhaustion and totalization in the circles of knowledge. These circles, unlike Hegel's perfectly circular conceptions of spirit, fail, minutely, to come full circle (222). I think this notion is strikingly suggestive in the current Powys context—not only inasmuch as it adumbrates a special hyperonthology for the odd displacement of communication that John Cowper focuses in his misreading of Oliver's letter, but also inasmuch as it rehearses the writer's disruption of the ontotheological circle when he speaks of Sylvanus and Marret: something was, we may recall, "*chipped off*" from the "rounded completeness . . . of the Eternal" (*WeS* 503).

12. Wilkinson, "The Letters of Frances and Jack," p. 56.

13. For further discussions of this issue, see my two essays, "John Cowper Powys and Ontotheology," *The Powys Review* 21 (1987–88): 35–48, and *"Owen Glendower: Love at the Margins of Being," The Powys Review* 23 (1989): 48–60.

14. Most of this paper was read at the annual conference of *The Powys Society of North America*, at Hofstra University, Long Island, in early June 1987. As I emerged from Penn Station one afternoon during the conference week, I did so with the hope of possibly finding some nearby mailbox for my odd postcards back to Europe. At precisely this moment, I was infinitely shocked to discover that I was standing below the mightiest post office I had seen in my life. The tremendous motto stretching (it seemed to me) half a mile across its facade arose in front of me as society's defiance of the notion (see note 11) of the precariousness of all communication. But perhaps the two opposed notions of the *rounds* of communication are not so incompatible after all. On the one hand there is our sense that the most firm circles of communication are stricken by the fatal possibility of a cruel miscarriage; on the other hand, it is the very possibility of that risk that inspires us to complete the orbit of what we have to tell and deliver.

The "Dark Gods" and Modern Society:
Maiden Castle and *The Plumed Serpent*

Peter G. Christensen

John Cowper Powys's novels have been rediscovered, but surprisingly they have not stirred up much debate in academic circles. The 1985 Inaugural Conference of the North American Powys Society at Colgate University was not particularly beset by conflicting interpretations of Powys's work, and yet, I ask myself, when we turn to the published criticism do we find the consensus shattered to some extent?

As I read *Maiden Castle* (1936) for the second time,[1] I was struck by the character of Enoch Quirm, who claims to be an incarnation of Uryen, also known as Bran the Blessed in Welsh mythology. I saw certain major correspondences between this novel and D. H. Lawrence's *The Plumed Serpent* (1925). First, in Lawrence's novel, Don Ramón claims to be an incarnation of the god Quetzalcoatl, the plumed serpent. His friend Cipriano refers to himself as another god, Huitzilopochtli. In each novel the repressed past of a nation (the Celts crushed by the Anglo-Saxons and the Aztecs crushed by the Catholic Spanish) is raised to public consciousness. Second, many of the characters in *Maiden Castle* have a strong attraction to Uryen: Dud, his son; Nancy, his wife; Thuella, his neighbor; and Wizzie, Dud's lover. Yet all of these characters also are repulsed by the peculiar old man. In *The Plumed Serpent*, the protagonist Kate Leslie has an ambivalent attraction for both Ramón and Cipriano, who eventually becomes her lover.[2] Through these character relationships both novelists discuss patriarchy, an idea that Lawrence, but not Powys, favors. Third, Lawrence's Aztec revival is bloody and proto-fascistic, whereas Powys makes no suggestion that worship of the Celtic deities should become a ritualized state religion. Powys tries to show that humankind is better off developing the interior life rather than turning to politics. For Lawrence, all of society must be changed to improve each individual's lot.

Although *The Plumed Serpent* has always been a hotly debated

157

book, the subject of many essays, chapters, books, and dissertations, I wondered if *Maiden Castle*, which treats many of the same themes, had generated much interest, particularly in the figure of Uryen, the most disturbing and vivid character in the novel.

The answer was yes, and a long line of critical comments proved indispensable for considering how Powys was using *Maiden Castle* to respond to *The Plumed Serpent*. G. Wilson Knight, Powys's friend, in *The Saturnian Quest* (1964) does not provide a complete analysis of the novel, but sees Uryen as "Powys's attempt to personify a wisdom or wise-being which is death as well as life; animal and the inanimate as well as man; a, or the, creative principle, wronged by four thousand years of misguided progress."[3] H. P. Collins, writing in 1966, is not fond of the novel, but finds that Uryen is "largely a reincarnation of primordial forces."[4] The following year, Uryen was only Nancy's "dreadful old husband" for Kenneth Hopkins,[5] who does not believe that the novel resolves any of Dud's problems.

Jeremy Hooker (1973) shows a biographical connection between Uryen and Powys. He points out that it was Sir John Rhys's 1891 *Studies in Arthurian Legend* that provided Powys with the documentation about Uryen's identity. This book had been very influential on Powys during his college years at Cambridge. For Hooker, Dud overcomes Uryen's mistake in believing that there is a "barrier that only the psychosensual force of unsatisfied desire can break through."[6] The search for life beyond life only leads to death. Jean Markale, in "Powys et le Celtisme" (1973),[7] is more sympathetic to Uryen, because the novel's women suggest to him variants on women from Celtic myth, thus partially substantiating Uryen's belief in the Celtic present.

The banner year of Powys scholarship, 1973, also saw the two best readings of *Maiden Castle* thus far. Glen Cavaliero focused on the theme of the novel as follows:

> In these two aspects of the novel, the story of Uryen and the story of Wizzie and [Dud], are to be found its twofold nature. It is a drama about self-enclosure and the impact upon it of another person; and it is the portrait of the human desire for power.[8] (94)

The strength of Cavaliero's interpretation comes from the attention he pays to the education of its central character. Dud No-man is "left alone with his solitary sensations; but he is wiser for his life with Wizzie, and aware that society as much as solitude is necessary for his well-being" (96). Cavaliero quotes the key lines of the novel— Dud's thoughts about his father Uryen on the last page:

And an apathy, a numbness, a strange quiescence descended upon D. No-man; not the same apathy that had been weighing him down all these last days, but the apathy that comes on a person when his soul, removing itself to a distance from his body, faces without flinching but with an immense weariness the long ascending path up which it has to drag that mortal companion of its wayfaring. Which of those two—his mother, with her inhuman egoism or Mona, with her weird unselfishness—held the secret that prevailed? Well! He must go on as best he could in his own way. He must be decent to Nance. He must be faithful, after his fashion, to Wizzie. He must hold fiercely to all those "sensations" of his! It was no good. He could *not* live, as this dead man [Uryen] had done, in a wild search for the life behind life.

One life at a time! But neither would he close one single cranny or crevice of his mind to the "intimations of immortality" that in this place and at this hour were so thick about him. (496)

Cavaliero recognizes that Uryen's beliefs can neither be denied nor confirmed, and that Dud must escape self-centeredness by living in a dialogue with all the contradictory views of human nature expressed around him.

In contrast, John Brebner decenters the story from Dud's personal progress. According to him,

There are clearly three different viewpoints about time being examined: Uryen representing the mythic past; Dud the historic past, and Wizzie the future. Thus, Uryen is identified with Maiden Castle and its gods, Dud with the Dorchester of the Romans (Durnovaria) and of Mary Channing; Wizzie with the movement of circus-life and with America. These levels are cleverly interrelated by a number of triadic similarities. . . . Their interests are reflected in their lives as religion, speculation, and performance: a trilogy of negative, neutral, and positive elements. This, then, is correlated to racial, social, and personal *motifs*. Uryen is the voice of racial inheritance, the spirit of a people intent on giving meaning to life; Dud is preoccupied by the injustice of Mary Channing's execution; Wizzie acts. She is the key to the whole *ensemble*.[9] (148–49)

For Brebner, the novel cannot be reduced to the education of Dud No-man. First, Dud not only learns from those around him, including Uryen, but he will look after the widowed Nancy and Lovie, Wizzie's illegitimate child, which also counts. Second, the reader must create a synthesis of the three main characters, and Dud must create a synthesis from his experiences with Uryen, Wizzie, and all the other secondary characters.

In an unpublished paper dated 1979, Denis Lane offers a view of Uryen and Dud based on the Saturnian myth.[10] He stresses that as Dud moves toward integration (with which Cavaliero and Brebner would agree), Uryen does not remain static, but regresses and disintegrates physically. Uryen is truly one of the dispossessed, because Bran the Blessed is a Celtic manifestation of Saturn.

Morine Krissdottir (1980) pays special attention to all of Powys's Magus-like figures and concludes that "Dud's Platonic philosophy is . . . echoed in Uryen's teachings, but in a magical form" (114).[11] Both apparently believe that all reality is insubstantial and that the soul is detached from matter. Krissdottir identifies Dor Marth, which Dud associates with Uryen, as the dog of Gwyn-ap-Nudd, the Hunter of Dead Souls.

In 1983, Ian Hughes suggested that once a restored version of *Maiden Castle* is published the relationship of Uryen and Dud to the minor characters will appear transformed.[12] About one fourth of the novel had been carelessly deleted by the editor, Quincy Howe. The secondary characters suffered most drastically. In a second article a year later, Hughes indicated that the Uryen theme had not been present in the discarded, but important, first drafts of the novel, now in the Bissell collection.[13] Hughes now has an accurate version of the novel ready for publication.

The Powys Review, no. 13 (1984/85), which contained Hughes's second article, is a special issue devoted to *Maiden Castle*. In her editorial, Belinda Humfrey notes that Hughes's version will restore the word "Uryen" to "Urien," a "name which in the light of the Blakean verbal tricks of this book, suggests that he is really nothing (Rien)."[14] Humfrey is very sympathetic to Dud in his conflict with Uryen. For her, Uryen "seeks to revive the ancient Powers of the dead within himself by exploiting the impotent love of people close to him: he would 'put out the sun'"(4). Uryen's power is "the very opposite of the Wordsworthean 'power', dependent on love of the green earth, which Powys comes close to invoking through No-man" (4). Ultimately, from her perspective, Uryen is a "pitiable but definitely *comic* Satanic figure" (6).

Angela Blaen, in a brief article on "Maiden Castle and the Celtic Calendar," stresses the importance of it being Candlemas when Uryen reveals to Dud that he is his father.[15] The cycle of the Celtic year provides reference points for the novel that suggest the continuing relevance of the Celtic past to the present. As Blaen states, "[t]hroughout the events of Candlemas Day, images of birth, life, death, and procreation abound, as if stressing the universal nature of Dud's experience with Uryen" (33). The relevance of the Old Calendar to the plot, I would conclude, can only make us more sympathetic to Uryen, for whom the ancient past is eternally present.

Susan Rands is mainly concerned with Powys's treatment of fantasies, particularly sexual ones.[16] She believes Uryen's fantasies are quite mad, but what really counts is that Dud does not take them as such. He thinks they make sense, based on Uryen's personal past and his readings in mythology. Her Uryen is hardly a villain, for he can heal the sick (Nancy), and he endures much pain, finally mistaking Wizzie for his lover Cornelia (Dud's mother), and asking her for forgiveness.

Margaret Moran also does not judge Uryen harshly.[17] For her, Uryen is the ultimate reader. His life is very similar to that of the other characters, who also live through books. Teucer Wye, with his ever-present volumes of Plato, and Wizzie, who reads cheap, dreadful novels, also are bound to a life seen through books.

It is apparent now that Uryen is an extraordinarily complex character and perhaps a substantially more provocative creation than Don Ramón in *The Plumed Serpent*. A thumbnail summary provides us with the following views of Uryen: the creative principle (Knight); a reincarnation of primordial forces (Collins); Nancy's dreadful husband (Hopkins); a philosopher with a mistaken view of a barrier beyond this life (Hooker); one of several figures in the novel based on Welsh myth (Markale); a man on a mistaken quest for life beyond this life (Cavaliero); an incomplete third of the cosmic whole (Brebner); a disturbing representative of dissolution and death (Lane); a representative of Dud's philosophy in its primitive form (Krissdottir); a Blakean figure, comically Satanic (Humfrey); an archetypal father in a cycle of recurrence (Blaen); a madman redeemed by powers of healing, suffering, and the desire for forgiveness (Rands); and a man animated by the fictions he reads (Moran). In short, if earlier Powys critics had juxtaposed their views of Uryen with one another, an exciting debate would surely have developed.

Although I must express my own ideas of Uryen in my comparison of *Maiden Castle*, it would be simplistic to expect my readers to approach my judgments with no sense of the complexity of the issues involved. Although *Maiden Castle* does not refer explicitly to Lawrence as it does to *Faust, Part II*, *The Mabinogion*, the poetry of Taliesin, *The Mayor of Casterbridge*, and the essays of John Rhys, we know from Ian Hughes's work on the discarded drafts that Powys was thinking of Lawrence when he wrote the novel. Describing Dud, Powys wrote in the discarded opening:

> His employers found this detachment of his exactly suited to their purpose. He never drank. He never went out with girls. He never quarrelled with the customers or made inconvenient alliances with them. He never

gossiped. He never took sides over politics. He never discussed religion. He even refrained from telling people what they ought, as intellectual persons, to read. He sold Miss Braddon with as much gusto as Miss Stein and Edgar Wallace with as much aplomb as D. H. Lawrence.[18]

By this date, Powys already had made a major statement on Lawrence, which appeared in a collection of essays on *Sex in the Arts* in 1932. Powys discussed sex in "Modern Fiction" and turned to Lawrence after his discussions of Proust, Dreiser, and Joyce. Although Powys seems most interested in *Studies in Classic American Literature* and *Lady Chatterley's Lover*, one does get the feeling that Powys has read extensively in Lawrence's work, including *The Plumed Serpent:*

> In its stoical and almost ferocious stripping off of the trappings of our bourgeois civilization, Lawrence's athletic and proletarian Eros might, one feels, serve many of the purposes of the great Russian Proletcult. But Englishman from the Midlands as he is, his poetic prejudice against industrialism and machinery makes this "figure against the sky" of his erotic dreaming more anti-social than any dictatorship could possibly tolerate; and it has been this anti-social element in him, this misanthropic Return to Nature, that always led him to hanker after the free ranch-life of Mexico and New Mexico, vast spaces and horizons, where his "dark gods" encounter something reciprocal and corresponding in the solitary eagles and serpents of the descendants of the Lost Atlantis.
> It is a far cry from Staffordshire and Nottinghamshire and Derbyshire to the altars of Quetzalcoatl. . . .[19] (54)

Powys, who published a romance on Atlantis in 1954, saw clearly the relationship between Atlantis and Lawrence's idea of Mesoamerican civilization. Indeed, Atlantis is referred to in *The Plumed Serpent,* and Michael Ballin has suggested that it was the writings of Louis Spence in *The Occult Review* that brought Lawrence to connect the religion of Quetzalcoatl with the religion of the lost Atlantis.[20]

Powys mentions Lawrence's "dark gods" six times in the essay and finds Lawrence's attempts to revive them as totally misguided:

> We have all made the mistake—in fact, it is one of the ways in which posterity will recognize our generation—of assuming that this eminently moral way of being libidinous *ex cathedra* is the same thing as being what we are accustomed to call 'pagan.' Nothing could be farther from the truth. Anything less 'pagan' than the feverish and frantic gravity with which Lawrence goes to work to transform his "dark gods" into a New Religion could hardly be imagined. One has only to turn over

the pages of Apuleius, no very hard-boiled pagan, to find this out. And yet, though it is easy, from an irresponsible profane viewpoint, to make sport of all of this, our psychoanalysis-bewitched era has undoubtedly achieved certain deep and permanent insights for the eroticists of our race. And among us all no one has dived deeper into these sub-Atlantean secrets than D. H. Lawrence. (54)

For Powys, Lawrence's paganism is false because it is willed a very telling critique of Lawrence's reasoning, because he was always denouncing the will that left people incapable of enjoying life, other people, and sex. Nevertheless, Powys gives Lawrence credit for his studies of the sexual antagonisms between men and women, particularly with respect to the masculine "soul" in women and the feminine "soul" in man (54).

None of the three previous attempts to compare Powys and Lawrence in detail considered this essay. G. Wilson Knight, in addition to his scattered mentions of Lawrence in *The Saturnian Quest*, discussed the two authors together in three of the five essays on Powys contained in *Neglected Powers* (1971)[21] and in "Powys and the Kundalini Serpent," one of at least eight other uncollected essays on Powys by him.[22] In this essay, Knight finds the Yoga Kundalini Serpent idea "a power of men lodged at the base of the spine and rising to fertilize the mind and body" (37), present in *Wolf Solent* and *A Glastonbury Romance*, on the one hand, and *The Plumed Serpent* on the other. However, Knight then indicates that Powys did not like Lawrence's Red Indians (the ones associated with Kundalini). Knight quotes from Powys's *Autobiography* (1934):

> Sometimes I pretend to myself, that I, who have always aimed at being a "magician" beyond every other aim in life, have really learnt a few occult secrets from the spirits of the Red Indians, this most original and formidable among all the children of men.
> I still regard Longfellow's *Hiawatha* as an exciting and thrilling poem; and I differ completely from D. H. Lawrence in my choice among Indians, *My* Indians are the Red Indians of the East, not the Indians of New Mexico, or Old Mexico, or any other Mexico. It is an inconsistency in me, being the idol-worshipper that I am, but all the same when it comes to Indians I prefer heroes who worship, as my father taught me to do, a Great Spirit whose breath bloweth like the wind, to artistic tribes who worship Quetzalcoatl and his feathery snake. (XI. 548)[23]

From these three mentions by Powys of D. H. Lawrence in the early 1930s, we can conclude that Powys felt a need to offer a corrective to Lawrence's views, and that Dud in the discarded opening of *Maiden Castle* was being gently mocked for the indifference with which he could treat the provocative Lawrence.

Three essays of *Neglected Powers* champion Powys's vision of life over Lawrence's. In "Lawrence, Joyce, and Powys," Knight asserts that Powys has a greater range in *A Glastonbury Romance* than Joyce in *Ulysses* or Lawrence in *The Plumed Serpent*. Knight finds that "Powys's general worldview concentrates heavily, though not exclusively on the powers coming from below in man and on the inanimate lower life-forms in nature, with a kind of mystic sensuality blending Wordsworth, Joyce, and Lawrence" (154). However, Knight concentrates on the symbols of the serpent and the grail, and he does not attempt to compare pre-Columbian Mexico as seen by Lawrence with Arthurian Britain as seen by Powys. In "Mysticism and Masturbation," Knight contrasts Powys's favorable view of masturbation with Lawrence's terror of it. Lawrence's lyric poems are compared with those of Powys in "The Ship of Cruelty." Knight prefers "The Ship" by Powys to any of Lawrence's poems. Because Lawrence concentrated so heavily on dualities of all sorts, and Powys saw the universe in less schematic terms, I sympathize with Knight's belief that Powys had a more wide-ranging understanding of life than Lawrence had.

Although Powys criticized Lawrence in the 1930s, he was surprisingly more sympathetic by the 1950s. In "Phoenix and Serpent," Glen Cavaliero indicates that in 1955 Powys wrote to Louis Wilkinson of his "terrible devotion" to D. H. Lawrence. In 1956, Powys commented to Nicholas Ross that "what D. H. L. stood for" was "JUST what I then and *still* 'stand for'" (51).[24] Cavaliero then categorizes many differences between the two authors, showing that Powys, unlike Lawrence, was not interested in political Utopias—especially of the Quetzalcoatl-religion variety, I would add. In line with Knight, Cavaliero points out that Powys did not reject "sex-in-the-head."

Linden Peach, turning only to two works of nonfiction by Powys (*In Defense of Sexuality*, 1930; and *A Philosophy of Solitude*, 1933) concludes similarly that Powys "places more emphasis than Lawrence upon the power of the mind and believing that man is a solitary animal he is adamant that solitude is essential for the development of one's innermost self" (39).[25] Dud No-man is the solitary hero, and he must discover the acceptable level of his solitude. In *The Plumed Serpent*, the protagonist, Kate Leslie, also has the same problem. After hesitating, she decides to becomes the lover of the Indian general Don Cipriano, who is also Huitzilopochtli, an Aztec divinity. Dud, with less hesitation, decides to take the twenty-one-year old circus performer Wizzie Ravelston as his lover. When the novel opens, Dud has lost both his parents and his wife, Mona, in an epidemic ten years before. He moves to Dorchester, where they are buried, and goes to their graveside for the first time. The narrative begins with a pervasive sense of death, sorrow, and loss, as Dud meets Nancy Quirm, who is mourning her son Jimmy at the cemetery.

Although loneliness is associated with death, we find that Dud also had lived in such an interior fashion that his life has suffered for it. He did not have any sexual relations with his wife, but has had an intense erotic involvement with his memory of her. Dud's story is that of a man who must come to grips with the dead, and in this framework Uryen is the main problematic figure, because he is a symbol of both life (as Dud's father) and death (through the images of decomposition that surround him). Whether Uryen will be a help or a hindrance to Dud's personal integration is an important theme of the novel. For Dud, Uryen is the "semi-mortuus rex," but this term cannot really be understood until we examine the way in which Dud looks at death:

> If our survival of death, he had come to feel, depended on the intensity with which we lived our individual life, the intensity with which we grasped life's most symbolic essences then it was "the Woman from Wales" [Dud's mother] who was most likely to dodge annihilation; whereas if our chance depended on the power we develop for sinking our individuality in others' lives, why then it was the dead Mona who had the better start. (*MC*, 21)

These two criteria need to be weighed again at the end of the novel with reference to Uryen. Yet, despite the great impression Uryen has made on him, Dud only thinks of his mother and wife as the people capable of directing him in the future:

> Which of those two—his mother, with her inhuman egoism or Mona, with her weird unselfishness—held the secret that prevailed? (*MC*, 496)

It seems probable that Uryen has succeeded in both categories, because he both has lived intensely enough to believe himself a god and has brought Dud to the resolution that he must not live looking for a life beyond this one.

Uryen's claim to be a god must be understood in relationship to Dud's ideas on immortality and annihilation:

> "I haven't cried for [Mona] once," he mused, "since she died. All Souls' day it is! The right day for me to go to her. *Are* they gone

forever—those two, or is one gone forever and the other, by some magic in her way of life, *not* gone? Why should survival of death be universal? Why shouldn't there be an 'art of survival' to which some souls find the clue and others not?"

And there came over him, as the sun of this "pet" day once more shone into his room, the old dark Homeric conception of death, with that terrifying multitude of the spirits of the dead surrounding us in their pitiful half-life and liable, on this day of their Cimmerian remembrance when the minds of the living turn so desperately towards them, to rise thronging up: *ethnea myria nekron*—"the myriad tribes of the dead, with a terrible cry!"

But it *could* not be like that, not just like that, he told himself. Anything were better than that, even total and absolute annihilation! (*MC*, 21)

Death may be bitter, but Dud concludes that annihilation is preferable to the half-life of the spirits of the dead. Thus he has an innate predisposition against Uryen, whom he characterizes tellingly as "semi mortuus." Uryen for Dud takes part in the life of the half-dead, and ultimately he would prefer a Uryen who is either all dead or all alive. In Dud's world, the relationship of survival from one side of the grave to the other is part of a continuum of the questions of incarnation (survival of the essence of a being from one body to another) and survival by "sinking our individuality into others' lives." After-life, incarnation, and memory are all relevant concepts in thinking about Uryen's immortality, and Dud's closing thoughts about his wife and mother indicate that he, perhaps from an Oedipal position, does not want his father haunting him philosophically or personally after his death.

In *The Plumed Serpent*, we also find the protagonist confronted with claims of divinity, and once more this protagonist is obsessed with death. Kate's second husband, a leader in the Easter Rebellion, has died, and Kate has left her children by her first marriage and her mother behind to take a Mexican vacation. She finds, however, that Mexico is the land of death, par excellence:

Kate could so well understand the Mexican who had said to her: *El Grito mexicano es siempre el Grito del Odio.* The Mexican shout is always a shout of hate. The famous revolutions, as Don Ramón said, began with *Viva!* but ended always with *Muera!* Death to this, death to the other, it was all death! death! death! as insistent as the Aztec sacrifices. Something for ever gruesome and macabre.

Why had she come to this high plateau of death? As a woman, she suffered even more than men suffer: and in the end, practically all men go under. Once, Mexico had had an elaborate ritual of death. Now it has death ragged, squalid, vulgar, without even the passion of its own mystery. (50)

Death in Mexico is connected with the memory of the hideous Aztec sacrifices; the aftermath of the Revolution, still continuing partially; and the disgusting ritual of the bullfight Kate attends in the first chapter.

Kate needs to overcome all this death, and she will have to decide if the religion of Quetzalcoatl revived by Don Ramón can offer this salvation. As compared with *Maiden Castle*, this novel implies a cleaner split between the living and the dead. Death equals annihilation, yet there is also death-in-life, which is the state most Europeans and many Indians are in, as Kate sees it. She must find out if the revived Quetzalcoatl religion is different from both Aztec barbarism and modern dictatorship. Thus she wavers continually over supporting the new movement. After all, she sees Ramón and Cipriano's band of cohorts execute the men who tried to murder Ramón.

Dud also must decide whether Uryen's deathlike appearance conceals something life-giving. When we first meet Uryen, we see him through Dud's eyes:

> He was a big heavily-built man, a good deal older than Dud, and what chiefly impressed the latter about him were the majestic proportions of his head and of his swarthy features. Mr. Quirm's features were indeed nothing less than tremendous. Brow, nose, mouth, chin, all were modelled on a scale of abnormal massiveness that would have been awe-inspiring if the man's eyes had been different. But Mr. Quirm's eyes were dull, lifeless, colourless, opaque, They were empty of every gleam of human response. They neither softened nor warmed; they neither lightened nor darkened—they were simply *there*, as if someone had found a great antique mask with empty eye-sockets, and had inserted a couple of glass marbles into the holes. His head was covered with small, stiff, black curls, and so low did these curls grow on his brooding forehead that Dud was reminded of some gigantic bust he had seen once, but whether Greek or Roman he could not remember. His dominant impression of the man, as he recalled it afterwards, was of a half-vitalized corpse, a being that "but usurped" his life, a semi-mortuus, an entity only "half there." (55).

In this memorable description, an equation is set up between three items that are only "half there": the antique mask, the bust, and the half-vitalized corpse. The art objects remind us of other eras in the world's history and set up Uryen's connections with an earlier age, whereas the corpse directs us toward the idea of the future dissolution of Uryen's body. Even as he serves up his healing potion to Nancy, who has suffered a heart attack near the town cenotaph, he smells like a corpse (56).

When Uryen sits in his armchair, Dud likens him to a "Beast in a Cage" (58), an image that connects him to Dud's statue of the Dor-Marth that he construes as Malory's 'Questing Beast,' and which is etymologically associated with death. Furthermore, Nancy confesses to Dud that her son would still be alive if she had not married Uryen.

In *The Plumed Serpent*, Don Ramón first unequivocally declares himself Quetzalcoatl in the ceremony that rededicates a church once consecrated to Catholicism. Ramón's wife, Carlota, a fervent Catholic, is destroyed completely by this event and dies shortly afterward. Kate, who attends the church service, is able to see that Ramón's assumption of the nature of Quetzalcoatl has killed something inside him—love:

> Kate looked up in consternation at Ramón. He had dropped his arm, and stood with his hands against his thighs, like a statue. But he remained with his wide, absorbed dark eyes watching without any change. He met Kate's glance of dismay, and his eyes quickly glanced, like lightning for Cipriano. Then he looked back at Carlota, across a changeless distance. Not a muscle of his face moved. And Kate could see that his heart had died in its connection with Carlota, his heart was quite, quite dead in him, out of the deathly vacancy he watched his wife. (377)

Although both Kate and the reader realize that Ramón has destroyed part of himself, Kate eventually turns her sympathies away from Carlota. Most readers, even L. D. Clark, one of the strongest defenders of the novel, agree that Lawrence has gone too far in discarding Carlota as an out-of-date representative of past values.[26]

We do not see the interior life of Don Ramón any more than that of Uryen, and we must discover from their speeches and actions how they interpret their own divinity. In *Maiden Castle*, there is always the possibility that Uryen is a madman and the chance that Dud has exaggerated his negative qualities.

Before he spends his first night with Wizzie, Dud is disturbed by a vision of Uryen appearing before him:

> And then, without a second's warning, the enormous sallow countenance of Mr. Quirm of Glymes materialized between him and the open door. Vague, nebulous, darker than the darkness, the man's lineaments wavered, fluctuated, solidified, and then faded away. But even as they

faded Dud's original impression of the fellow's eyes returned upon him. They were devoid of every kind of expression. They were part of the feeling he had had just now, they *were* that feeling, that the whole place, with his whole day, All Souls' Day in Dorchester was *unreal*, unreal with a dissolution that would turn it to dust under his feet if he moved an inch. (*MC*, 107)

Uryen is both more than real, because he can appear in a vision, and less than real, because the whole day may be a mistaken illusion. This strange appearance of Uryen contributes to Dud's new view of him when they meet for a second time at Glymes. Uryen becomes a kind of Celtic divinity to Dud even before he reveals himself as one.

> "There!" thought No-man, who was watching Uryen. "I believe I saw the fellow's eyes come to life!" What rushed into Dud's head as he noted this change was the curious phrase *rex semi mortuus* which he had once come across in some work on the religion of the ancient Celts. "That's what he is!" he said to himself. He's a *rex semimortuus*, He's a corpse-god!" (166).

On their first encounter, Uryen appeared to Dud as a half-dead man, but now he is both a king and a god, because his eyes have come to life. Later that evening, in a room smelling of rotten apples, Uryen gives Dud the statue that serves as a companion piece to Dor-Marth, and begins to reveal himself, but Dud cuts him off before Uryen speaks the following words:

> "Just think of it, lad," went on the other, "Mai-Dun, Poundbury, Maumbury Rings, all coming slowly back to life! I don't mean the dead in them,". . . . (174)

At this point Dud resolves he must never look for the life beyond this life. This is the same belief that he confirms on the closing page of the novel. The reader realizes that Dud will not try to break through, because it makes no difference whether there is something beyond or not. Both possibilities are too frightening.

> The impulse to go further in his thoughts, to go *the one step further*, had become for him like a menace that *had* to be obliterated, suppressed, reduced to nothing. The second it heaved up, pushing him forward, he retorted by a quick mental act of deliberate negation. It was as if he set a machine at the back of his mind automatically working, with

a dark, secret hammer, that fell with an interior thud—"down, down,
down!"—at each stir of that suspected impulse. (174–175)

Although Dud has already decided not to "break through," only
later, when he and Uryen go out to Maiden Castle, does he begin
to reveal himself.

> "What I mean is this," the man went on. "All extreme emotions reach
> a point where you can't distinguish between pain and pleasure. The suffer-
> ing is intense; but something in you rushes towards the suffering, opens
> its arms to the suffering. Now, lad, you must know it is not given
> to everyone to feel what I'm talking about. At its intensest it comes
> when love and hate are one. It is terrible then. It is a feeling so terrific
> that it often ends in madness; but if it doesn't end that way, it ends
> in *breaking through*. You must know, lad, that there are secrets only
> revealed to magic. I don't mean physical magic; I mean *spiritual* magic.
> And this kind only comes when the emotion of love-hate gathers to
> a point that's terrible. And you must know too that it only comes when
> the passion remains sterile. Any fulfillment dissipates its power. Nothing
> but unfulfilled love, love turned to hate, can beat hard enough upon
> the barrier of life, can beat hard enough what separates us from the
> secret till it breaks through! It's like despair, lad, *that's* what it's like;
> it's as strong as despair. Of course it means abominable pain. I mean
> *mental* pain, of course, though there's a frightened pleasure mixed with
> it too, and few can endure it. (248)

Uryen's combination of mental pain, spiritual magic, and sterile passion is an abomination to Dud, who objects to the notion that mental
pain can be worse than physical pain. However, it never occurs
to him that, stripped of the vocabulary of magic, his father is offering
him a version of salvation through mental suffering. Dud has no
major physical maladies in the novel, and it is clear when the narrative
closes that he has been saved for a life of full humanity through
his recent mental sufferings over Wizzie and Uryen. In the long
run, Uryen's ideas cannot be simply dismissed.

Uryen goes beyond a sufferer; he sees himself as a sacrificial victim.

> "I became convinced, not from any revelation, you understand, but be-
> cause of this *necessity* I'm under of bearing the pain of the world, the
> pain of what beats against the wall, that in one incarnation after another
> I've been the same Power! And do you want to know *what* Power I've
> been, lad?" (251)

It is impossible to clarify where this "necessity" comes from, but there is always the possibility that Uryen feels someone should bear the pain of the world and redeem it, because the world, in his eyes, is radically fallen. His own life has been unhappy since his orphaned youth, and he dies thinking of his lost Cornelia. If we consider unfulfilled sexual desires and unrequited love as the givens of his later life and not as goals toward which fulfilled sex and requited love should be diverted, then Uryen's ravings make more sense. His Power has not been gained through seeking but through finding some meaningful form for his disappointments. He continues telling Dud:

> "I've been the Power that's older than all this damned sunshine, the Power that's older than all these new gods, the Power that's deepest of all, for it's got Death in it, as well as life. It's this Power—the Power that works in me, lad, the Power that I *am*—that beats in its pain against the wall of the world. You can cry out, lad, if you like, that it's all fantasy and illusion, you can cry out that your excavations set it at naught; but I tell you that sooner or later you'll know it as I know it! I tell you it's in all the pain of the world where love turns to hate and beats against the wall! (252)

Uryen does not claim to be the only one to possess the Power. Possession has both elicit and democratic sides to it. Others may gain it—others who have passed through the crucible of pain. For these people, history, as it is commonly understood, is a distortion that conceals the continuity of Power. Uryen only hints about these other gods:

> I tell you *we*, I and others like me, are the gods of Mai-Dun—the same yesterday, today and forever. There's no one God, lad. Lay *that* up in your heart. Things are as they are because there are so many of us; and as fast as some create, others destroy; and a good thing too, as the Son of Chaos cries out in *Faust!* (250)

In total contrast, in *The Plumed Serpent*, being an Aztec god does not establish the same continuity with the past. There have been no incarnated gods since the Spanish crushed the Mexican natives. Revival of the old religion is seen in terms of joy, and suffering is going to be ended for everyone. Mexican Catholicism is considered morbid, and so Quetzalcoatl will have cheerful and colorful ceremonies to transform the land of death. In addition, the Quetzalcoatl state makes Ramón feel better about himself and his role as a Mexican.

There is never any suggestion that Ramón is mad, but it is not easy to establish how he believes in his divinity. Surely, he has not been brooding over it for years as Uryen has done, and the idea does not emerge from personal disappointments of great magnitude. On one level, Ramón is obviously an opportunist with a private army on hand and a policy of manipulating the local people as he wants. There also is, however, another sense in which he is not lying. He is the form that Quetzalcoatl must take in the twentieth century. Through an act of will he becomes an incarnation of the god, although he is not actually the god in the traditional sense. He is much more of a god through recourse to symbolism than Uryen. Ramón sees ritual as important to the notion of godhead, and at the rededication of the former Catholic Church Ramón, amid much ceremony, assumes his Quetzalcoatl state. In his initiatory speech, he proclaims the kind of access other people also have to divinity status:

> For man is the Morning Star.
> And woman is the Star of Evening.
>
> I tell you, you are not men alone.
> The star of the beyond is within you.
>
> But have you seen a dead man, how his star has gone out of him?
> So the star will go out of you, even as a woman will leave a man
> if his warmth never warms her.
> Should you say: *I have no star. I am no star.*
>
> So it will leave you, and you will hang like a gourd on the vine
> of life
> With nothing but rind:
> Waiting for the rats of the dark to come and gnaw your
> inside.

(340)

That Ramón's religion is based on symbolism is clear through his designation of men and women as stars. There is a life behind this life into which humans can thrust themselves, a world of symbolic relationships. To get there, one has to break through Christianity, whereas for Uryen, "breaking through" means escaping the historical timeframe.

In *Maiden Castle*, unlike *The Plumed Serpent*, Christianity is never at issue, whereas Platonism, communism, and fascism are considered as approaches to life. Christianity has no spokesperson. By implication, for Powys, it has little hold on the deepest part of man, whereas Lawrence perceives it as having a stranglehold on man. Uryen's defense of the Power in Celtic mythology is not aimed as much against the Christianity that buried it from view as it is against the world of death, nature, and evolution.

Powys must have felt that one of the internal weaknesses of *The Plumed Serpent* is that at the end of the novel the Quetzalcoatl religion becomes the state religion of Mexico, in what appears to be 1923! Even in Nazi Germany, Christianity was not undermined or overthrown in this fashion.

When Kate decides to become Malinche, goddess consort of Cipriano/Huitzilopochtli, she decides to break through into the new order. Dud, as we have seen, believes that breaking though is a disastrous error. Each narrative centers on the response of the protagonist to the "way" proposed by the god-figure. In *The Plumed Serpent*, the world is pervasively religious. God is both immanent and transcendent, and the question is finding the right religion that will grant most access to God. *Maiden Castle* does not begin with the assumption that there is any god at all, and when Uryen proclaims there are many gods, his frame of reference is at odds with everyone else's in the novel. As in *Weymouth Sands*, nature may be only a veil in front of a void. In Lawrence's world the wonders of nature are living manifestations of God's presence, but Dud can only wonder if there is something transcendant in the wind at Glymes.

Dud does not see Uryen's ravings and collapse before his death. He only knows second hand about his father's self-doubts. In *The Plumed Serpent*, Ramón does not have self-doubts about his divinity. It is Kate who communicates her doubts to the reader.

In his last big speech, Uryen tells Wizzie and Thuella everything that Dud has missed in his ignorance:

> . . . "and what those fools can't see, and what my son *won't* see, is that the Power of the Underworld that our old Bards worshipped, *though it was always defeated*, is the Power of the Golden Age! Yes, it's the Power our race adored when they built Avebury and Maiden Castle and Stonehenge and Caer Drwyn, when there were no wars, no vivisection, no money, no ten-thousand-times accursed *nations!* They twisted it all round later, the sly children of gold and of burning, turning the dew of darkness into evil, and Bran the Blessed into a demon; but the Power that rushes through me when I go out *there*"—and he gave a jerk of his shoulder towards Maiden Castle—"the Power that I *am* under my name Uryen lies too deep for them to destroy. Whether I'm Uryen or not—'for all my mind is clouded with a doubt'—this *Hiraeth* of my race, this baffled, this thwarted, this hopeless desire, that from the beginning

of all things has defied morality, custom, convention, usage, comfort, and all the wise and prudent of the world, can never be destroyed out of the human heart now it has once appeared! (467)

Uryen would have no use for a free Welsh nation, because nations do not make any sense to him at all. Conversely, in *The Plumed Serpent*, the Quetzalcoatl religion is specified as the redeeming force for death-oriented Mexico. Kate, as a Celt (Irishwoman), is drawn to the Mexican religion, for Lawrence sees both Celts and Indians as more insightful than Anglo-Saxons, who have little blood knowledge. In contrast, the Celtic Uryen views his own ethnic heritage as part of a universal Golden Age. It is not the exclusive property of one people.

Wizzie dismisses Uryen's final ravings as not only the product of a troubled mind, but a troubled *male* mind. She has been infatuated with him for almost a year, but his disintegration repels her, and she comes to believe that the only woman that Uryen ever really thinks about is Dud's mother. For her, women have more innate knowledge of life than men, and god-talk is basically a male hysteria.

Kate Leslie also has a feeling of revolt against men's views, but she hesitates to act on it. She has the wisdom to see that Ramón's religion is entirely patriarchal, and that even if she is the goddess Malintzi, it is the gods who call all of the shots. Unfortunately, Kate does not like most women and has an exaggerated fear of returning to a Europe filled with middle-aged women hunting for masculine prey from salon to salon. She ultimately decides to continue with her marriage to Cipriano, although she knows he is Ramón's puppet. Her fate is truly a sad one, for there is no man around to treat her as a real equal. As Judith Ruderman says, explaining Kate's dilemma:

> The postures that men and women must take in the church of the living Quetzalcoatl, and that Kate Leslie and Cipriano assume in their marriage ceremony, require the woman to stoop and kneel, the man to stand erect; these ritualized positions invert the positions of the characters in works like *The Lost Girl* and are meant to correct the modern-day ascendancy of the Magna Mater that *The Lost Girl* depicts. For it is not simply woman who has assumed the power role but woman as Mary or Queen of the World: she is the real target of Lawrence's spleen in the novel. Kate has been worshipped as a queen by her previous husbands, both of them blue-eyed, ineffectual men like Basil in *The Ladybird;* now the black-eyed men, like Count Dionys in that novella, are ready to reassume their proper leadership role after pulling woman down from her pedestal.[27]

In *The Plumed Serpent*, Lawrence makes it clear that marriage, with man in the superior position, is the ideal relationship. In *Maiden Castle*, Thuella and Wizzie run off together to America in what is clearly a lesbian relationship. No disapproval is cast on them. One of the most impressive passages of the novel describes the two women sleeping next to each other:

> But the secret of that great underworld sea, into the bosom of which, at that hour, after the tumult, so many human consciousnesses, from Portland Bill to Stonehenge, had sunk, was independent of the demon-shoals of dreams that troubled it. It was an element *sui generis*, an unfathomable dimension peculiar to itself, the everlasting *other side* of the turmoil of life, a state of being that resembled death in one of its aspects and life in another; and was indeed life with something removed, and death with something added. And though independent of those troublesome shoals of demon-fish that dart through it, wretched intruders, phantom half-lives, chaotic eidola from the muddy inland streams of consciousness, this great undersea takes many shifting lights, many variations of density and volume, from the accidents of time and place and neighbourhood. To a girl asleep by a man those mysterious waters are not the same in their lulling flow as to a child asleep by its parent. A woman asleep by another woman draws from this mysterious sea ebbings and flowings of magnetic currents different altogether from those that reach her when she lies by a man.
>
> The same unfathomable redemption lulls and smoothes her, but the mystic chemistry of that sublunary immersion, that baptism in the flow of this life-death, has its own peculiar quality, a quality as different from the other as the nearness and neighborhood of a man is different from the nearness and neighborhood of a woman.
>
> It was not till after they had slept for several hours that, awake together in the darkness, Thuella told Wizzie her great secret. (MC 475–76)

Powys offers women not just happiness, but redemption as well, away from the world of men. Dud has always felt that men intrude in the world of women and even goes so far as to postulate parthenogenesis as the proper manner of giving birth:

> "*Parthenogenesis* is the natural thing! That's why the act of love is monstrous and ridiculous. Lust isn't comic. Lust is grave and sacred. And there's nothing but poetry in conception. It's the act of paternity that's so horribly humorous. Monstrous and comic. That's what it is. An interference with the beautiful processes of parthenogenesis." (MC 174)

Although Dud's comment is a humorous one that reflects his sexual inhibitions, it has a more serious side. Here we can see a connection with Uryen's desire that sex be kept sterile for man to "break through." Uryen is a larger than life father and lover (of Cornelia), but he does not promote a patriarchal world. Instead, he exposes the patriarchal hold of the fascist state:

> "What I would like to ask Mr. Wye," said Uryen suddenly, and something in his tone—perhaps the intonation of man about to speak to men on the subject of politics—caused Mr. Cumber to assume his most alert office expression and grow serious, "is whether you mightn't maintain that the Fascist movement in the world to-day is a reaction from Matriarchy?" (MC 226)

The Quetzalcoatl movement is one such reaction against matriarchy. In it the goddess Malintzi will not have the status that was once accorded to the Virgin Mary.

Neither Uryen nor Dud offers a plan for how a modern nation should be run. They have a completely apolitical view of life; several other characters do not. Teucer Wye is an old-fashioned liberal, his son (Dunbar) is a fascist, and his daughter's boyfriend (Claudius) a Communist. Another viewpoint is expressed by Mr. Cumber, the capitalist. Because much of the material about these characters still has to be restored to a new edition of *Maiden Castle*, it is hard to be sure what Powys meant to do with the political discussions of the novel. As it stands now, I believe *Maiden Castle* suggests that man is better off attending to the interior life than to politics. Dud does not come to any political awakening, and Powys does not consider this as part of his failings. We should note, however, that beginning in 1936, when he began to receive letters from Emma Goldman in Spain, Powys became more interested in politics and for a time had a pronounced sympathy for the aspirations of anarchism.[28]

In Powys's world, Uryen and Dud can afford to be apolitical because the British government poses no great threat on their freedom. The government remains unseen and nebulous. In *The Plumed Serpent*, revolution has been a reality for the decade since the overthrow of Porfirio Diaz. Ramón, a landowner, lost much of his wealth under the socialist land distribution at the beginning of the Revolution. Under Cipriano, he has an army ready to do his bidding. The novel does not indicate what kinds of government policies he will endorse now that the Quetzalcoatl religion is the state religion. Ramón believes that religion should be communal and ritualistic. In *Maiden Castle*, there is no need for ritual or state religion. Any religious experience is personal and private.

For Lawrence, the path of reaction is the way to salvation. Mexico has historic roots that must be tapped. Socialism is a new European import, and it must be rendered as inconsequential as possible. It is not hierarchical enough, and it promotes disorder.

In the Stanley Baldwin era, revolution at home is an impossibility, and Uryen considers the excavation of Maiden Castle by Robert Wheeler to be a form of reaction.[29] The past, he believes, cannot be restored through archaeology. As a god, Uryen is the past as presence, and he thinks of Wizzie as an incarnation of the goddess Ceridwen. However, Uryen dies, and Wizzie leaves for the New World. The vestiges of the Golden Age are lost.

For Powys, wisdom lies in understanding human limitations; for Lawrence, in the awareness of man's possibilities. Kate wonders how she can act most sensibly. Dud wonders if the world can make any sense at all. Kate hopes that a fulfilling love will save her. Dud is saved by Wizzie, although their love fails to fulfill the deepest needs of either.

Both Powys and Lawrence knew that all gods seem to incite rebellion. Uryen is a tremendous threat to Dud simply as his father. As God the father, he can only crush his son, regardless of the truth of what he says. Kate also finds that gods are rulers. Goddesses are just consorts. She consents outwardly, but inwardly she still has a rebellious nature. Whether father or husband, the god is a threatening figure.

For Powys, Lawrence's "dark gods" do not simply offer too much reactionism and too much violence, but too much assurance as well. In Lawrence's novel, godhead is pervasive in the world and waiting to be tapped. Powys offers us the world of matter infused with Uryen's cries of pain.

Notes

1. John Cowper Powys, *Maiden Castle* (London: Macdonald, 1966). All subsequent references are cited parenthetically in the text by page number. The Picador edition of 1977 has similar pagination. The earlier editions were by Simon & Schuster (New York, 1936) and Cassell & Co. (London, 1937).

2. D. H. Lawrence, *The Plumed Serpent* (Cambridge: Cambridge University Press, 1987). All subsequent references are cited parenthetically in the text by page number.

3. G. Wilson Knight, *The Saturnian Quest* (New York: Barnes & Noble, 1964), p. 55.

4. H. P. Collins, *John Cowper Powys: Old Earth-Man* (London: Barrie and Rockliff, 1966), pp. 133–38.

5. Kenneth Hopkins, *The Powys Brothers: A Biographical Appreciation* (Rutherford, N.J.: Fairleigh Dickinson University Press, 1967), pp. 191–94.

6. Jeremy Hooker, *John Cowper Powys* (Cardiff: University of Wales Press, 1973), pp. 68–74.

7. Jean Markale, "Powys et le Celtisme," *Granit* nos. 1/2 (Autumn-Winter 1973): 246–63.

8. Glen Cavaliero, *John Cowper Powys: Novelist* (Oxford: Clarendon Press, 1973), pp. 93–102.

9. John Brebner, *The Demon Within: A Study of John Cowper Powys's Novels* (New York: Barnes & Noble, 1973), pp. 141–53.

10. Denis Lane, "The Vital and the Perverse in Powys's *Maiden Castle*" (Paper presented at City University of New York Conference on Myth, New York, March 1979.)

11. Morine Krissdottir, *John Cowper Powys and the Magical Quest* (London: Macdonald & Jane's, 1980).

12. Ian Hughes, "A Poor Ragged Maiden: The Textual History of *Maiden Castle*," *The Powys Review* no 12 (1982/1983):17–25.

13. Ian Hughes, "A Virgin with No Name: The Beginnings of *Maiden Castle*," *The Powys Review* no. 15 (1984/1985):14–21.

14. Belinda Humfrey, "Editorial," *The Powys Review* no. 15 (1984/1985):1–10.

15. Angela Blaen, "*Maiden Castle* and the Celtic Calendar," *The Powys Review* no. 15 (1984/1985):32–34.

16. Susan Rands, "*Maiden Castle:* Symbol, Theme, and Personality," *The Powys Review* no. 15 (1984/1985):22–31.

17. Margaret Moran, "Animating Fictions in *Maiden Castle*" (Paper presented at the First Conference of the Powys Society of North America, Colgate University, June 7–9, 1985).

18. Hughes, "A Virgin with No Name," p. 16.

19. John Cowper Powys, "D. H. Lawrence," *The Powys Review* no. 16 (1985): 52–54. This article is reprinted from John Francis McDermott and Kendall B. Taft, eds., *Sex in the Arts: A Symposium* (New York: Harper & Row, 1932), pp. 57–63.

20. Michael Ballin, "Lewis Spence and the Myth of Quetzalcoatl: D. H. Lawrence's *The Plumed Serpent*," *D. H. Lawrence Review* 13 (1980):63–78.

21. G. Wilson Knight, *Neglected Powers* (London: Routledge & Kegan Paul, 1971).

22. G. Wilson Knight, "Powys and the Kundalini Serpent," *Contemporary Review* 233, no. 1350 (July 1978):37–44, 92–100. See also the following essays by Knight: "Man's Total Nature: An Analysis of Powys's *The Complex Vision*," *Mosaic* 10, no. 2 (Winter 1977):97–107; "John Cowper Powys and T. S. Eliot," *Contemporary Review* 228, no. 1321 (February 1976): 73–84; "Powys and Death," *Contemporary Review* 227, no. 1317 (October 1975):219–20; "John Cowper Powys as Humorist," *Contemporary Review* 222, no. 1285 (February 1973): 78–83; "Powys on Death," in Belinda Humfrey, ed., *Essays on John Cowper Powys* (Cardiff: University of Wales Press, 1972), pp. 189–204; "Cosmic Correspondences," *The Times Literary Supplement*, 11 October 1957, reprinted in Robert Blackmore, ed., *Powys to Knight: The Letters of John Cowper Powys to G. R. Wilson Knight* (London: Cecil Woolf, 1983); "Sadism and the Seraphic," in Belinda Humfrey, ed., *Recollections of the Powys Brothers: Llewelyn, Theodore, and John Cowper* (London: Owen, 1980), pp. 226–37.

23. Knight, "Powys and the Kundalini Serpent," p. 43.

24. Glen Cavaliero, "Phoenix and Serpent: D. H. Lawrence and John Cowper Powys," *The Powys Review* no. 2 (Winter 1977):51–58.

25. Linden Peach, "Powys, Lawrence, and a New Sensibility: A Reading of Two Neglected Prose by John Cowper Powys," *Anglo-Welsh Review* no. 59 (Autumn 1977):32–41.

26. L. D. Clark, *Dark Night of the Body: D. H. Lawrence's "The Plumed Serpent"* (Austin: University of Texas Press, 1964), p. 67.

27. Judith Ruderman, *D. H. Lawrence and the Devouring Mother: The Search for a Patriarchal Ideal of Leadership* (Durham, N.C.: Duke University Press, 1984), p. 144.

28. See David Goodway, "The Politics of John Cowper Powys," *The Powys Review* no. 15 (1984/1985):42–53.

29. Robert Eric Mortimer Wheeler, *Maiden Castle, Dorset* (Oxford: Oxford University Press, 1943).

Animating Fictions in *Maiden Castle*

Margaret Moran

In 1938, the year after the publication of *Maiden Castle*, Powys paid tribute to the astonishing power of books in his introduction to *Enjoyment of Literature*.

> Though books, as Milton says, may be the embalming of mighty spirits, they are also the resurrection of rebellious, reactionary, fantastical, and wicked spirits! In books dwell all the demons and angels of the human mind. . . .
> Here are the poisons to kill, the drugs to soothe, the fire-water to madden, the ichor to inflame, the nectar to imparadise![1]

Although *Enjoyment of Literature* is a book about books, Powys's fictions also meditate on the intense and varied results of reading. Through their dependence on analogy and allusion, all his stories insist that both life and art derive complex resonances from participation in traditions. Many of his characters acquire inspiration, solace, and perturbation from their involvement in the written record of human experience.

If Powys's people acknowledge the significance of their shared cultural heritage through their tendency to reenact patterns from past masterpieces, several characters also provide testimony to the influence of books by speculating about the probable impact of their own writing on their intended readers. Among the most memorable of these would-be authors is Williams Hastings of *Ducdame*, who thinks of his volume as a "nihilistic catapult" to be hurled "at the citadels of life."[2] The old crone, Betsy Cooper, takes so seriously the attribution of malignant force to his "categorical Domesday Book of all life's progeny"[3] that she predicts: "Till book be burned no child'll be borned!"[4] Underlining her concern is the claim of the rustic character, Mr. Pod, "'Tis this book-writing what do worrit quiet-lived folks."[5] One of the most troubling worries assigned to the hero of *Wolf Solent* is his complicity in the production of Urquhart's perverse book. Urquhart, in his turn, has allegedly been corrupted (along with his servant) by the bookseller, Malakite, "whose books do larn 'em their deviltries!"[6] In *Maiden Castle*, Powys continues to use a central character engaged in a creative endeavor. There, Dud No-man writes a historical romance championing Mary Channing. Because his work is in defense of a murderess, he too transgresses against the ethical code conventionally endorsed by society.

Perhaps partly in reaction against the emphasis of the great Victorian critics on literature's capacity for amelioration, Powys insists that the latent magic of the printed page can also be released with disturbing or corrosive results. Powys may have echoed another of Milton's sentiments:

> For books are not absolutely dead things, but do contain a potency of life in them to be as active as that soul whose progeny they are; nay they do preserve as in a vial the purest efficacy and extraction of that living intellect that bred them. I know they are as lively and as vigourously productive as those fabulous dragon's teeth; and being sown up and down, may chance to spring up armed men.[7]

In spite of the continuity of Powys's exploration of the importance of books, the near contemporaneity of *Maiden Castle* and *Enjoyment of Literature* suggests that they share a special concern with the potency of literature. Even more than the previous stories, *Maiden Castle* relies on characters who embrace literary or legendary mentors deliberately. Using several individuals who have selected their own models and even gone so far as to "steal" names for themselves,[8] he has discovered a striking method of giving an illusion of autonomy to his imaginary creations. The paradox is that here a sense of vitality is endowed on his characters by their own self-conscious alignment with other—usually invented—beings. In those instances in which inspiration is taken from historic figures, the effect is surprisingly the same. Teucer Wye noted: "*I* take Plato in a way peculiar to myself as an absolute skeptic, so uncertain about everything he could afford to turn God and Immorality into poetry, and the Soul and Love into fairy-tales" (143). Books of any kind prove capable of sustaining life-illusions, of allowing a reader to "swell" his identity into a larger-than-life existence. Like the child Lovey, who treats a scrap of paper as if it were her baby, the readers within *Maiden Castle* vivify the printed page, only to find their own experience enlarged.

Because the selection of exemplary books is not forced upon the people in any obvious way, Powys feels free to voice skepticism about the appropriateness of their choices. In this way, Powys continues his practice after *Ducdame* of advocating seriously very odd ideas and simultaneously engaging in self-mockery. Uryen Quirm makes the outlandish claim that he is the reincarnation of an ancient Welsh divinity about whom he read in books by Sir John Rhys. The author dissociates himself from responsibility for the accuracy of Uryen's divine pretensions by two removes. Rather than defending him with unqualified authorial support or allowing him to appeal directly to our sensibilities, Powys presents him through the perspective of other characters. Because their responses are ambivalent, the reader is allowed to interpret Uryen's vision of himself either negatively as a mirage or positively as an illustration of man's capacity to enter into a pre-existing myth so that it may be shaped to his own needs.

In the daring of conception and the skill of execution, Uryen's portrait deserves an honored place among the group of quasi-divine characters Powys has invented, including Geard of Glastonbury and Sylvanus of Weymouth. But he differs prominently from them by being a world-renouncing figure who is without their missionary zeal. The truth he has discovered is mainly a matter for private contemplation, not promulgation. The attribution of this reticence to Uryen probably owes something to Powys's view of the Welsh personality as *"less advertised* less *public,* less *revealed* in their secret soul than any other race in the world—except the Chinese."[9] In any case, Uryen is made so averse to publicity that the role of speechmaker, a function he is far more qualified to perform authoritatively, goes to Teucer Wye by default when the Grand Discovery is viewed. When driven by dire economic necessity, Uryen offers some articles to Mr. Cumber's newspaper, but being oddly sensitive (for an immortal) to the world's mockery, he believes this attempt to share his theories has exposed and destroyed him. If his story is to be told, a bard is needed to celebrate his existence for him. Like his prototype, Uryen is a supporter of poetry and a fit subject for literature, but he is unable to function in the intermediary capacity as an author.

Instead of being an author, Uryen is made the ultimate reader who shows very literally our vital dependence on story. Through Uryen's circumstances, Powys is able to show that even the most wildly improbable fiction can have an animating power over life. That Uryen should be used as the major vehicle to explore the complex relationship between the reader and the narrative is the more remarkable because we are discouraged at every turn from seeing overt resemblances to ourselves in his weird personage. Arousing by turns veneration and revulsion, Uryen seems to have no need of the reader's pity or association. What is involved, then, is something quite different from direct identification or empathetic involvement. Instead, we are forced to recognize that our relationship to him is analogous to his connection to old Welsh literature. Our act of faith in granting a special sort of existence to the character Uryen Quirm has its equivalent in his own abandonment to the figures of mythology.

What prepares for Uryen's role as the reader's representative is that the very first particular offered concerning him establishes him as one obsessively devoted to books. "My husband is a reader. . . . Our place is nothing but books," Nancy tells Dud. In his first encounter with Dud, Uryen shows himself so devoid of polite amenities that he ignores Dud completely in favor of his reading. Dud thinks of him as a welter of antiquarianism, a sedentary bookworm who lolls on his sofa day and night. Still, Dud is intrigued by him, partly because he is familiar with Dud's own historic fictions. Uryen himself is always acknowledging that the reading of ancient texts provided him with conformation of what he intuited about his purpose and life's meaning. Indeed, his faith in the power of the printed word is such that he believes "that if he could tag together a sufficient weight of legendary allusions to immortality in the old books it established a strong probability in its favour" (236). As long as he can maintain the certainty that fictions can be lived (even in the hereafter), he flourishes; but the loss of his faith causes his death. Therefore, although he is patently an invented being himself, he is used to dramatize the supreme necessity of story as a shaping influence over life.

All art puts the reader into a relationship that differs only in the intensity and the duration of the commitment from Uryen's espousal of his mythology. Uryen speaks to Dud of his gods:

> They'd have their reality, not the reality of the mole on your belly, lad; but they'd have their own *kind* of reality. . . . I tell you, lad, there are a thousand realities in life that aren't, and never *can* be, 'bed-rock realities,' and yet they're well worth pursuing. (234)

The same might be said of the reality Uryen acquires in the reader's mental life. What a reader wills and what a reader imagines become a mysterious part of what is. Using the contemplation of ancient myth, Uryen has found a kind of immortality. Through his pursuit of the necessary fiction, he has made himself a contemporary of time itself. He offers, therefore, in symbolic form, the gains literature can provide to its absorbed and dedicated readership. He also demonstrates how episodes in literary works merge into the action of lived experience.

Conspicuous for its absence among the many impressive claims

Uryen makes for the value of reading is the mention of moral change. Quirm's early life is so deeply enshrouded in mystery that attempts to measure the alteration of his ethics prove so impossible that they are rendered an irrelevant consideration. As an orphan without known parents, he seems to have sprung *ex nihilo* from olden times into the present. In spite of all Nancy's efforts to discover something definite about him, she admits to knowing virtually nothing concerning his background. Her inquiries in Shaftesbury yielded little but cryptic hints and rather sinister innuendoes. Told only that Enoch was said to have been taken for adoption from a Welsh tramp by Mr. Quirm, Nancy was left with the impression that her informers were deliberately misleading her. "They looked repulsively malignant, at least one old man did, when they told me this, as if they knew better; but I don't know what they were hinting at," she tells Dud. (159) In such passages, Uryen is given an obscure but fateful past appropriate for a hero or an occult divinity in a myth.

Because his mythological equivalent is in one of his attributes the god of carnage, this destructive capacity must coexist in Uryen with his benignity. He has the power to heal using some secret herbal concoctions that have a curative effect on his wife, Nancy. But in some unexplained way he is made culpable for the death of Nancy's young child, Jimmy. His latent violence is further demonstrated in his nearly fatal attack on Old Funky. Like his prototype, then, he is the king of the sunset realms of death and the imagination. He is a character who can provide both menace and comfort, and arouse in others both exictement and repugnance. He may be compassionate enough to take on the pain of the world, but he is also, by his own admission, ruthless enough to sacrifice a woman and abandon a child without any moral qualms. Sinister without being sadistic, Uryen has so far transcended normal ethical distinctions that good and evil are meaningless terms.

Uryen's alignment with a very recondite myth contributes significantly to the risk Powys took in his portrayal. In some ways, this venture goes beyond even the claim of *A Glastonbury Romance* that its characters are affiliated directly to the grail legend. However extreme may be the demand that the people be seen as reincarnations of the participants of the Arthurian story, that requirement at least permits us to use a familiar mythical system. Similarly, the biblical and classical parallels found throughout Powys's canon, although individually they may at times be quite *recherché*, are at least derived from within a well-known frame of reference. The arcane certainly has been used before, but it never has been so central.

Previously, we have always been able to come prepared in some measure for the posture we will be expected to adopt toward a character who behaves like Merlin, Arthur, or Christ, or toward one who is called Persephone. In contrast, intimacy with Celtic mythology cannot be assumed to be part of the cultural equipment that even the educated reader brings to his experience of English literature. In choosing deliberately to derive inspiration for Uryen Quirm from an occult divinity whose provenance is within an esoteric tradition (albeit one that was eventually incorporated into the Arthurian legend), Powys forces his readers to experience a mysterious relationship to a mystery. Because the average reader has little or no preconception about how a character named Uryen might be expected to behave, he can be unpredictable and unfathomable.

In Uryen Quirm's speeches, he documents himself by alluding freely to the books of Sir John Rhys in which background information about his namesake can be found. But even when Rhys is duly consulted, the inexplicable elements associated with this Celtic hero do not dissolve; rather, a rationale is provided for our bewilderment. Rhys explains that the enigmatic nature of the tradition to which Uryen belongs is an indigenous attribute of that culture. Stories that were mysterious initially were made more so by the way they were imparted through the ages. Various redactors transmitted the legends by freely adapting and embellishing their sources. No doubt the liberties taken are partly attributable to the desire to be inventive, but sometimes they were caused by ignorance about the significance of details found in the original. With the passage of time, obscurities multiplied. If the puzzling reference was retained, the mystery was more deeply entrenched. But if it was omitted or tampered with, the inner coherence of a passage was jeopardized. Rhys quotes Matthew Arnold as having observed in a lecture on Celtic literature "how evidently the medieval story-teller is pillaging an antiquity of which he does not fully possess the secret. . . . In the medieval stories of no Latin or Teutonic people does this strike one as in those of the Welsh."[10] The result is that even readers like Arnold and Rhys, who are most expert at making inspired guesses to unriddle the many puzzles, are often perplexed. Therefore, the mystification of the common reader is scarcely surprising.

The fact that there is inherent cause for wonderment in Uryen's story works to Powys's advantage. His adaptation of what is known about this Celtic divinity to a modern context is admirably done, and the fragmentary state of the information about the original Uryen has allowed considerable scope for Powys's creative imagination. Uryen's physical attributes reveal him as a figure of such colossal proportions that his claim to semidivinity cannot be lightly dismissed.

With his towering lineaments and tremendous face, he commands attention and respect from the first encounter. To conform to the description of the complexion of the original Uryen as "ardu, 'black, dark, or dusky',"[11] he is said to have "swarthy features" (55) or a "dusky physiognomy" (247), and he is frequently given the epithet, the Black Man of Glymes. As a divinity who embodies the natural cycle of life and earth, Quirm is given features of vegetative and animal realms as well as those of the human species. His head is said to be like moss, his breath like "an emanation from long-dead seaweed" (461). He reminds Dud of "a great sweltering toad" (56) or a "strange beast" (58). The most impressive physical evidence for Uryen's status, however, is provided by the mark of Brân, the Crow, which he bears on his chest. This distinguishing sign of his identity as the reincarnation of Uryen conforms completely to Rhys's description of his namesake.[12]

On the basis of corporeal characteristic alone, Uryen demands to be regarded as both human and something else. When Nancy Quirm says of her husband, *"He's* not a simple man. He's *more* than a man"* (60), her bitterly sarcastic remark carries a descriptive weight. What she regards as delusions of grandeur are made to seem not altogether unjustifiable assertions. Like the other quasi-divine characters in Powys's canon, Uryen's majestic nature is incongruously intermixed with comic traits. Uryen, for example, prays while immersing his head ritualistically in water, but he is chary of using water for ordinary hygiene. Uryen has to function simultaneously in mundane and heroic spheres. Although Uryen is a divinity who is in touch with dreadful supernatural forces, he must also perform within a familial and social context, though not without considerable dramatic tension. He claims to be a reincarnation of a Welsh mythological figure, but he also is able to attend a sophisticated literary luncheon at the Antelope Hotel. If he presents himself as a gigantic form looming out of the distant past, he is also incongruously harassed by mundane financial worries and vexed by minor irritants, like not having his tea prepared for him at the proper time. He voices his mystical pronouncements while clothed not in resplendent vatic robes, but in an old, malodorous sweater. In him the extraordinary has been domesticated, or the ordinary has so submerged itself within the mythical that the effect is the same.

Enoch Quirm adopted the name Uryen after the birth of his son, thus making himself, as it were, self-begotten and self-baptized. He discovered his own destiny by finding a word for himself that corresponded perfectly to what he was and would become. A single word, therefore, is proven to be capable of altering an entire life by allowing the liberation of the self through language. But the name was originally meant for Dud No-man. When this name occurred to No-man's mother in a dream, she wished to call her son by this magical chance word. The plan was thwarted by the anticipation of Smith's fear of the potency of the name. "Elijah would as soon have had his son called Satan as called Uryen and of course you passed as *his* child" (243).

Denied his rightful heritage by Smith's opposition, Dud had the freedom to name himself as a child. Dud's choice of his own name was another act of self-delineation and self-acceptance. For "a nameless bastard, whose mind was so morbid, and whose virility was so weak, that he could neither 'love' as other men or feel angry as other men" (121), the selection is in complete accord with his nature. In applying his cryptonym, Dud aligns himself with a comic grotesque figure popular to folk tradition. In the Renaissance, Nobody was a scapegoat who was forced to take the blame for mishaps when all present pretended innocence. Pictured often as "a ragged, bespectacled figure, often with a padlocked mouth to indicate enforced silence, and surrounded with a heap of broken objects," Nobody was a clumsy and ridiculous caricature.[13] Dud's inability to control inanimate matters may owe something to his affinity to this creature. His kettle is certain to spill its water, and bits of sponge in his basin can be counted on to resist all his efforts to catch them. In addition, the tendency of the other characters, most notably Jenny Dearth, to blame Dud for the results of his well-intentioned meddling in their problems may have been inspired by this caricatured scapegoat.

Although he is inept and quaint, there are aspects of Dud's nature that are genuinely heroic rather than clownish. The mysterious circumstances of his birth force him to embark on a quest for his true identity as a disinherited prince might do in an old tale. For a character involved in this archetypal search, the initial anonymity is apt. There is a sense in which Dud deserves to be associated with the story of "Odysseus's encounter with the Cyclops" (18). Modestly, Dud denies any affinity to this wily hero; yet there are elements in his experience that have a legendary dimension. Through his reluctant acceptance of Uryen as his father, he regains his lost heritage. Early in the book, he told himself "a childish story about his father being some great Welsh nobleman, who claimed to be descended from Sir Pellenore" (128–29). When he discovers that this fantasy is closer to the truth than he ever could have expected, he resists Uryen by scoffing at his notions. However much scorn Dud may heap on Uryen, he sees in his father a magnified version of his own propensities. When he argues with Uryen at Maiden Castle, he is appalled to notice that he has been forced "to become like his father even in the act of denouncing him" (149). Only at the end of the book is he able to admit freely to Nance that he shares with Uryen the desire to live "more in the great cosmic forces . . . than in ordinary human interests" (496). Although he has reservations, Dud carries the effects of his father's reading into his own generation.

The supporting characters also seek guidance from books about how to give order and direction to their lives. Opportunities thereby are created for still further exploration of the ways in which reality imitates art. Wizzie derives her standards of decorous feminine behavior from her reading of pulp fiction that is represented by the cleverly titled *The Adventures of Lily Turnstile*. By emulating the heroine's wiles as they are set forth in "the discoloured pages of this unliterary pamphlet" (288), she endeavors to arouse and maintain the interest of her own infatuated suitors. For his part, Roger Cask credits the turning point in his life to a reading of Lord Shaftesbury. From this example, Roger determined to become a philanthropist, a preposterous ambition because he lacks money. Fitting the book to the individual seems crucial. Teucer Wye tries desperately to be patient with his daughter's behavior by rationalizing that Thuella suffered an involuntary exposure to Homer during her prenatal life: "I read Homer in *those* days, when her mother was carrying her, and I was always quoting him" (65). After the disappointment arising from the imposition of this apparently inappropriate influence, Teucer has had recourse instead to Plato. He illustrates the necessity of books for life in a literal and comic way through his fetishistic requirement that a copy of the *Phaedrus* be placed in his right pocket and the *Timaeus* in the left one. In addition to giving physical comfort, these texts have soothed his spirit by providing answers for every crisis in his life. When he decides to advise his favorite daughter, Jenny, about her treatment of Roger, he tells Wizzie about his preparations: "I've been thinking what to say for a whole week; and I've got the passages marked" (411). Ironically, the test of sincerity demanded by his daughter is that the only books he now cares about be burned. To pass on the wisdom he has gleaned from ancient teaching, he is forced to destroy the source of his own consolation and self-definition. He speaks of "these books, which are my life" (415). Shorn of his exalted reason for being through direct contact with great ideas, he comes face to face with his own banality.

Literature and daily life are engaged in a creative interplay, not confined to their separate spheres. In varying degrees and with diverse results, everyone lives by and through books. (The exception that proves the rule is the character, Dumbell, whose home is noteworthy for its absence of reading material.) In other ways, the lines of demarcation between art and life are blurred to pursue Powys's ongoing concern with the interconnection between the imagined and the real. To this end, the common-sense distinction between the level of reality normally attributed to real people and characters in books is deliberately made indefinite. Thus, Dud can think of Hardy's characters as if they had actually wandered through the Dorchester streets. This assumption lies behind the remark made about the gargoyle head presently adorning the old brick entrance to a meeting house on Glyde Path Lane. The head is said to have "occupied in poor Trenchard's time a different position from what it did now" (263). When Dud contrasts his own behavior in buying a "wife" to that of Henchard in selling his, he makes the comparison as if he and Henchard had an identical ontological status. For the reader of their respective stories, the two do indeed share the same kind of existence. But usually Dud, obeying fictional conventions, thinks about himself as if he were an actual person and the reader willingly connives in the deception. By treating his own existence as comparable to that of Henchard, he must either be drawing attention to the artifice involved in his own being or endowing Hardy's character with an extra-literary validity. References to Hardy's statue also stress the reciprocity between art and life. Although his statue is present most palpably at an important Dorchester intersection, it also is a reminder that the place has been provided before with a collateral artistic reality as the setting for his fiction. Hardy himself, in artistic replication, is now a part of that very landscape, the perception of which he altered permanently through his Wessex fiction.

Throughout *Maiden Castle*, Powys refers to Dud as both "our hero" and "our friend." These designations show him to be simultaneously the product of artifice and a being real enough to be a companion to author and reader alike. Even the name No-man may be intended to draw attention to his position as a character rather than as an actual person. The ambiguity is pursued in the way Dud is made to think about himself, his friends, and the subject of his own quasi-historical book. When he considers how he would manipulate events if he were telling his own story, he forces acknowledgment of his own fictional status as if he were a character in search of an author. A large part of the book is exactly the autobiography Dud might have written if he were not currently so preoccupied with his own tale about Mary Channing. For this historical fiction, Dud derives inspiration from his "real" companions and his real environment.

In particular, Wizzie teaches him lessons in feminine psychology that he applies to his portrayal of Mary. His art is enriched by his observation of reality. But his absorption in the story of Mary is so intense that Wizzie is right to regard her as a rival. When Nance says to Dud, "And don't forget to show Wizzie that house where you lived when you were Many Channing's friend" (435), she voices her knowledge of the extent to which this eighteenth-century subject had acquired an existence in which Dud is an active participant.

Although his perception of his peers usually involves recognition of their substantiality, he also experiences occasionally (like other Powysian heroes before him) "a queer impression that he too, and Nance—and all of them—were characters in a play" (275). This sense of unreality is juxtaposed to a microscopically exact observation of the physical minutiae of the individuals in his world. There is, for example, a certain absolute rightness about focusing attention on such empirical details as the small gray louse on Old Funky's forehead or the stain on Wizzie's circus tights that is shaped like the figure eight. These acute natural descriptions give Dud's companions a solidity of specification; yet they also strike him in other circumstances as creatures out of fairy tales. At certain times, Thuella has qualities that are suggestive of a Lamia, Old Funky of an ogre, and Wizzie of an elf. Of course, no one is more important than Uryen in drawing attention to the way the boundary between reality and art can vanish. When he recounts to Dud the events of his early life, his story seems closer to literature than actuality. His recital of incidents seems to his son to be a self-created legend or "exactly the sort of tale that a wayfarer on the high way would tell" (243). Even as Uryen's name sounds ridiculous and affected to Dud "like the name of a person in a book" (231), so do the happenings of his life take on a fabulous, invented configuration.

Attention is drawn further to the fictional status of the people when speculation is offered about how other authors would have treated them. At Hardy's statue, Dud wonders whether this great writer would have found Thuella or Wizzie a more intriguing subject. When Thuella and Dud visit Scummy Pond, Powys interrupts the description to imagine how they might have fared in the pages of other books.

The magnetic interchange between them was rendered more complicated though not less exciting by reason of their dangerous position above the "scummy pond", into whose dark water it is certain that John Bunyan would have precipitated them both, and out of whose green slime it is equally certain that Dante would have called forth a cartload of horned devils, of scratching, biting, scaly devils, of foul, stinking, obscene devils, to switch them off to hell.(212)

In passages such as these, notice is attracted to the author's omnipotence over his characters' personalities and destinies. No matter how lifelike and self-directed fictional people may seem, they are circumscribed by authorial control.

Insofar as a distinction is admitted between literature and life, it is found less in the implausibility of the content than in the formal pattern imposed by the author's control. In the absence of the solace provided by this arrangement, the accidents and sorrows of reality are more acute in the living than in the telling. Dud thinks:

> How grotesque . . . are the situations we get into! I must remember this in the story of my Mary. People in books are luckier than in life. Every life, if the truth were known, contains experiences of a monstrous grotesqueness. (211)

The comment is more striking because it comes from a writer who is engaged on a biography of a woman who committed murder and suffered public execution. Dud is stricken by the rejection of his book on Mary because he hoped to make her live again and to redress her wrongs through his writing. Books, through the efforts of their authors and the engagement by their readers, have a revitalizing effect on subject and recipient alike.

There is special fitness in arranging for *Maiden Castle* to open on All Souls' Day and to end one year later with another visit to the cemetery. In the beginning, Dud comes to life on this day in two ways. After paying a visit to his dead, he is prepared for entry into the land of the living by the guidance of the cemetery woman, Nancy Quirm. He undergoes an emotional awakening from the state of oblivion in which he had spent his last ten years. His personal experience of reanimation is paralleled in that he is simultaneously beginning to seem real to his reader. On the following second of November, he will "die" as a character when his story is concluded. Many ambiguities, however, do complicate this general pattern. Although Nancy encourages Dud to set free his dead so that he may live more abundantly, she has a frail heart and lives constantly with the threat of her own annihilation. Moreover, it is she who takes Dud to meet Uryen, the *"rex semi-mortuus,"* the "corpse-god" (166). Clearly, Dud's rebirth into new vitality also involves a closer acquaintance with the reality of death. There is also life to be discovered in his figurative extinction as a character in the final chapter. In his last words, he affirms his commitment to ordinary existence and his determination to be watchful for "'intimations of immortality'" (496).

In addition, as the story of Uryen has demonstrated, although they seem to share in the mortality of men, there is a sense in which characters in literature enjoy a special sort of imperishability. Insofar as Uryen exerts his power over his readers' imagination, Uryen is made to live again. The answer to the question posed by the epigraph, *A vyd vyth Uryen arall?* (Will there ever be another Uryen?), is that by acting as a liaison between modern man and ancient culture, Quirm causes Uryen to have a new advent each time his story is read. And through the artistry of Powys's romance, the same kind of serial immortality is available even to a character who styles himself so unprepossessingly as Dud No-man. As Uryen says, "It's all in the books" (252).

Notes

1. John Cowper Powys, *Enjoyment of Literature*, (New York: Simon and Schuster, 1938), pp. xii–xiii.

2. John Cowper Powys, *Ducdame* (London: Village Press, 1974), p. 413.

3. Ibid., p. 417.

4. Ibid., p. 408.

5. Ibid., p. 418.

6. John Cowper Powys, *Wolf Solent* (Harmondsworth, Middlesex: Penguin, 1976), p. 176.

7. "Areopagitica," *John Milton: Complete Poems and Major Prose*, ed. Merritt Y. Hughes (New York: Odyssey, 1957), p. 720.

8. John Cowper Powys, *Maiden Castle* (London: Picador, 1979), p. 60. Subsequent references are cited parenthetically by page number.

9. John Cowper Powys, *Obstinate Cymric: Essays 1935–47* (London: Village Press, 1973), p. 54.

10. John Rhys, *Celtic Folklore: Welsh and Manx*, 2 vols. (Oxford: Clarendon, 1901), 2:551.

11. John Rhys, *Studies in the Arthurian Legend* (Oxford: Clarendon, 1891), p. 256.

12. Ibid.

13. Frank Kermode, ed., "Additional Notes" to William Shakespeare's *The Tempest* (London: Methuen, 1968), p. 169.

The Lie of the Land, or, Plot and Autochthony in John Cowper Powys

Richard Maxwell

It is customary for readers of John Cowper Powys to see him as an escapist, a naïf out of his time. In recent evaluations, this impression has been used to several ends. When John Bayley describes Powys as a "domestic" novelist, he is working against the sort of interpretation that would associate the writer with Dostoyevsky, Rabelais, and other outsized geniuses; he is arguing that Powys's real talent is for depicting the intimate life of "a small historic town," and with it—to quote the title of Bayley's essay—"Life in the Head." When Vernon Young asserts that Powys "never saw the world in which he lived," that he "retreated throughout our mid-century," the implication is quite different. Young is offended by the thought that Powys might be a major British novelist; he wants to get him off the list of candidates for this position, and does so by making him out a gutless crackpot, the village idiot rather than the village chronicler. One might say that Bayley and Young disagree about everything concerning Powys—except his propensity for seeking out remote, sheltered places and associating his literary efforts with them.[1]

Unlike these essayists, I will not attempt a grand survey of Powys's fiction; what follows no doubt will take the duller form of an essay for scholars. Some of my observations, however, may be helpful to those who attempt the magisterial note in the future. There is a good deal that is right about the picture of the novelist looking for a corner where he can hide and enjoy himself while forgetting the impingements of the twentieth century. As the hero of *Ducdame* (1925) muses, "Better, far better, to live harmlessly in some quiet untroubled place, watching season follow season, month follow month, aloof and detached; leaving the breathless procession of outward events to turn and twist upon itself like a wounded snake." But for every such passage in Powys's work, there is another like this one, also from *Ducdame:* "It's the fact of one's knowing every stick and stone in the background of events that gives to events their heightened value. To get the passing of time one has to possess a dial, as it were, on which the hours are marked."[2] The spirit of place excludes time (that twists "on itself like a wounded snake"); the spirit of place makes time and its passage perceptible, allowing us to discover "events" that would otherwise remain invisible.

These statements do not necessarily contradict each other. There is a certain kind of Powysian narrative where events emerge from place but issue in peace: plot is subdued by the spirit of Glastonbury, Weymouth Sands, Maiden Castle, or the Vale of Edeyrnion, as though it were possible to live an eternally serene moment, a moment that somehow includes narrative unpredictability and suspense while keeping it under control. The novelist thus finds a way to remain at rest within an exciting world. I will pause over one artful example of this compromise from *A Glastonbury Romance;* however, my principal interest will be elsewhere. The dominance exerted by a mythical spirit of the place, a *genius loci*, can be challenged by "authochthonous aboriginals": monstrous creatures who have sprung from the soil and thus can combat the *genius* on its own terms. A plot that includes authochthons can wake up virtually anyone, disrupting any chance of forgetfulness and escape. The act of disruption turns out to be one of the novelist's most fruitful subjects, allowing him and his characters a passage back to the mainstream (or perhaps the nightmare) of history. This is clear especially in *A Glastonbury Romance* and *Porius*, books in which a revolt of autochthons establishes the independence of plot from place. Powys proves less the village idiot, or for that matter the village chronicler, than he seems.

1. *Hic Jacet*

Powys claimed that *A Glastonbury Romance* (1933) was written to convey the "personality" of a "place," "the life of a particular spot upon the earth's surface."[3] The quality of this life is defined in an early chapter titled "Hic Jacet," in which the novelist describes a tea party at the house of Euphemia Drew, just across from the ruins of Glastonbury Abbey. Mat Dekker, the Vicar, recites an inscription that sums up much of the Abbey's claim to notoriety: *"Hic jacet sepultus inclitus Rex Arturus in Insula Avallonia."* A touchy conversation ensues over the subject of Arthur's grave. Is the Once and Future King indeed buried in Glastonbury, the Isle of Avalon, and if so is the location of his tomb known? John Crow, skeptic and outsider, irritates his hostess by citing a Welsh Triad that affirms general ignorance on this subject. "'Not *know* where it is?' she said sternly. 'Fiddle-de-dee! we *all* know where it is! It's under that broken arch'" [i.e., in the ruin across the street].[4]

Crow persists. If he is trying to antagonize Miss Drew, an enthusiastic believer in local myths, he succeeds; he also turns up a pair of clues to Glastonbury's personality. The first clue concerns the Latin phrase *Hic jacet*. Crow recalls some other "jingle" to which these words belong. "Mat Dekker smiled sadly. 'You mean *"Hic jacet Arturus, rex quondam, rexque futurus"?'* . . . 'Most of our Glastonbury sayings have to do with some sort of *'Hic jacet,'*" he concluded rather wistfully." The second clue is less obvious. Crow asks whether King Arthur is "the most deeply rooted superstition that this place represents." Sam, Mat's son, stirs uneasily. "To definitely challenge the whole *genius loci* seemed to Sam's simple mind as much a lapse from Nature's ways as it would have been to allow a minnow to perish for lack of fresh water" (119–20). The reference is personal, and, as we will later see, crucial. Powys's *Autobiography*—published a year after *A Glastonbury Romance*—relates how young Johnny is caught by his father transferring tadpoles from deep ponds to shallow puddles. In Powys's narration, the father does not seem to comprehend the deliberate cruelty of his son's gesture, because it is so foreign to his own nature. By a regrettable coincidence, father displays immediately to son his personal "deeds of devastation," the unconsciously cruel "hewing and wounding" of a laurel tree. Powys comments: "Oh how hard it is to live in Arcadia and not meddle with *some* species or other of autochthonous aboriginals!"[5]

The clues elicited by John Crow will lead us in two different directions. If we draw out the significance of *Hic jacet*, we end with a comprehensive theory about the personality of Glastonbury and a narrative that extols the virtues of peace, escape, and rest. If we pursue the question of which inhabitants are aboriginals—a question suggested by Sam's thought about minnows as well as by Mat Dekker's historical speculations on the same topic—we discover a flaw in our comprehensive theory (120). This flaw creates its own story, whose import is quite different from that of the first.

It is best to begin with *Hic jacet* and let the puzzle of autochthony arise a little later. A few minutes after his scandalous performance at Miss Drew's party, John Crow watches the sun set over "the lowest pastoral country in the land of England . . . it was nothing else than this very low-lying character of the country that made it such a fatal receptacle fot the superstitions of two thousand years. Into this blue-purple vapour, into the bosom of these fields lower than the sea, floated, drifted upon the wind, all those dangerous enervating myths . . . This place must be charged, 'thick, and slab,'

with all the sweet-sickly religious lies that had ever medicined the
world . . . [lulling] to sleep the mind of the generations!" (121–22)
Much of the novel develops from the punning implication that there
are several sorts of *Hic jacet.*⁶ Here lies. Translated into English,
the phrase refers to altitude and topography; it also suggests untruth
and is also associated (cf. the Latin) with lying in slumber or death.

The topographical meaning is explained further a few paragraphs
later. "Creative energies" have poured into Glastonbury for several
millenia. By the "psychic channels" of renown, poetry, and individual
experience, the *genius loci* has come to be what it is (125). The
notion of a channel that conveys energy downwards and inwards
is to be taken figuratively, but it also has a literal application that
shades back into the figurative one. As Mary Crow comments, "They
call ditches about here by some funny name like that. No! Rhyne,
that's it, not Rhys" (124). This word "rhyne" recurs frequently.
Like the mention of minnows in shallow water, it has personal
reverbations for Powys, whose first sense of irretrievable loss—he
claims—came from reading Aytoun's "The Passage of the Rhine."
In Aytoun's poem, it is the exiled Highlanders of Prince Charles
who cross the great river. After reading their history, Powys discovers
a peculiar Celtic emotion, an inward turn after defeat "like water
seeking its level."⁷ So, when John Crow is first approaching Glastonbury, "He experienced a pang of sadness . . . a thousand old impressions of Isle-of-Ely dykes, called up, out of deep-buried race
memories, by the ditches, or 'rhynes,' as they call them, of the
Isle-of-Glastonbury" (108). Exiled from Norfolk, Crow feels the loss
of his native soil in his first experience of rhynes—low-lying channels,
yet unlike his native ditches. The rhynes make him homesick. At
the same time, they draw him (as they have drawn so many others)
toward the magical place that lies directly below him.

"Sweet-sickly religious lies" provide a further gloss on *Hic jacet.*
Glastonbury is a "vortex" from which many cults "sucked their life-
blood" (125). This vortex, or whirlpool, does the swallowing but
in its turn is fed upon by its prey. This process of mutual exploitation
has continued until there are many layers in the Glastonbury tradition.
The pageant that occurs at the book's center begins with Arthurian
lore, works its way back to the crucifixion, and is supposed to end
in a presentation of Cymric (Welsh) mythology: Taliessin, Druids,
and others. As the pageant suggests, Glastonbury has become a historic palimpsest. Its lies may not originally have had much in common. Powys writes that the Grail, the Absolute, had "attracted these
various cults to itself with an indifference as to their divergency
from one another that was almost cruel" (756–57). Taken together,

however, the cults create an unmistakable atmosphere: the livid blue vapor that characterizes Yr Echwyd, "the Land of Glamour and Illusion"[8] (755).

The *genius loci* of Glastonbury is associated with another kind of lying: lying down, repose. In its most intense form, such repose is brought about by the Holy Grail, an image of happiness that governs human fantasizing on this spot. The grail offers "an absolutely New Thing—sobbing happiness—black—earth—rain—dew— peace—" (163). Illusion leads to blissful forgetfulness.[9] It is ultimately this prospect that lies in Glastonbury. Several chapters after "Hic Jacet," the capitalist Philip Crow flies over the area in his airplane. Philip Crow is the novel's great doer; he is the embodiment of restless, enterprising energy. When he watches from a height, his tendency to think of power, of imposing his will on a passive substance, is exacerbated. "Philip recognised the general lie of the land tonight and its natural landmarks more quickly than most passengers would have done in one of their first ascents" (231). All the same, something is missing from his perception of Glastonbury. "It was of the planetary earth . . . not of any calm earth-mother, lying back upon her secret life, that his mind was full" (231). The earth mother and her receptive repose are reduced to insignificance; Philip thinks that he works upon a neutral substance, so misses the trancelike lying that pervades the *genius loci*.

Perhaps it is clear already that among the meanings associated with *Hic jacet*, the third has a privileged position; that it is, in effect, the goal toward which the others lead us. This impression is confirmed by the book's central plot, in which Powys follows the career of Johnny Geard, Glastonbury's mayor. Geard wants to tap the energies of the *genius loci* and thus transform his town into a great religious center. I have no intention of following his project through all its crises. It is enough to suggest that at every great turning point in Geard's quest, the three kinds of Glastonbury lie are a shaping presence, with the third, the possibility of rest, held out as a final good. The appropriate end to Geard's efforts occurs when a flood engulfs the low-lying land. Geard resolves to die in the flood and thus, by his own logic, gain more life. Powys describes him deliberately swallowing enormous quantities of the salt flood as he goes under "in the exact space of water that covered the spot where the ancient Lake Villagers had their temple to the neolithic goddess of fertility" (1117). During his last moments of consciousness, Geard stares at Glastonbury Tor, which seems to turn into the Holy Grail. His final memory is of "lying in the green spring grass." The scene and the novel conclude with a tribute to the fertility goddess Cybele, "that beautiful and terrible force by which the Lies of great creative Nature give birth to Truth that is to be" (1120).

Geard's striving toward rest has a privileged position in *A Glastonbury Romance*, but it does not, as Powys says, "cover the whole field."[10] Owen Evan's pursuit of the Grail stands in a more problematic relation to *Hic jacet* and its unfolding implications. Evans, a clandestine sadist horrified by his own desires, craves parthogenesis: a self-birth, a cleansing of the mind, which he hopes the Grail will afford him (149, 150). At one point Evans repeats to himself *"Hic jacet Arturus . . . Hic jacet . . . Arturus . . . Hic jacet . . . hic"* (183). As the magic phrase fades, it evokes an obsession so powerful that it dissolves the materials on which it works. Evan's mingled fear and desire of the Grail turn into a fear and desire of its source: the autochthonous aboriginals of Glastonbury, descendants of those conquered races who were either driven west to Wales or lingered on obscurely in Somerset. Evans is aboriginal in this sense: like Mrs. Geard, he belongs to the line of Rhys (the name that Mary Crow mixed up with rhyne). Most of the autochthons, however, come from the poorest classes of Glastonbury. Throughout the novel, Powys carefully characterizes Glastonbury indigenes as a miserable *lumpenproletariat*.[11] It might be assumed that these indigenes embody the spirit of the place as do the literally autochthonous figurines of Arthur, Merlin and others made in the municipal factory from Somerset clay. This is not exactly true. Relations between the autochthonous poor and the *genius loci* are strained. Like "imprisoned Titans" the "real People of Glastonbury" are ready "to break forth in blind scoriac fury" against the powers that be (561, 567). The autochthons supported the bastard Monmouth, they rioted with Jack Cade, they sheltered Owen Glendower, and "waylaid the lovely queen of Rex Arturus himself" (562). Their antagonism is so powerful because it comes from the center, the originating mystery, of the *genius loci*. "That impoverished and mutinous population in the slums" thus becomes the great anomaly of the novel—and a special problem for Owen Evans (756).

At first the hostility of the autochthons emerges indirectly: for example, at the novel's midpoint when Geard's Glastonbury pageant is performed. The pageant has three parts: it begins with Arthur, moves back to Christ, and ends with the ancient, autochthonous, mythology. The first section is almost broken up when the aboriginal population nearly murders Lord P., a spontaneous expression of hatred against "everything in these people's lives that they had suffered from" (569). Only Geard's direct intervention preserves a semblance of order. The second section ends abruptly for a similar reason.

Evans, who is playing the crucified Christ (and thus directing his sadism against himself) has a horrible vision of all the suffering that has ever occurred in Glastonbury. A divine voice mumbles incoherently. "'It is God and He is lying to me,' thought Mr. Evans. 'He is lying to me. People lie to the condemned for whom there is no hope'" (618). Evans collapses and the pageant ends without reaching the third section.

Perhaps the most striking point about the pageant is that it both calls up and suppresses the autochthons: it rouses them to revolt during the Arthurian tableau and turns back from the presentation of their ancient lore—the lying lore from which the *genius loci* sprang— when Evans drops on his cross. A sinister logic begins to develop here. It develops further during a later chapter, "Nature Seems Dead," that describes the night of 10 December in Glastonbury. On this date, "what really came back . . . were the *dreams* of the conquered, those disordered, extravagant, law-breaking dreams, out of which the Shrines of Glastonbury had originally been built" (756). Powys distrusts dreams. The blessing of the Grail is vouchsafed to those who lie obliviously, "carrying those carefree foreheads deep down under the sacred waters of Yr Echyd." It is a disturbing anomaly for the Grail lore to appear in dreams, another one of those lies that forbids rest (cf. God whispering to Mr. Evans). What does it mean to remember a magic forgetfulness? Powys writes eloquently on this paradox. The autochthonous legends of Glastonbury "seem to recede and vanish away even as they are named among us, like creatures of a blundered incantation." The old stories are called upon but assume a monstrous, confusing, and supremely disruptive form. We can neither banish nor face them. Powys thus reveals a conflict not so much between the Grail and its enemies—although this remains his putative subject—as within the *genius loci* of which the Grail is the expression. The Grail was created to banish pain. On 10 December, pain breaks through the illusions of Yr Echwyd, the reality overtaking the myth it fostered. What finally returns that night—the most extravagant and law-breaking dream of all, stranger than Philip's fantasy of killing inefficient workers, stranger than Persephone Spear's dream of dancing around a tree that also is a cross, stranger than John Crow's dream of urinating into the Holy Grail—is the horrible Finn Toller. Once invoked, Toller will lead Mr. Evans to his great moment of temptation.

Weak, slobbering, and wolfish, a natural victim as he is a natural aggressor, Toller finds his appropriate partner in the only inhabitant of Glastonbury socially lower than himself. The madwoman Bet Chinnock convinces him to commit a murder. Toller then involves

Evans in the project by dangling before him the prospect of seeing
a man's head crushed with an iron bar. At this late stage, the pathos
of Powys's conception comes home. The novelist has invented a
character obsessed by the ancient lore of his ancestors but also obsessed by sadistic revery. Together the two obsessions produce a
trap in which Evans struggles. He lives a nightmare in which thoughts
of the Grail prompt despair rather than rest. Thinking about the
iron bar, Evans enters a tavern in which "there was not a man
. . . who had not come to *forget his troubles*" (1006). After Evans
purchases a "tumbler of pallid gold" (Our Special), he chooses to
share this grail of forgetfulness with Toller, who whispers that the
murder with the iron bar is imminent (1009). A scene within the
scene recalls the issue of autochthony: Dave Spear, leader of a new
Glastonbury commune, is nearly assaulted by the "Glaston folk"
who resent his dogmatic political theorizing. Spear argues for a sort
of abstract autochtony ("the human race, sprung from the earth,
returning to the earth, loving the earth") in a future in which there
will be no more Glastonbury, only a united human race (1017).
Although Spear has no sadistic impulses, his utopia sheds light on
Owen Evans' fight with himself. In his own way, Evans also has
depersonalized the autochthonous. His fascination with the iron bar
and its wielder is "surrounded by a vacuum of anonymity" (1019).
The iron bar will merely demonstrate "the law of gravitation" (1021).
That same law creates a down-dragging force, a "pull of cosmic
entropy" that draws Evans to the spectacle of a crushed human
brain. His sadism pushes Evans toward a depersonalized autochthony
(caricaturing what he sought in the old legends); his conscience pulls
him back to a world of personality, his own and the town's.

Evans partly escapes the temptation created by his blundered incan-
tations. He wants to meet Toller on Tor Hill and watch the murder.
His wife Cordelia (Geard's daughter) realizes that something is wrong;
she keeps him from his appointment using a seduction whose grotesque qualities Powys underlines. "She began feverishly stripping
off her clothes. He followed every movement of her hand with those
burning eyes, under the shadow of that bowler. His coat was buttoned
up tight under his chin" (1034). She keeps Mr. Evans from witnessing
the murder—it takes place all the same, though the wrong man
is killed. (Finn Toller, the murderer, dies a few moments later,
pushed from Glastonbury Tor by Mad Bet.) The lovers arrive on
the scene too late to prevent any of this. Mr. Evans "stared round
him till he caught sight of the iron bar . . . he went over to where
the body was lying [and] gazed at what was revealed" (1053–54).
It is not Mr. Evan's sexual nerve that is stimulated; that part of

his obsession is gone forever, along with most of his will and intelligence. Cordelia remains endeared to him "in the way mothers are endeared to a deformed or an idiot child" (1055). Her "savage maternal protectiveness" supports Mr. Evans's now ineffective search for the Great Good Place, Esplumeoir, to which Merlin disappeared.

It would hardly seem that there is anything pleasant to say about Mr. Evans; he suffers the saddest fate in Glastonbury. How then can I account, therefore, for the exhilaration that his adventures prompt in me? A direct contrast between Evans and Geard may clarify such feelings. A Grail quest arising from flaws in the *genius loci*—contradictions that Geard's charismatic presence obscures—will create a distinctive atmosphere. Initially, Evans seems a marginal case, but Powys's emphasis on his sufferings and especially his placement of Evans as the crucified Christ of the pageant demonstrates this character's importance. Evans bears the weight of the contradictions evaded by Geard. The lie of the land no longer conducts the quester toward a region of permanent sleep, no longer implies that all important decisions have been made already and that he must wait merely for the right turn of the pun, the proper mood for the *genius loci*, to swallow peace. Instead he reaches a crisis, an extraordinary development for this book of livid blue vapors. The system generated by *Hic jacet* is shattered so that he must decide something on his own. Evans is not the only one in Glastonbury that bears this burden, but he bears it most fully. That he fails to complete the Grail Quest is not so important: what counts is the sense of a plot that breaks from the *genius loci*, revealing it in a new light. Against the background of the book's narrative logic, Evan's story is an extravagant, unpredictable phenomenon like the autochthons with whom he is involved.

This sort of analogy will be explored further in *Porius*. The novelist searches for ways to assimilate the autochthons and their claims into his exploration of the *genius loci*. He wants to reconstruct something like the progress of Johnny Geard, from the lie of the land to semantic lies to lying at rest, but to reconstruct it so that he can come to terms with autochthony. The effort expands Powys's already generous frame of reference: it means less emphasis on "sweet-sickly religious lies" that are designed to yield rest and forgetfulness; it means more emphasis on law-breaking lies connected with a permanent remembrance of pain and also with excessive, violent narrative. Following a narrative of unforgettable pain and a disastrous meddling with autochthonous aboriginals, how can we lie restfully? Porius will discover a solution to this dilemma the hard way, when he finds himself in a story much like that related by "The Iron Bar."

2. Cave

The action of *Porius* (1951) is confined to the Vale of Edeyrnion, an area in northern Wales that Powys imagines as it might have been in the year 499 A.D. The novel's opening pages describe Porius surveying the Vale from above. It is "still covered by the aboriginal forest" but bears a name of Roman derivation ("Eternus"). No less than Glastonbury, Edeyrnion is an historical palimpsest. The Brythons (Celts) were transplanted there by the Romans. Before the Romans the Gwyddylaid (Scots) held sway, and before them the Ffichtiaid (Picts) and the Forest People (Iberians) had Edeyrnion to themselves, except for the legendary "aboriginal giants."[12] These giants or Cewri—who may still survive in mountain caves, who may come out on occasion to eat corpses—were the real autochthonous aboriginals of Edeyrnion. Their relation to this place, to the story that Powys draws from it, and to our eponymous hero, will be a crux in *Porius*.

Readers of Powys know his fascination with giants: for example, with the Cerne Abbas giant marked on the Dorset landscape. We also recall that the iconography of giants and the gigantic is not a Powysian invention: it has a history that the novelist respects even as he adapts it for his own purposes. Susan Stewart has argued that giants are originally associated with "an overabundance of the natural . . . the gigantic unleashes a vast and 'natural' creativity that bears within it the capacity of (self-) destruction." Such giants give shape to the earth by their movement across it; in some folk tales giants literally mold landscapes: building mountains, carving valleys. However, this excessive nature is not present only within landscape; it also takes narrative form. A story about giants is a whopper—the sort of life defined by fantastic, unexpected twists.[13] Giants are that version of the autochthonous in which the connection between the lie of the land and the lie of exaggeration is most obvious and most unavoidable.

Stewart says little or nothing about our third term, rest; aside from Blake's sleeping Albion and Swift's sleeping Gulliver, giants might not be considered a terribly restful topic. This issue is raised at an early point in *Porius;* its difficulties are expressed by a word related to the *Hic jacet* of *A Glastonbury Romance*. Porius, who has recently turned thirty, belongs to the romanized elite of the Vale. Years before the beginning of the novel's action, he went with his Roman grandfather Porius Manlius to search out an appropriate resting place for the old man's ashes. They explored a wild area that reminded the elder Porius of his own ancestral estates; he thought the neighborhood appropriate to his interment but had to control his "dread . . . lest the old local divinities, turned now by the new faith into evil spirits, but acknowledged to be more potent in this part of the country than anywhere else in Britain, should disturb his rest" (83). Autochthony, locality, and rest draw together in such a way as to exclude outsiders or invaders. The genius of the place is stubbornly indigenous—which means that it offers peace only to its own kind. The *genius loci*, therefore, is represented less well by *Hic jacet* than by a word that Porius and his grandfather encounter on several graves: "*cave!* beware!" attached to the patronymic inscriptions of other Roman colonists. Perhaps these syllables name a family; perhaps they are intended to scare away intruders. Perhaps, although this thought is not yet articulated, the intruders in question would include those corpse-eating giants who are thought to lurk in caves.

The child and his companion argue over *cave* as they return "from their final choice of an unappropriated resting-place." *Cave* remains on young Porius's mind. Eventually he puts it to a "secret use": he expands it into his own word, cavoseniargizing. This coinage is intentionally absurd, Powys tells us. Our hero thus expels any hint of mysticism from it (403). Cavoseniargizing denotes a moment when the gulf between body and soul is temporarily resolved. Soul remains suspended above body, but is "able to follow every curve and ripple of . . . bodily sensations" (83). "To feel this first and last sensation of the human body and soul in harmony you had at once to unite things and isolate things, to immerse yourself in things and to escape from things. It was anything but easy" (84). Cavoseniargizing is a stunt; is is also a way of relaxing by reconciling oneself to existence on earth without losing one's mental powers, one's special identity.

The suggestion *in* the word is that this compromise could somehow emerge from our reaction to the autochthonous. An absurd idea, no doubt—yet it may linger in our minds, because Porius's obsession with the Cewri is emphasized throughout the novel. He has a Roman grandfather on his mother's side, but on his father's side matters are different. His paternal great-grandfather (Edeyrn, also the name of this place) married an aboriginal giantess; not only did the marriage break a racial taboo, it also prepared the waning of the ancient matriarchy still influential among the forest people (308). Porius wants to return to this earlier phase in political and social consciousness. If he had seen his grandfather's mother Creiddylad, perhaps he might have done so. When she "gave suck" to her son, she must have taught him "some old Cader Idris trick of lifting this jealous past and crazy future off their feet while you hugged the present" (139).

It is rather difficult to visualize this feat: do you lift the past and future with one arm while hugging the present with the other? Porius's murky thought is in character, however. We have already seen him lift an importunate Arthurian envoy off his horse and hold him up like a doll; soon he will hug Myrddin Wyllt (Merlin) while that avatar of Cronos goes into a trance that summons up all time (24, 58). Despite his short stature (he is well under six feet), Porius has inherited the strength of a giant, which he wants to use mentally as well as physically. From Creiddylad he could have learned this ultimate form of cavoseniargizing: immersement and escape together, escape from the flow of time into the moment, into the sensations of *now*. Falling asleep at the end of the first day narrated in this novel, Porius asks an elaborate question that is almost a myth in itself: "Could a man with the blood of the giants in him embrace air, water, and fire as though they were a cloud, and embrace them without ravishing or devouring any beautiful goddess, as he was accustomed to do with the elements in what he called his 'cavoseniargizing'?" (146; cf. 411). Whether such an embrace is possible is an abiding mystery for Porius, a mystery that a confrontation with giants perhaps would solve for him.

Porius's yen for the "true aboriginals" of Edyrnion continues to haunt him (490). He can speak of it to no one; it remains a secret along with cavoseniargizing. The reason for Porius's reticence about the giants is explained in a passage at the end of chapter 10, in which the Henog (Chief Storyteller) from Arthur's Court interrogates a dying hermit about the "old incestuous gods of magic and illusion" worshipped by the forest people (389). This ancient religion— identified with figures from *The Mabinogion* like Gwydion, Math and Arianrod—has become "a dark horrible sensitive bruise . . . a bruise upon which [Christianity] was forever pouring oil and spreading the poppied ointment of oblivion." Powys adds that the forest people have embraced Christianity, embraced it with their souls to escape a heathenism inappropriate to their pacific natures. This embrace is the opposite of the one Porius would learn from Creiddylad, a non-Christian figure if there ever was one—and yet there is a parallel between his dilemma and that of the forest people. They are reluctant even to name the old gods, fearing that this blundered incantation "might bring down some appalling disaster" (390). Porius has the same kind of *tynged* or "neurotic inhibition" against discussing the giants.

This passage is virtually a gloss on the search of Porius and his grandfather for a burial place; we now understand how it is that the gods of illusion can be transformed into evil spirits and why their indigenous influence should be feared. If even the stalwart Roman feels such trepidation, then it must be drastically intensified among those nearer to the native culture. If like Porius or Mr. Evans, we desire as well as fear the repressed beings, our dilemma is intensified. One character alone is exempt from such inhibitions. The Henog comes from another part of the island where the old gods had a happier aspect. He is gathering material for a book about the struggle between Pryderi and Gwydion. No one else would have chosen this forbidden subject. The Henog plods forward, in his competent, pedantic, and occasionally inspired manner. He surrounds his stories with a kind of abstract space. As Porius reflects much later, "in the eternally empty space round him he sees the perfection he aimed at and gives himself the credit for having attained it; and maybe, in some cosmic ideal sense he *has* attained it" (543). Porius sometimes envies the Henog his detachment. Porius's relation to the Vale of Edeyrnion—his imagined and desired connection with aboriginals—will not allow him this freedom. In Porius's mind there is no "cosmic idea"; there are solely the oppressive circumstances of the place and its intricate history.

Porius desires to break the tynged; his doing so seems plausible to him, mainly in those moments when he has almost but not quite lapsed into sleep (in other words, when he is nearest to the state that the giants embody for him). That a waking, acting Porius should meet giants is another matter. It is not even clear to Myrddin Wyllt, thinking on his own remembrance of an "enormous earth-mother," that such encounters can occur outside the world of narrative so neatly arranged by the Henog (282, 284). Once or twice Powys hints that "the treacherous shimmer of fabulous invention" threatens accomplished chroniclers like the Henog with all their presumed "devotion to truth" (574). In this case, truth is a largely aesthetic fabrication; it is what can be made to seem probable or better yet inevitable by the appropriate disposition of narrative materials.[14] Once something *has* happened a particular way, then it *must* have happened that way: so the storyteller would have us believe. Could one tell a story another way, presenting it as a break with the probable or the inevitable? This method is suggested by one of Powys's favorite phrases, associated in *Porius* with the teachings of the heretic Pelagius. Porius tells himself stories, meaning that he envisions his liberation from present circumstances "not by a deep effort of will, or by a frantic confession of human frailty but in what Brother John insisted was the true Pelagian method; by letting his soul imagine his rescue by his friend, the south-wind, the wind that came from Cader Idris!" (140; cf. 63). The south-wind has sought out "the deepest hiding-

places of the giant-children of the Cader." Telling oneself stories
is not a scrupulous but a gigantic or extravagant act. It is a way
of bringing into one's life that unknown quantity that lurks in caves
and gives us an ultimate cavoseniargizing.

Powys tries to prepare for something that is going to happen in
his own novel; in a sense, happen to him as well as to his characters.
He will break the laws of probability within whose bounds he has
barely stayed thus far. Preparation for this moment is elaborate,
a summoning of images, ideas, and situations that might seem disparate. Porius has just had sex with his new wife Morfydd; he was
unable to keep his mind on what he was doing. Waking from sleep
he hears rumors of the Cewri's arrival. He determines to come upon
them at Craig Hen, a "spot of holy terror" associated with "the
wicked enchanter Gwydion, who killed Pryderi" (508). At the same
spot, moreover, Medrawd (Modred) has been hiding while trying
to win the support of the local peoples who *called themselves Cymry*
(514). The Cymry are drawn from those "ordinary inhabitants" who
are neither Roman nor allied with Romans, "us who have been in
the country from the beginning and yet now have to serve others"
(380). Medrawd wants to be recognized by them as successor to
Arthur, something that would appeal to pre-Christian tradition, because matriarchal descent is through the females and Medrawd is
Arthur's nephew. As these details accumulate, we may suspect that
the crucial connecting theme is autochthony: who was here first?
how does native tradition shape or not shape successive layers of
history? how do sexual, metaphysical, and political experience relate
to the aboriginal presence in Edeyrnion? One last allusion—one last
frame of reference—confirms the pertinence of such questions. Porius
realizes that the giants are near when he smells them. "It reminded
him for instance of the smell of the tadpoles—especially when they
were dying or dead—which he had carried as a child to certain
wayside puddles at the foot of the Gaer" (507). Porius or Powys
is once again about to meddle with autochthonous aboriginals.

A few moments later, the Cewri can be seen through the mist.
The father—the Gawr—carries the half-devoured body of the young
warrior whom Porius had snatched off his horse a few days before.
Porius focuses on the daughter who follows. Merely a glance between
them does what he had long hoped for from his second Creiddylad:
"so increased the division between his mind and his body that his
mind had suddenly felt powerful enough to put an end once and
for all to the disconcerting *equality* between these two antagonists;
powerful enough to assert itself once for all as the dominant partner. . . . . His mind felt as if it had become a new creature . . .

taking hold of its lumbering brother-in-arms to use that simple companion for purposes that must seem to it both fantastic and obscure" (512). After experiencing this stepped-up version of cavoseniargizing, Porius wants more. He loses the giants momentarily while he investigates a sobbing in the mist; it proves to be his father's servant Afaggdu, lamenting his role in Modred's scheming with the Cymry. Then the young giantess appears before him, "loosening her belt of plaited reeds in the immemorial gesture of feminine complicity and consent" (517). Their coupling demands Herculean energy from Porius, but it is "accomplished at last . . . and over Porius's sense there floated that same ineffable Cewri-scent." The giantess intones a "mystical saying": "cariad-digon," love is enough (519).

If the chapter ended here, Porius would be represented as having accomplished a return to autochthonous origins, a leap of imagination in which mind really does take over, the lie of the land becoming the lie of fantastic narrative becoming the lie of peace. We would have a revised version of Mr. Evan's Grail Quest in which the autochthons, instead of forbidding rest, make its accomplishment possible. "Sweet-sickly religious lies" would have been replaced by the lie of gigantic narrative. This kind of revision, however, does not prove so easy; Porius's postcoital reveries are soon interrupted. The father of the giantess tracks down the couple. He uproots a tree and begins swinging it at Porius, who is saved when his Creiddylad interposes herself between the combatants. "One of the most hammer-like bulgings of that knotted root struck her on the side of the head. . . . Broken bits of her skull, to which were adhering blood-soaked strands of yellow hair, hung down against her shoulder" (521). Catching up his daughter's body, the Gawr throws a horrible curse at Porius, then retreats along his original path with his opponent in pursuit. Porius wants to reclaim Creiddylad's corpse, but before he can make an effort the giant leaps into a deep tarn. A minute or two later, the bodies come to the surface. "At first he tried to separate and distinguish the two pairs of up-gazing eyes; but he soon reached the conclusion that all he could really see were no eyes at all, only a mixture of yellow hair and grey hair swaying like a submerged tangle of weeds amid clots of blood" (523).

I don't know if interpreting this scene is possible or desirable. There are many things to say: once they are said, we may feel like starting over again. A perhaps esoteric detail will illuminate Porius's meeting with the Cewri. Sir John Rhys's *Studies in the Arthurian Legend*—Powys's favorite book on Arthurian matters—reminds us several times that Creiddylad and Cordelia are versions of the same name.[15] This odd parallel can lead us on to trace the marked structural

similarities between "The Iron Bar" in *A Glastonbury Romance* and
"The Cewri" in *Porius*. A maternal woman, Cordelia/Creiddylad,
undresses for a man. The man is obsessed with autochthonous aboriginals ambiguously destructive and creative. His mating with her somehow releases him from the obsession, but there is a nightmarish
sequel, when an iron bar or a tree trunk wielded by one of those
same aboriginals misses its intended mark and smashes someone
else's head. The killer falls to his death from a great height. The
obsessed man is mentally shattered by the blow, but his memory
will remain with him.

In *A Glastonbury Romance*, it takes seven characters to act out
this story; in *Porius* it takes three. Compression is accompanied by
a change of emphasis. Mr. Evans will never attain "Esplumeoir."
Porius can do something with the memory in his head besides suffer
under it. As he leaves Craig Hen, he discovers (much as Evans
did during his crucifixion) that his pain has become a person to
whom he can speak. His reaction is that he amuses himself by playing
with the pain and eventually applying it like medicine to the wound
inside his mind. The image of the dead giants is further accepted
after Porius is back in the cell of his dying hermit teacher. The
Henog is there, telling one of his perfectly arranged tales. When
the wife of a visiting doctor goes into labor, "it soon became clear
that if the Henog could turn the Brother's cell into a negligible
portion of a vast dome of empty space in which the story of Gwawl
wrote itself upon the air, Nesta ferch Aulus [the midwife] could
turn it into a traditional lady's bower of Ynys Prydein, devoted
to the natural functions of birth, of life, of sleep, of death" (546).
Porius witnesses the birth of a child, "nor was it long before he
was looking, as he had looked once before, that day, through a
mist of water and wet hair and torn flesh, at a human head smeared
with blood; only it was one head now and not two." The infant's
name is Magog and his older brother's Gog, which makes the identification with the Cewri a pointed one. Gog and Magog are the Apocalyptic giants who were supposed to be led by Satan in a war against
God. They entered into British lore via Geoffrey of Monmouth;
according to Geoffrey they were taken prisoner by the founders of
London and chained to the city's gates where they acted as porters.
Porius has lost the old nature giants; he gains in their stead tamed
Gog and Magog. This miniaturization of the confrontation with elemental powers suggests a transformation of his recent experience.
He pauses in a world in which not only stories but elemental facts
of birth and death gain meaning from a humanly maintained context.

The baby's voice is lifted up "like the shriek, Porius thought, of a filmy-winged bat from the fathomless darkness outside, caught in the confines of a human cave" (547). Nature is assimilated by culture, *cave* by cavoseniargizing and then by the civilized cave—the "bower"—of shelter and comfort. Love is not enough, nor is the peace that Porius felt with that ultimate mother-figure Creiddylad. There is nothing like sleeping with mother to foster the impression that self-creation, parthogenesis, is attainable; however, even autochthons do not spring literally from the earth (unless they are the clay statuettes of the Glastonbury factory), and even giants submit to the constraints of generation and generations. The rupture in time and space when Porius meets the Cewri was exhilarating. Now he must learn how to sustain it in a composed dimension, as though some of the tall tale's raw freedom could be brought back to the familiar domestic world and even while being changed by it used to change it.

The absorption of the giants into the novel's world is not worked out exclusively through Porius's mind; there is a political side in which the Cewri are replaced by the Cymri; the "true possessors of these woods" by people who came after but who claim in their own right to be autochthonous aboriginals. We might borrow a term from the preface to *A Glastonbury Romance* (written soon after *Porius* was published): whereas the Cewri are natural autochthons, the Cymri are "autochthonized," transformed into indigenes by long residence and then by a rebellion against the elites who have dominated Edeyrnion since the giants disappeared (xii). Understood thus, autochthonization is a theme throughout *Porius* but especially toward the end. I would cite the paragraph-long sentence that ends chapter 21, "The Aboriginals": the sentence begins with Myrddin Wyllt crying *"Cymry"* and ends with the echoes of that word following the Cewri "whence and whither these monstrous shapes of the true aboriginals of Ynys Prydein had, as so many now believed, actually come and gone" (490). The juxtaposition between Cewri and Cymry is a pointed one, and not just phonetically. A few years before he published *Porius*, Powys had contrasted those "typical Celts" of Ireland who "succeeded in killing off, along with their snakes, all their aboriginals" with the Welsh who survived *as* aboriginals by a kind of cultural introversion or incest.[16] *Porius* works toward a similar but more sophisticated reading of aboriginal autochthony. No culture is entirely innocent, however peace-loving. Every aboriginal claim replaces a prior aboriginal claim: one might even extend such generations to the Cewri, who superseded a race of terrifying dragons.[17]

Powys's political fable works closely with his psychological one. Incest is an attempt to get back to origins, to become a child in the mother's embrace even while asserting a sexual claim over her and (by implication) a claim of power over the land. Efforts of this kind are useful only if their limits are understood. Powys tries to suggest the appropriate limits by establishing a new perspective on fights about possession and priority, about who was here first. He insists that the *genius loci* is a problematic creation. The closer we get to it, the more we try to encounter it as a reality, the more its contradictions must be confronted. Along with Creiddylad comes the Gawr, along with the rest-inducing earth-mother the jealous father. Then we find ourselves involved in the moral dilemmas of cruelty—not so much sadism, the desire to inflict pain that burdened young Johnny Powys when he lifted the minnows out of their pond or Owen Evans when he thought of the iron bar, as a sort of unintended and blundering destruction. It is closer to when Powys senior hewed and hacked at the trees, as when the Gawr accidentally killed his daughter, as when one claimant succeeds another in familial or political conflicts.

For Porius, this unintended infliction of pain is the crucial issue. He didn't mean to cause the death of the giants or the extinction of their race, but he feels responsible for doing so. The novelist approves his hesitations: lying at rest needs the counterforce of remembrance. In a section of the novel that Powys cut under duress, "yet another Cewri utterance . . . the last he was ever destined to learn" approves his decision to serve Arthur in the wide world—i.e., to leave the Vale with which he has been obsessed. If the original chapters 27 and 28 were restored, the reader of *Porius* could trace more completely how the memory of the giants, the resting place of Porius Manlius (to which the action returns), and Porius's ability to distance himself from Edeyrnion are interconnected.[18] Even as the novel stands, we understand this. The lie of extravagant narrative has transformed Porius's relation to the lie of the land. Having experienced the spirit of the place in its crudest and most terrifying form— having told himself the most law-breaking story he can imagine—he returns to the realms of law and culture, but returns a different person than before. It is worth recalling John Crow's somewhat muddled departure from Glastonbury, in which the question of whether one should stay in the magic spot or leave it is equally important but confronted less satisfactorily. If *Porius* repeats plot elements from *A Glastonbury Romance*, it repeats them with a difference of substance. Departure from Edeyrnion, unlike departure from Glastonbury, is represented as an advance in a hero's sophistication, in his ability to think about the world and act within it, rather than as an imaginative defeat for him. Having grasped the nature of the Vale, Porius is released to other places.

3. Blundered Incantations

There remains some doubt about the kind of novelist Powys was; about the terms, that is, on which we are to value him. Vernon Young is half-right when he suggests that "Powys retreated throughout our mid-century" because Powys certainly wanted to retreat—only his great novels kept turning him toward unsettling confrontations. Similarly, John Bayley's more positive remarks contain an important truth about the novelist. At times he is the intimate, domestic writer that Bayley wants him to be, except that the domestic idyll contains within it an epic that always gets loose at some point. Glastonbury or Edeyrnion—these little, out-of-the-way retreats—prove to be where history is occurring. (Porius doesn't have to leave Edeyrnion to feel that he is at the center of an historical struggle; he has to abandon an *idea* of Edeyrnion.) The conflicts within the *genius loci* prove to be the conflicts of time; the serpent twists upon itself right here, thrashing until we cannot ignore it any longer, until narrative is less an adumbration of place than an exposure of the falsehoods whispered by the *genius loci*.

Perhaps the confusing point about Powys is that he uses myths as a way to think about human predicaments within history. The great modernists, writers like Eliot, Pound, and Yeats, exploited mythology so brilliantly that mythical thinking became a major category—perhaps the major category—for reading literature. Ready or not, everybody sailed to Byzantium. (I hope the reader will take this flippant remark as an excusable piece of shorthand.) The result was that we ended up with increasingly ahistorical modes of criticism—Northrop Frye in the fifties and Claude Levi-Strauss in the sixties and early seventies are only the two most recent examples. In Frye or Levi-Strauss's schema, mythical thought and historical thought are at odds. To read Powys, we would need a criticism sensitive to myth but capable of situating myths in relation to the movements of time, the strains of history. Sometimes I think that the best comment on Mr. Evans's "seduction" by Cordelia or Porius's meeting with Creiddylad might be Levi-Strauss's famous analysis of the Oedipus story, in which autochthony plays so crucial a role;

but in an important way, Powys has outdistanced Levi-Strauss, for he includes in his tale the politics of autochthony, and this Levi-Strauss cannot bring himself to do.

Today it requires no particular courage to suggest that criticism needs its historical dimension. This position is almost too fashionable for its own good. On the other hand, defining Powys's fluctuating love-hate affair with the larger movements of history will continue to require a good deal of tact. One last example may help toward a summation. Porius's final accomplishment within the Vale is to rescue Myrddin Wyllt, or Cronos (god of time), from what seems to be eternal imprisonment. Considered as a piece of storytelling, this is not quite a denial of myth in favor of history; after all it is the myth that is rescued, whose reality is affirmed. But neither is the myth allowed to float (or sleep) in the eternal space favored by storytellers like the Henog. A myth of time has to exist within time. The balance between myth and history created by this narrative turn is extraordinary—unless we are reading John Cowper Powys and then it can be understood as typical. No one else but Powys does just this sort of thing, or thinks just this way. The quality of mind, of invention, and of imagination in *Porius, A Glastonbury Romance,* and Powys's other great books is something his readers cannot afford to gloss over, either by declaring him a crackpot or by making him out as more like other writers than he is. After the modernist debauch, Powys weighs myth and history on the same scale and chooses to judge the former by the latter. Could it be that the moment for reevaluating this novelist, and indeed for learning from him, has arrived?

Notes

1. John Bayley, *New York Review of Books* (28 March 1985); Vernon Young, "The Immense Inane," *The American Scholar* (Spring 1986): 255—both pieces occasioned by the Harper and Row reprinting (1985) of *Wolf Solent* and *Weymouth Sands.*

2. John Cowper Powys, *Ducdame* (New York: Doubleday, Page & Co., 1925), pp. 301, 391.

3. John Cowper Powys, "*Glastonbury:* Author's Review," originally printed in *The Modern Thinker* (March 1932); reprinted in *The Powys Review* no. 9 (1981–82): 7–9.

4. John Cowper Powys, *A Glastonbury Romance* (London: MacDonald, 1966), pp. 118–19. Subsequent references are cited parenthetically by page number.

5. John Cowper Powys, *Autobiography* (New York: Simon and Schuster, 1934), p. 3. R. P. Graves comments on this incident in *The Brothers Powys* (Oxford:

Oxford University Press, 1983), p. 5; on Powys's relationship with his father, also see David Cook, "The Autobiography of John Cowper Powys: A Portrait of the Artist as Other," *Modern Philology* 72 (August 1974):30–44.

6. On the shaping role of wordplay in *A Glastonbury Romance*, cf. Ned Lukacher, "'Between Philology and Psychology': Cronos, Dostoievsky and the Language of Myth in John Cowper Powys's *A Glastonbury Romance*," *The Powys Review* no. 9 (1981–82):18–25. Also pertinent is *The Language of Allegory: Defining the Genre* (Ithaca: Cornell University Press, 1979), in which Maureen Quilligan discusses "the generation of narrative structure out of wordplay" (22).

7. Powys, *Autobiography*, p. 24.

8. Cf. John Rhys, *Studies in the Arthurian Legend* (Oxford: Clarendon Press, 1891), p. 259: "For the name of that realm is *yr Echwyd*, the evening and the dusk, the twilight which is essential to the illusion and glamour on which this whole cosmos of unreality is founded."

9. For Powys's sympathy toward this idea, see his *The Art of Forgetting the Unpleasant* (London: Village Press, 1974).

10. Powys, "Glastonbury," p. 8.

11. Some of the major passages ignored or barely touched on in this essay include 924 on Sam Dekker's encounter with workers at the factory, and 997–1000 on Paul Trent's encounter with Morgan Nelly.

12. John Cowper Powys, *Porius: A Romance of the Dark Ages* (London: MacDonald, 1951), pp. 1, 2. Subsequent references are cited parenthetically by page number.

13. Susan Stewart, *On Longing: Narratives of the Miniature, the Gigantic, the Souvenir, the Collection* (Baltimore: Johns Hopkins University Press, 1984), p. 73. Cf. Powys's perface to *Lucifer*, written about 1956 (*Lucifer* [London: Village Press, 1974], pp. 14–15), on the "pre-natal terror" of "remote" "gigantic" forms of the past, "whose huge chaotic struggles with one another" constitute a "weird, grotesque, monstrous, miraculous story."

14. The Henog's present confusion about what is happening contrasted with what has happened is established early in the novel: see especially p. 85. His use of artifice is emphasized throughout: the omission of chapter 31, "The Little One," is regrettable on this account, for it contains the comedy of the Henog's intrigues against another storyteller, Cretinloy, intrigues that involve scheming fabrication used as a political tool. See Joseph Slater's summary of the incident in *The Powys Newsletter, Porius Issue* 4 (1974–1975):41.

15. *Studies*, p. 36: "Creidylad or Cordelia, daughter of ILud of the Silver Hand;" (322): "The daughter's name does not appear . . . though in other hands it has yielded the well-known name of Cordelia."

16. John Cowper Powys, *Obstinate Cymric* (London: Village Press, reprint ed., 1973; originally published 1947), p. 12.

17. When the Gawr dives into the tarn, he lands in an "earthquake-sculptured Avanc," the jaws of a stone dragon (523); Porius on several occasions thinks of himself as an avanc.

18. For a summary of the missing chapters, see *The Powys Newsletter, Porius Issue*, pp. 37–39.

Porius and the Cauldron of Rebirth

Michael Ballin

The image of the cauldron expresses Powys's most mature perception of the nature of that process of perpetual change that we call history. The dynamic alternation of the forces of creation and destruction, in Powys's view, is the essence of the historical process that provides a continuous pattern in history. This pattern enabled Powys to perceive a continuous unifying link between the twentieth century and the distant past. Moreover, this motivic pattern of death and rebirth unifies narrative action and character relationships in *Porius*. Justice needs to be done to the unified vision of this novel that has been sometimes unjustly criticized for its sprawling length. A consideration of the full text, rather than the abridged published version, in the light of the motivic pattern, reveals the fundamental coherence of Powys's conception.

Powys had been concerned with the philosophy of historical change since *A Glastonbury Romance*, but he explores this philosophy much more comprehensively in the historical novels of his maturity. *Porius*, the most mysterious of his historical novels, looks back to that first *magnum opus;* in fact, the relationship between the two novels is clarified by Powys's comments in his preface to *A Glastonbury Romance*, written in 1953 after the publication of *Porius*. It is significant that Powys alludes to the motif of the cauldron, first in its Christianized form of the Grail, and then in the "de-sublimated" pagan version of the grail, the cauldron of rebirth.

After proclaiming that the heroine of *A Glastonbury Romance* is the Grail ("Its hero is the life poured into the Grail"), he refers to the pre-Christian faith of Glastonbury as founded on the cult of the earth goddess who "had her cauldron of the food of life safely guarded in our island of the West, where Kronos still waits under forest heaped upon forest and mountain piled upon mountain his final release from the tyranny of Zeus, and where that other cauldron, the cauldron of rebirth, alternates between salvation and destruction as the fatal zodiacal cycle revolves on the pivot of the everlasting mystery."[1]

The Grail quest was used as an important thematic and psychologi-

cal motif in *A Glastonbury Romance* at a time when Powys was interested in twentieth-century anthropological interpretations of the Grail
such as those of Jessie L. Weston or T. S. Eliot in "The Wasteland."[2]
A mystical interpretation of Christian motifs such as resurrection
or crucifixion was still of interest to him. But in *Porius* we note
that the pre-Christian tradition of the two cauldrons of death and
rebirth have replaced the Grail; the allusions in *Porius* to the Fisher
King have the orgiastic significance of fertility myth and fertility
rites that promote rebirth and renewal through physical passions
and instincts. Powys's allusion to the pagan figure of Kronos is
also significantly linked to the cauldron of the food of life, because
Powys similarly links Myrddin Wyllt in *Porius* to the cauldron rebirth
process and the mysteries of time. Thus "Cronos" is the title of
the last chapter of *Porius*, and Myrddin is presented as the Celtic
equivalent to the Greek deity of time, buried beneath the summit
of Y Wyddfa to await a rebirth into a nontyrannical and benevolent
age.

The cauldron image is derived from *The Mabinogion* and embodied
the highest wisdom of the aboriginal Welsh tradition in Powys's
eyes. The main features of the cauldron legends are usefully brought
together by Sir John Rhys, who was a staple source for Powys's
knowledge of Celtic traditions. Rhys comments on the presentation
of the cauldron in *The Mabinogion*—especially in the stories of Bran-
wen and Culwch and Olwen—and in the Taliessin poems.[3] In the
story of Culwch and Olwen, Arthur makes a journey to Hades to
bring away the cauldron. This association links the cauldron with
death (i.e. the journey or descent *to* Hades) and rebirth (the ascent
from Hades). The stories of Bran utilize the cauldron as a rebirth
agent in war, because the cauldron can revive the corpses of soldiers.

Powys thus defines the historical process as a movement between
the poles of life and death impulses, both of which have to be accepted
as part of reality. Powys's essay "Pair Dadeni" in *Obstinate Cymric*
is an important source for understanding the significance of the cauldron image. As well as exploring the cauldron as an image of death
and rebirth, Powys also relates the international destruction that
accompanied the second world war to a similar impulse of mankind
toward death in the Dark Ages. Moreover, Powys identifies all of
Celtic mythology, epitomized in *The Mabinogion* with the expression
of "all manner of *magical mixings up*—I can use no other expression
—of life and death and death with life; so that on all sides we
grow aware of half-alive things and of half-dead things, of life vanishing as the death mists rise or fall, of birth appearing even from
the lap of death."[4]

These essays, written between 1935 and 1947, are deeply influenced by the background of the second world war, and they closely precede the writing of *Porius*. Powys describes the war as the most evil period in mankind's history since the Dark Ages. In this way he establishes a unifying link between the period of *Porius* and contemporary experience and is able to use Celtic myth both to distance contemporary horrors and to place them in the context of the previous experiences of mankind. Racism and authoritarian fanatacism are common to the Dark Ages and to the twentieth century. Powys also proclaims that the political tyranny of the present is unique in history—but with the exception of the period of the battle of Badon in the Dark Ages. In accord with his interest in linking past and present, Powys creates a superficial narrative action for *Porius* from the threat of a Germanic invasion of Britain and the imminent destruction of its Romano-British culture, which preserves the remnants of a previous aboriginal wisdom.

In this way Powys forges an original link between the past and present in *Porius* and deepens the reader's consciousness of the nature of the historical process. His concern with this process is still the same as it was at the time of writing *A Glastonbury Romance*. In that novel he used the legends of Glastonbury and the Grail—which reach back into dimmest recesses of time—to explore the transition between the organic world of the "Magian" John Geard and the technological, "Faustian" modern world of Philip Crow. This transitional feature of our modern experience is again part of a rhythm of history that alternates between salvation and destruction. Moreover, Geard is a prototype of the Myrddin Wyllt of *Porius* in the respect that, like Myrddin, he commits voluntary suicide, an act seen as a way of embracing death in the name of life that is carried out, significantly, in a spot marked as a fertility temple by the lake villagers.

In *Porius*, however, the perspective is reversed; the present is perceived through the spectacles of the past, as the reader is plunged into a specific portion of the Dark Ages past right at the outset of a crucial transitional period for the history of Britain and medieval Europe. Powys makes clear, however, that the past is nevertheless linked to the present as he argues that the sixth century and the twentieth share the same versions of the experience of creation and destruction. This link enables Powys to present a quasi-Hegelian perspective of history. Hegel emphasizes the idea of cultural change as a process of birth from death: in the *Philosophy of History* he says, "while change imparts dissolution, it involves at the same time the rise of a *new life*. That while death is the issue of life, life is also the issue of death."[5] Powys's motif of the cauldron of rebirth objectifies and humanizes a somewhat abstract historical vision that Powys usually rejected.

The function of the myth of the cauldron, therefore, is to place the historic process within the envelope of an eternal process through which mankind fulfills his destiny. Spengler's *The Decline of the West* had helped Powys to form his historical philosophy; and so he can be seen to share with Spengler an interest in the idea of analogous cultures and the parallels between past and present. These parallels reinforce his dynamic perception of history in which the past is implicit in the future and the future in the past.

When writing *Owen Glendower*, Powys had tried in his book *Mortal Strife* (1942) to help his British public assimilate the crisis of a possible Germanic invasion. As a consolation to readers who were finding ways to endure the harsh realities of the war, Powys suggested that a new human condition of wholeness and unity, different from the typically modern Faustian individualism, was soon to be realised. He quotes Berdyaev's assertion that the world is moving towards a new Middle Ages. For Powys, therefore, the twentieth-century rebirth process is a movement into the culture that the civilization of *Porius* is leaving. In alluding also to the wisdom of Heraclitus that "all flows away," Powys asserts that "we must include death as well as life in our inmost being" (78).[6] Powys expounds on the motif of rebirth, death and birth again, from all perspectives in this book: the earth itself "heaves, yawns, fumes and shudders, bringing forth death but bringing forth also Death's twin, the unknown body of never-before-seen life" (8).

The darkness of the world war is thus assimilated positively, although Powys simultaneously describes Hitler as a black magician who had hypnotized his innocent German followers "into a horrible Renaissance of the Dark Ages." This Satanic rebirth helps Powys to distance current horrors by presenting their medieval equivalent. Powys's description of the rebirth in the twentieth century of "superstitious, sanctimonious and fantastical awe" that is "the most dangerous aspect of mysticism" (203) applies closely to the Christian church in *Porius* under the aegis of the priest, Minnawc Gorsant. Thus *Porius* expresses Powys's central philosophy of history–that it is a continuous process of transition from the death of the old to the rebirth of the new. Although Powys uses the Dark Ages to reflect the British experience of potential invasion and racial conflict, he also strives to present a vision of history as an eternal process in which the seeds of the present are seen to be unfolding within the past. To find a form that can capture such a bird's-eye view of the past in the context of the present afforded a challenge to Powys to create anew the form of the historical novel itself.

Throughout his life, Powys nurtured a consistent passion for the antiquarian for its own sake. His feeling for the past, incarnated in its ruins and physical remnants, is apparent in most of his fiction. He was also an avid reader of historical novels and mentions Ainsworth, Scott, and Thackeray's *Henry Esmond* in his letters. He even claims in one letter to Boyne Grainger that he gained inspiration in his writing of *Porius* from an article in *The New Yorker* on the recreation of a special brand of antique furniture.[7] Powys's recreation of the Dark Ages is achieved in the same fashion as the craftsman's recreation of artifacts of the past. The process of *recreation* is different from that of *imitation* of an existing original. There is room in the process of creation for a creative adaptation of the past in the light of the present.

What Powys valued in both the American antique chair and the created world of *Porius* was what he termed an "artless innocence." The distant Dark Age period embodied values that we now have forgotten about or repressed—values resident in an aboriginal culture existing in a precivilized state. Powys had employed in *A Glastonbury Romance* what Eliot had found to praise in Joyce's *Ulysses:* a continuous parallelism between contemporaneity and antiquity. But now the Past is to be presented in its own right, drawing upon what has gone before and fulfilling its Destiny in terms of the present which is to be. History is therefore not confined to the telling of facts and the determination of chronology; in fact, Powys's novel contains mostly nonfactual material along with much of the fabulous and fantastic, such as giants and magicians and, in one momentous event, an owl transformed into a maiden. But the idea of history is never forgotten. The figure of the magician-prophet Myrddin Wyllt is counterbalanced by the Henog, who is himself a chronicler of history. (Such antiquarian figures are present in Powys's novels from Urquhart in *Wolf Solent* to Owen Evans in *A Glastonbury Romance* and Dud and Uryen in *Maiden Castle*.) Thus the perspectives of the prophet of the future and the chronicler of the past and present reinforce one another. Romance, imagination, and myth are therefore all the expression of history and, conversely, history can be reexpressed as myth. The fabulous and the historical are aspects of one another. Consequently, the endless bubbling of the cauldron of rebirth is a fitting symbol for the myriad possibilities for evolution from the seeds of the Past; for history is nondeterministic and ever ready to renew itself.

Powys's analysis of the nature of civilization allows him also to assert the values of Life and Freedom while admitting the realities of death and destruction. Powys defines civilization as the marriage of rational culture and aboriginal nature—the latter is the source for the former. Powys took from H. J. Massingham's *Downland Man* the notion that civilization had begun in Britain as a peaceable agricultural order that had migrated to Britain from the shores of the Mediterranean. These peaceable peoples had built the great monuments at Stonehenge and Avebury. Massingham believed that these ancient inhabitants from Iberia were the protagonists in a story which has "direct and living contact with the civilised life of today."[8] Massingham emphasized that *history* is "a much more complicated affair than the onward and upward ideas of evolutionists give credit for." The barrows of ancient Britain contain no weapons; Massingham argued, therefore, that war was not natural to primitive society but was a "by-product of the first civilisations of the world in their later phases." In answer to the notion that War is the parent of civilization, Massingham asserted that "war was never the agent of civilisation but of barbarism; it was civilisation which was the agent of war" (305). But Powys used Massingham's perspective positively. Civilization may drift towards decay but in doing so it encounters the life-giving forces of its primitive origins.

Powys does not only use the motivic pattern of death and renewal to explore a philosophical view of cultural change; he also applies the pattern as a unifying device at all levels of narrative including ritual action, character development, and dramatic presentation of psychological experience. Brochvael and Morfydd are examples of characterization that expresses the pattern of renewal and rebirth in terms of psychological experience. They are two centrally important characters because they try in the most heroic way to create a cultural rebirth from the death of the old. Brochvael is also distinctive because, as a representative of an older, classical civilization, he both perceives the specific dangers to freedom in classical restraints and preserves a link with the aboriginal culture. The contrast, but also the living links, between cultural and aboriginal aspects of the self are presented through Porius and Morfydd. The structural and thematic unity of the novel is obscured, however, if we read it mainly as being personal biography of its protagonist. Powys's unifying conception is conveyed through the presentation of the cultural and personal context of Porius's inner realization of freedom. His character is essentially bound up with those of all the other major characters of the novel, but Morfydd and Brochvael, more than any others, are characters who are essential in order to complete the historical and visionary pattern that *Porius* presents.

Morfydd, for example, is one of the strongest characters of the novel. Her strength takes many forms, bearing testimony to the potential for woman to be free and responsible in a very modern way. But character also has a cultural significance. For example, her decision to subdue her racial differences and, as a part Gwyddy-laid girl, to join with the Romanized Brython in a pact that is meant to serve Porius's interests, is presented as "a daring and dramatic course of action" that gives Morfydd a feeling of "a tremendous crisis" (193).[9]

In chapter II of the published text, a chapter which bears her name as its title, Morfydd determines to meet with Princess Euronwy and join forces with her, despite her customary opposition to her, to support Porius. To guarantee that Princess Euronwy keeps her word, Morfydd's idea is to cement the bond between their two contrary souls with a pact made on the things each holds most sacred—a vow, in this case, upon the altar of Christ and the relics of Rhitta Gawr, the legendary aboriginal leader. The solemn contract symbolizes a momentous marriage of Romanized Christian and aboriginal values, a conjunction of civilization and culture that marks a crucial stage in the development of civilization.

The typescript of *Porius*, which contains sizeable portions omitted from the published version of the novel and some passages not found in the holograph text, gives to the Derwydd these comments, addressed to Brochvael:[10]

> We certainly live, Derwyddon, Tywysogion and Guerin-druids, princes and people . . . in the most exciting times the world has ever seen. What world shaking events, what settings and risings of Zodiacal aeons, what sinking into irretrievable downfalls, what mounting into unbelievable restitutions. (464)

Morfydd's initiative in bringing about the coalescence of aboriginal and civilized values through her acceptance of the marriage with Porius provides a cultural rebirth from this crisis, and that she would be the occasion of it corrects the subservient and passive role of woman in the old order. ("'He' - 'them' - that's the way it always is! 'They' go and we wait and wonder" (203) Euronwy complains.)

Morfydd's proposed marriage to Porius is one mode of action that establishes rebirth and continuity in civilization, whereas Brochvael's acceptance of a dangerous quest is prefaced by Prince Einion's lament for the end of Rome:

The age of our Brythonic glory is over . . . Why shouldn't it be? Isn't the glory of Rome over? . . . Sidonius may pretend his bishops of Rome are carrying on the Roman Empire. I tell you whatever they're doing . . . They're not doing that. *Rome's done for.* (367; italics mine)

Brochvael journeys to the sacred fountain to keep Porius there because Einion has precipitated an attack by the forest people. The journey is the occasion for Brochvael's serious engagement with destiny in which he furthers the union of culture and civilization and establishes the dependence of the House of Cunedda on the primeval.

In the course of his quest he encounters the Gwyddl girl, Sibylla, who appears at the end of the Morfydd chapter in the typescript. As mistress of Einion and teller of the tales of Iscovan, the hero of the forest people, Sibylla links Gwyddl, Cuneddan, and Derwydd racial strains.

Brochvael befriends Sibylla because she has been cast off by Prince Einion. She offers Brochvael a temptation to turn from his path of duty and penetrate the Derwydd lair. This penetration of the most secret nerve center of civilization by the overcivilized Brochvael is a crucial stage in the rebirth of civilization through contact with culture. On his way to the Derwydd lair, Brochvael brings to the surface his buried aboriginal and Gwyddl sympathies. When Sibylla spits on a twisted tree stump with a demonic shape, Brochvael perceives the necessity to resist a perception of the world that reflected the stark moral polarities of either Christianity or Mithraism. He thinks, "Why should I love or hate anything or anyone? I am myself; they are themselves; an unfathomable multitude of creatures in an unfathomable multitude of worlds!" (237). Nevertheless, he is conscious of the incongruity of his presence in the Y Bychan Mound when he witnesses a chess game between the Iberian Druid, his brother, and two servants, one an oversexed aggressor against Sibylla. Brochvael asks himself what a fellow student of Sidonius of Auvergne could make of such a situation which would challenge the imagination of an Ovid. Nevertheless the reality of aboriginal culture challenges in a real way the values of Rome; Brochvael recognizes that the weird scene may be the occasion of a "contest upon which the fate of the whole tribe of Cunedda . . . might ultimately depend" (243). In fact, the rebirth of civilization must be attained by achieving a delicate balance between the forces of culture and civilization.

Powys makes the Y Bychan Mound a central symbol of the meeting of antagonistic forces; in addition, the mound is the central location and symbolic focus of the chapter, not included in the published

text, "The Little One." This episode in chapter 14 of the published
text, "The Derwydd," prepares the way for the novel's occult conclusion that celebrates the renewal of cultural life. Brochvael may clutch
the image of the head of the emperor Hadrian in an effort to free
himself from the atmosphere of the aboriginal world, which to him
was the essence of "all he instinctively detested, of all that was
occult, obscure, and treacherous, of all that was obscene, unclean
and barbarous" (256). But, Brochvael is forced to join in a ritual
communion before he leaves, an act that represents a significant
stage in the process of cultural renewal.

The Derwydd dips his finger in the blood of his brother and
insists that Brochvael partake of it. Fighting his nausea, Brochvael
partakes of Llew's blood in an aboriginal rite that replaces the Christian communion with the magical ceremonies of the cauldron of
rebirth. The dual associations of the primitive rite parallel Morfydd's
conjunction of the rites of the Christian church and Rhitta Gawr.
A complex fusion of the aboriginal and the Roman, the Dionysian
and the Apollonian, prepares the way for the renewal of culture.

The reader experiences the unearthly rite undergone by Brochvael
as a prologue to the events of the central chapter of *Porius*, chapter
15, "Myrddin Wyllt." As the central prophetic figure, Myrddin brings
the novel to its climax and also embodies consistently the notion
of death and rebirth and the continuity of culture in time. The
Myrddin of Powys's imagination draws upon the traditional figure
of the Wild Man of the woods. This tradition may have suggested
to Powys Myrddin's distinctive ability to relapse back to the beginning of things and to tap knowledge associated with the goddesses
of the primeval cauldron. For example, when Porius first encounters
Myrddin and holds the entranced and collapsed magician in his arms,
he has a significant vision connected with the motifs of the cauldron.
Porius "[grows] aware of vast continents and countries and cities.
He was conscious of the unrolling of world-shaking events; of famines
and plagues, of battles and migrations, *of the births and deaths of
whole civilizations*" (58; italics mine). This vision of world history
is Spenglerian in scope and compounded of the ingredients of the
mystic cauldrons of destruction and creation. In chapter 15, Myrddin
encounters the mystery of death without fear, because he has conquered the fear of death during a visionary encounter with the goddess
Styx in her cave. Myrddin's vision at this point is all inclusive because
it comprehends time, the return of oppressors in cyclic time, as
well as death and renewal beyond death. Myrddin's vision of death
is unique: he has a first vision of Styx, the river of Hades, "the
face of Styx herself, eldest daughter of backward-flowing Ocean,

leaning out from her cave and peering down at him over her clenched knuckles through that grey ghost of an ash-stump" (284). Myrddin perceives that there is only one true reality; ". . . there remained but one thing, one thing only, in the eyes that stared down into mine over the grey ruins of that phantom ash. And that one thing was death. 'From death,' those eyes said, 'all that exists has sprung; and to death all that exists will return. Death was the beginning. Death will be the end. It will be the end of gods and men'" (285).

If history is to bear testimony to the continuity of the life principle, it must incorporate death within it; Myrddin faces the end of governments, gods, men, and the cycles of time. But immediately after he has uttered the fourfold incantation, "Death, death, death, death," the face of the daughter of Styx stares back at him with a sense of inescapable doom. Myrddin is consoled by the animal touch of a water rat, to remind him of life. Thus the historical vision has to place death in the context of life.

Chapter 15 presents a second mythic prologue to the death and rebirth theme. The structural centrality of the chapter is established by the description of the early Saturday morning carefully denominated "Saturn's Day or the Day of Cronos," and by the two locations—the first at the cave of Mithras and the second at the tent of Gwendydd and Nineue. These locations refer the reader back to the opening of the novel, which presented the meeting of Porius and Rhun, and later Myrddin at the cave and their encounter with the Mithraic mysteries explored through images of the god of Time. In this chapter Myrddin asserts his relationship to Saturn, Cronos, and the Titans. The exploration of the Cronos myth and the brooding over Time anticipates Porius's philosophical explorations of the mystery of Time in the final chapter, "Cronos."

Powys exploits the association of twilight with the worship of Mithras, a twilight god who combines the dualistic properties of evil and good, dark and light, and he evokes magically the special properties of this time of day. Twilight approaches imperceptibly with "a tragic greyness, far more death-like than anything to be found in the comfortable embrace and kindly oblivion of darkness" (260). But the really distinctive quality of twilight is expressed as a "death cold, corpse like, alien entity" that has newly arrived on earth from "heaven knows where." Powys concludes, "There is indeed nothing on earth more supernatural than the first light of dawn." The reader is invited to the presence of the "tragic elemental mystery play of Creation"—the Cauldron of Death and Rebirth itself.

After this mythic prologue to the death and rebirth theme, Powys turns to a more human level. The title of chapter 16, "The Youngest

Princess," is a meaningful paradox, because even the youngest of "the three aunties" has reached the advanced age of seventy-three. The princesses represent a historic tradition that derives its values from a Rousseauistic Golden Age in Africa. The tradition, much older than Christianity, is "at once anarchical and peaceful" (308). These matriarchal rulers epitomize the aboriginal culture that is on the verge of extinction, because the new Faustian and classical age is ready to be born.

The aunties' resistance to Roman Cuneddan rule had inspired their "treachery": an alliance with Colgrim, the Saeson, to oust Roman and Arthurian rule. Erim, the silentiary of their household, wishes to revive the old kingdom of Venodotia as a forest people's kingdom and is willing, like Hitler, to cooperate with Prince Medrawd in the extermination of Gwyddl Ffichti and the eviction of Romanized Brythons. However, the dream of Venodotia as a land of racial purity is happily not fulfilled, because the death of aboriginal culture is to be the occasion for the birth of a national entity devoid of sinister associations: the Cymry. This political rebirth realizes ideals of fellowship, community, and a sharing of power, ideals that Powys regarded as typically Welsh values and essential ones if the rebirth process is to continue in the twentieth century.

The lives of all three aunties, but especially Tonwen, dramatize a psychological and passional aspect of the rebirth process. Throughout his narrative, Powys has been careful to link the growing political crisis with the celebration of the orgiastic rites of the feast of the sowing. This fertility ritual is the source of the mystical motif of the Grail quest and, in Powys's view, the Celtic cauldron of rebirth was transformed into the Grail through assimilation to the Christian tradition. The Fisher King ritual, for example, is used in the narrative of *Porius* as a symbolic catalyst that forces the characters to realize their passional selves. Thus, Morfydd's semi-incestuous love of Rhun, Porius's passionate union with the female "Gawres" of his dreams, Erddud's incestuous passion for Brochvael, Tonwen's love for Cadawg, and Einion's for Sibylla all come to sudden fruitions in contexts of crisis.

Tonwen's passional rebirth is among the most significant examples of the rebirth process. When Tonwen makes her way to the cave of Cadawg, the disinherited chieftain, she arrives to find him engaged in a cauldron rebirth ritual that involves washing his hands with meal and water and drying them with fire. The aim of the ritual is "to get even with death," which he attempts by means of extensive preparatory rituals that are related to the death and birth process in the individual and political worlds. Cadawg, the pure aboriginal, stands for peace although he fiercely resists the violence associated with the Modrybedd's opposition to Arthur. But Cadawg celebrates other than political values in his love for Tonwen. With Tonwen, he embraces the "wild free natural reality" beneath the "conventions, symbols, logic, ritual, reason, *words*" (399) of civilization. Tonwen reveals to the emperor that the Modrybedd and the Derwydd are ultimately in decline. The Derwydd is the last of his line and has betrayed Arthur for Colgrim out of desperation. He says, "We are at an end, Amherawdr, and the Derwydd is at an end. When ruins fall they drag down with them many fresh and living things" (354). In this part of his narrative, Powys dramatizes the close interweaving of life and death; a civilization is saved from destruction by an aboriginal culture that also is dying.

If in the three aunties we "meet with things dying," Nesta, daughter of an ex-centurian Aulus, and Gwythr her husband, a Gaer messenger, present us with the "hope of things new born." In the chapter "The Doctor," they consult with Lot-el-Aziz about their infertility problem, a consultation that takes place at the marriage bed of Porius and Morfydd. Thus, through character and setting, Powys explores his deep cultural theme of rebirth from death. The portentous birth of a separate nation from the mixture of subject peoples to be governed by Arthur and to be saved from the Saeson accompanies a potential human birth. Although the aboriginals criticize the marriage of Porius and Morfydd as a political act designed to perpetuate their subjugation and a false fellowship with the Saeson, the reader, applying the perspective of subsequent history, knows differently. The new nation, the Cymry, is to be born as a result of Saxon invasions that have forced an assortment of tribes to conglomerate behind the mountains of North Wales.

The reader, however, is also returned to a preoccupation with death when Lot-el-Aziz informs Porius of the condition of Brother John, the aged religious instructor of Porius, who is in the last stages of cancer and who deals with his pain by holding a dialogue with an imaginary Pelagius. This death is also associated with a political crisis, a fact that Powys emphasizes in his original preface to *Porius*. There he describes Brother John as the focus of "hidden struggles of a social and a political nature, seething and swirling all the time around this very aged heretical hermit." Brother John's political or social role had been one of philosophical peace maker between the Romanized Brythons and the rebellious Gwyddl-Ffichti. His deeply felt Pelagian values of faith in the goodness of human nature were realized in the truly Christ-like peaceable values of the aboriginal characters. This optimistic ideology counters the Christian fanatacism of Minnawc Gorsant, and thus the Pelagian values of Brother John look forward to later versions of humanism by Erasmus, Rabelais, or Rousseau. Brother John's belief system reinforces the forces of creative renewal in the political action of the novel and establishes a tradition that can be drawn upon by future ages as well as by the post-World War II reader—or the reader in any age dominated by philosophical pessimism, fanatacism, or broken faith in the potential of mankind.

Brother John's relationship to the motif of cultural rebirth is both complex and established on political, religious, and mythological levels. His conversation with the Henog of Dyfed, for example, explores the Celtic inhibition about the exploits of Pryderi that is paradoxically related to the Celtic enthusiasm for Christianity. The repression of the Pryderi worship is presented as a kind of aboriginal cultural death; the death is a prelude, however, to a rebirth of such values on the psychic plane.

In *The Mabinogion*, the conflict of Pwyll and Pryderi against Gwydion is a struggle against "older, darker, less human deities of the magical north" (390). Powys took from Sir John Rhys this identification of Gwydion with Woden of the Teutonic peoples. Such a struggle was reborn within Powys's contemporary experience during World War II, and perhaps he perceived its origin to be at the aboriginal roots of Celtic mythology, deep within the unconscious of the race.

Taliessin's poetry also celebrates the birth of a new sensory humanism after the death of an era of guilt. Taliessin's poem in particular ushers in the hope of a new age embodying the cultural values distorted by certain aspects of the Christian faith. Taliessin's "almost babyish abandonment to pure unadulterated sensation" is pictured by Powys as a corrective for the rationalizing intellect dominant in Western thought from Aquinas to the twentieth century. Not only does the poem celebrate the end of an era, it also identifies the negative values emphasized by the Christian tenancy:

> The ending forever of the Guilt-sense and God-sense
> The ending forever of the Sin-sense and Shame-sense
> The ending forever of the Love-sense and Loss-sense

Guilt, sin, shame, and sacrificial charity have induced a death of the human spirit that is to be replaced by:

The beginning forever of the Peace paradisic
The 'I feel' without question, the 'I am' without purpose,
The 'It is' that leads nowhere, the life with no climax.
(417)

Myrddin explains to Porius earlier in this chapter that Christianity has created a revolutionary change; the complete reversal of that change will not be accomplished until the twentieth century formulates the existential values that Taliessin describes in these lines. The seeds of cultural revolution thus are sown within the context of the aboriginal wisdom also shared by Porius. Porius's "cavose-niargising" also celebrates the liberating power of "'Time free at last from its Ghostly Accuser / Time haunted no more by a Phantom Eternal'" (418).

This is an interesting reflection of Powys's own similar development. As early as *Rodmoor* (1916) and *Ducdame* (1925), Powys had created protagonists, such as Adrian Sorio and Rook Ashover, who dramatized a battle between life and death forces in the psychological arena. This conflict is presented in a way that human, psychological, and natural processes are linked with one another. As early as *Ducdame* and then progressively in *Wolf Solent* and *A Glastonbury Romance*, Powys has extended the frame of reference of the struggle within Man and Nature more consistently to History. These novels include antiquarian figures, amateur historians such as Urquhart in *Wolf Solent* or Uryen Quirm in the later *Maiden Castle*, presented in a sometimes ambiguous light. Those who cling onto or who are dominated by the Past hinder the process of growth and renewal for themselves and others. The antiquarian remains, and historic settings of these mature major novels are memorials for the characters of the continuity of experience in history as well as the ambiguous nature of the past.

The climactic place of Porius in this development is displayed in several ways: by the fresh urgency created by the situation of extreme historic crisis and by the exploration of the death and rebirth theme in *all* the major characters rather than in one single individual. The latter fact, especially, suggests that Powys is concerned primarily with the representation of a process of massive cultural renewal. The rebirth theme is explored in the experiences of the subsidiary characters of the novel but also in Porius himself, most specifically in the episode describing the death of the Gawres, the sole surviving female of the race called Cewri. In the typescript version, the episode receives its most heightened treatment because Powys describes the rape experience as a foreshadowing of the plunge of the Gawres into the cauldron-like lake.

During the rape (and it is significant that in the printed version Powys uses the words *rape* and *ravish*,[11] because some readers interpret the scene as an ecstatic union without the overtones of death and destruction that Powys builds into this episode in reaction, perhaps, against the traditions of romantic idealism), Porius sees "a swirling bottomless pool wherein there whirled round and round a terrible vortex of all the beautiful and horrible waves and eddies and ground swells of black blood and crimson blood mingled with slime and ooze and sea-weed like hair that cover the shoals and patches of the threshold of life." This description points to the way in which Powys effectively "de-sublimates" the image of the Grail Chalice, replacing it instead with the image of the cauldron of life and death that bubbles with the gross material as well as the spiritual or vitalistic principles of existence. From this death of the oldest culture of Ynys Prydein the new civilization will arise, but it forgets its basis in this "terrible vortex" of forces at its peril. I now turn to a discussion of the general significance of this theme.

Powys's analysis of the nature of civilization allows him to assert the values of life and freedom while admitting the realities of death and destruction. Civilization is created as a result of the marriage of rational culture and aboriginal nature; the latter is the source of life for the former. Thus, as civilization drifts toward decay, it encounters the life-giving forces of its "primitive" origins. H. J. Massingham's *Downland Man* had provided Powys with ammunition to attack the neo-Darwinian creation of a society that pitted the strong against the weak in a ruthless, competitive struggle for survival.

Sigmund Freud faced the problem of "natural man's" hostility to civilization as a repressive force. In "Civilisation and its Discontents," Freud says,

> But man's natural aggressive instinct, the hostility of each against all and of all against each, opposes this programme of civilisation. This aggressive instinct is the derivative and the main representative of the death instinct which we have found alongside of Eros and which shares world dominion with it. And now I think the meaning of the evolution of civilisation is no longer obscure to us. It must represent the struggle between Eros and Death, between the instinct of life and the instinct of destruction, as it works itself out in the human species. This struggle is what all life essentially consists of, and the evolution of civilisation may therefore be simply described as the struggle for life of the human species.[12]

According to Freud, the historic process is driven dynamically by hostility to civilization, because civilization is seen as a repressive force that stifles the instincts. Because civilization is built upon the renunciation of our instincts, it is the producer of aggression. Thus, "Eros" becomes "Thanatos," because the aggressive instinct turns inwards in a spirit of death and destruction.

In *Porius* the logical conclusion to a Freudian perspective on civilization as the product of repressed instinct is expressed through the death philosophy of Prince Medrawd. Chapter 24 of the published text, "Better Nothing than This," includes Medrawd's discourse to Porius about his "hate philosophy." Medrawd has gone further than any man before (one might suggest further even than the fated characters William Hastings of Powys's early novel *Ducdame* or the equally destructive Adrian Sorio in the earlier novel *Rodmoor*) in "the depth of his pessimism and in the desperation of his loathing of life." Medrawd expresses this loathing by his determination to bring all life to an end and, in his words, "the quickest of all ways to bring it to an end is *war!*" (570). In identifying Medrawd with the social or national drive toward war, Powys identifies war in turn with the death principle. The death instinct is expounded in Medrawd's proud boast: "I have condemned Life to die and I have appointed War its executioner. I am come that the world should have death . . . after life has disappeared . . ." (570). Medrawd is indeed an anti-Christ, like the monstrous beast in W. B. Yeats's "The Second Coming."

The path of Death, however, is only one of many that a civilisation, convinced of its integral relationships with the primitive rather than bent on its hostile repression, can follow. Powys thus provides a counter to Freud's pessimism and determinism as a result of his consistent bias against the disastrous social Darwinism of the nineteenth and earlier twentieth centuries. H. J. Massingham would have appreciated Powys's revelation in *Porius* that at the base of civilization there is a peaceable community unafflicted by the spirit of competition, aggression, and the neuroses of Sin and Guilt and devoid of the mass of aggressive conflicts depicted by others. As Porius exemplifies when he defies Nineue, Man can free himself even from Eros, to be reborn into a condition of genuine freedom that allows him to live life, even within the bounds of death, in a free and liberated spirit.

Powys includes another rebirth myth taken from the fourth branch of *The Mabinogion*, in this instance, which has the function of complementing the emphasis upon death created by Prince Medrawd. The Welsh legend, from the fourth branch of *The Mabinogion*, tells of

Blodeuwedd's conjuration from flowers by Math and Gwydion. In *The Mabinogion*, when Blodeuwedd betrays Math, she is transformed into an owl. But in Powys's presentation of the legend, the owl maiden appears after the terrible death and necrophiliac ravishment of Teleri by Medrawd in the face of the fanatical Christian followers of Minnawc Gorsant who were opposed to Teleri's Christian burial. When an owl appears fluttering in the twilight, Myrddin Wyllt seizes the creature and draws it under his cloak. He actually creates a feminine shape out of the owl, and this magical act can be interpreted as a rebirth miracle created in the twilight—time that fuses creative light and death-bearing darkness. The crowd watches the miraculous birth in a deepening silence, aware of the primordial elements of "water full of the mystery of life, save the waving torch fires, full of the mystery of death, save the earth herself, mother of both the darkness of life and the darkness of death" (654). In this episode Myrddin Wyllt seems to embody the creative power in Nature that reminds Man of his power to create and renew himself. Powys includes this rebirth myth as a direct response to Medrawd's enactment of a philosophy of death. Blodeuwedd appears in human shape in a process described as an "improper and unsatisfactory human birth." Moreover, this rebirth is also a rebirth of the very spirit of Teleri. When Morfydd, who is present at the miracle, looks into the owl maiden's face, she sees the image of Teleri in her eyes. She recognizes that "by recreating Blodeuwedd, the counsellor had in some queer way liberated the souls of all the Teleris in the world" (557). In addition to its philosophical portent, the episode is an overpoweringly feminist statement.

This miracle of life-in-death and life's subsequent resurrection also inspires political renewal because, as a direct consequence of the miracle they have experienced, the life-in-death cry of the forest people is heard. Powys comments, "In vain had the house of Cunedda with its association with the Romans, and later its association with the emperor, struggled to stamp out this life-in-death cry of the forest people!" (659). Moreover, the holograph text makes clear that there is an association between the forces of destruction and war on the one hand, and peace and recreative renewal on the other. The full text describes in detail Morfydd's struggle to regain the body of Teleri with the help of the dwarf Paun-Bach, and further makes explicit that Morfydd's liberation attains its complete expression in the struggle over Teleri with the priest who refuses her burial. The Blodeuwedd episode thus dramatizes the process of cultural, cosmic, political, and psychological renewal. Medrawd's desecration of death produces, paradoxically, the miracle of rebirth.

In the holograph and typescript manuscripts of *Porius*, there is another chapter that intervenes between "The Home Rock" and "Blodeuwedd" called "The Little One." The episode presented in this chapter is also structurally parallel to that of "Blodeuwedd," but here the focus is on Porius who is given another, parallel visionary experience to Morfydd's. The experience is another central exploration of the processes of death and renewal in a context more obviously male and political, but nonetheless still mythological in form.

Porius takes Amreu ap Ganion and Lelo, his wife, to the haunted chamber of the Druid beneath the mound of Y Bychan—a location that is fatefully associated with the opposition to Cuneddan rule and which Porius has encountered in the early episodes of the novel. In chapter 4, "The Tent," for example, the mound was described as "a rallying point for all such local rebels as not only hated the Romans but had small love for the house of Cunedda" (65).

The visitors to the mound discover a red-haired child, sitting on a chest and clutching the image of a terra cotta wolf cub. This child delivers a mysterious speech in the third person:

Y Bychan will not cry however much it hurts, but if you beat Bleiddyn Y Bychan will cry so loud it will bring the Derwydd out of his grave. And if you don't stop beating Bleiddyn, the Derwydd will give Bleiddyn the power to *bite your heart out.*

Porius feels a strange occult force binding the three of them together; he also speculates on the creation of the child and notes its appearance "Like an earth aboriginal." The Roman earth cub also strikes Porius by surprise, because Rome was the eternal enemy of Y Bychan. The child chants repetitively "Bleiddyn may rest in peace now" as Porius observes a fourth object, a chess piece that he identifies as a black bishop—but a bishop looking like "the hairy penis of the wolf cub." Porius again has the sensation of being bound with the others: child in contact with wolf cub, which in turn is in contact with the bishop. The child utters another portentous oracle:

When Bleiddyn is obeyed there'll be no difference between Brython and Gwyddl or between Ffichtiaid or Coranian. All will be equal. All will be one. All will be the same. It will be as if Bleiddyn had bitten their hearts out.

Porius's sense of being joined with his companions as if by an invisible cord is now accompanied by a precipitous transportation into another mode of consciousness. Then comes a climactic vision of a mound of dead bodies with a spear transfixing the heart of one to another, forming a hieroglyph of the first letter of Ynys Prydein. In his description, Powys identifies the figures as drawing together "all the desperate opposites of the world whose fanatic teeth are at one another's throats." Porius finally sees a child born from a heap of dead leaves; the child is surrounded by a body of white foam and the reader learns that "the foam is Y Bychan still a child."

This mysterious and mystic scene is a core image in the novel of the process of renewal of life from death—a process that Powys always identified as the central significant motif of *The Mabinogion*. The probable source of the child Bleiddyn and the child born from leaves amid sea foam is the fourth branch of *The Mabinogion*, "Math Son of Mathonwy." In this section of *The Mabinogion*, the story of Blodeuwedd is told. Math transformed Gwydyon and Gilvaethwy into animals for the rape of the virgin Goewin. A year later Math finds a wolf, a she-wolf, and a sturdy wolf cub at his door. Math says, "I will take the cub and arrange for his baptism, for the name Bleiddyn is ready for him."[13] (Bleiddyn is Welsh for wolf.) Math then wishes to take to wife the virgin Arianrhod, but Arianrhod steps over Math's magic wand as a test of her virginity. She fails the virginity test because she drops a child, a sturdy boy with thick yellow hair. Arianrhod runs away leaving Math another small bundle. Math arranges baptism for Dylan. When Dylan is baptized he goes to the sea, "and when he came to the sea he took on its nature and swam as well as the best fish." He is destined to die at the hands of his uncle. The small bundle is placed in a chest by Gwydyon, and a child is born out of it. The child is Llew, future husband of Blodeuwedd, who is also responsible for Llew's death. Llew, however, transforms himself into an eagle.

The complexity and confusion of the story cannot hide the recurring patterns of birth, death, and rebirth. The child Bleiddyn, born from animal shape, seems to be the counterpart of Blodeuwedd, who was made from flowers. As creatures of earth and the animal body, they both celebrate the earthly element as the unifying principle that joins man, nature, and the national or racial divisions that separate men. Transferred to Powys's novel, the rebirth motif in the chapter "The Little One" is expressed as a political union of discordant elements meant to replace political conflicts with peace. This reunification in terms of the earth, symbolized by the appearance of the dead bodies, is associated with the appearance of the rebirth symbol of the child born from the heap of dead leaves and surrounded by the body of white foam. The last element strongly links the child with Arianrhod's child, Dylan. Sir John Rhys identifies the two children of Arianrhod as the principles of darkness and light; Powys perhaps followed Rhys's lead in using them in *Porius* as concluding symbols of the unification of opposites that makes rebirth possible.

Powys's achievement in *Porius* is to unite an exploration of rebirth from death in the individual psyche with an analogous process in the whole culture. He expresses in his own fashion the urgent necessity for modern man to return to his origins within individual, national, and cultural contexts. The goal of this gigantic quest is to recapture the principle of spontaneous life. *Porius* is an historical novel that dramatizes and poeticizes a view of history as contemporaneous. The past does not recur mechanically, because the sixth century is different, indeed unique in human experience. But the sixth century is still present in the twentieth century as the twentieth century was implicit in the sixth—implicit, but not determined. The mythic and the imaginative qualities of *Porius* are still an expression of an imaginative, but historical vision expressed in what I maintain is a wholly new form of the historical novel.

Moreover, although Powys's vision is unique, it places him in relationship to the major writers of the twentieth century, such as T. S. Eliot, W. B. Yeats, or D. H. Lawrence, who had their own characteristic visions of the way civilizations decay and are reborn. Powys is closest perhaps to D. H. Lawrence—another ambivalent reactor to Freud. In *Fantasia of the Unconscious*, Lawrence expressed his interest in the rise and rebirth of civilizations:

> I like the wide world of centuries and vast ages—mammoth worlds beyond our day, and mankind so wonderful in his distances, his history that has no beginning yet always the pomp and the magnificence of human splendour unfolding through the earth's changing periods . . . nothing will ever quench humanity and the human potentiality to evolve something magnificent out of a renewed chaos.
>
> I do not believe in evolution, but in the strangeness and rainbow-change of ever-renewed creative civilisations.[14]

Fantasia was written after *The Rainbow* and *Women in Love*. The latter novel explored the destructive element manifested in the international environment of the 1914–1918 war. Lawrence dramatizes the turning of the erotic instinct into a death desire in the thwarted mechanical psyche of Gerald Crich. Gerald's destructive fatalism is contrasted with Ursula Brangwen's acceptance of the death rhythm and her recognition that to die is to move on with the invisible. Death is the unseen but final reality that gives rise to a new cycle of creation.

Yeats's visionary historical system drew upon Vico and Spengler, and in his poetry he explores the relationship between analogous cultures. Also, Yeats, like Powys, valued the Celtic mythological tradition and saw it as offering a path for renewal for twentieth-century technological man. In 1938 Yeats wrote in his essay *On the Boiler* that "Vico was the first modern philosopher to discover in his own mind, and in the European past, all human destiny. 'We can know nothing,' he said, 'that we have not made.'"[15] Poems such as "The Second Coming" or plays such as "Purgatory" present a prophetic vision of culture in the throes of destruction and hint at the possibilities for rebirth.

Even so, Powys's values may provide a safer and saner guide for the twentieth century than those of Lawrence or Yeats, even allowing for Powys's eccentricity! Perhaps because Lawrence and Yeats did not live through and beyond a *second* world war, they never became as alive as Powys did to the destructive role of power that Powys, through Myrddin Wyllt in *Porius*, isolates as the most damaging force in individual human and political relationships. It is assuredly the virtue of *Porius* that it addresses as a central contemporary theme: How can a culture renew itself and what processes within the psyche of the individual man or woman allow for recreation and continued growth? *Porius* is both a diagnosis and a criticism of Western contemporary culture, but at the same time the critical process opens up for the reader the potential for continued life and growth. Moreover, this diagnosis is presented in a form that is a unique blend of historical realism and romantic myth. Despite its sprawling length, *Porius* is a unified and richly orchestrated novel that makes a forceful, coherent, and humane statement about the potential destiny of humankind.

Notes

1. *John Cowper Powys, A Glastonbury Romance* (London: Macdonald, 1966), p. xii.

2. Jessie L. Weston, *From Ritual to Romance* (New York: Doubleday, 1957). Morine Krissdottir also emphasizes Powys's debt to twentieth-century anthropology in her arcane study, *John Cowper Powys and the Magical Quest* (London: Macdonald, 1980).

3. John Rhys, *Studies in the Arthurian Legend* (Oxford: Clarendon Press, 1981), pp. 10, 251.

4. John Cowper Powys, *Obstinate Cymric* (London: Village Press, 1973), pp. 85–86.

5. Hegel, *The Philosophy of History* (New York: Dover Publications, 1956), p. 40.

6. John Cowper Powys, *Mortal Strife* (London: Jonathan Cape, 1943), p. 80.

7. Powys described the article in *The New Yorker* for 30 July 1949, "The Reporter at Large: The Old Man's Chair," as a "great and very subtle achievement much more o much more than mere journalism." Powys also claimed to have learned from it "for my long, long, long, long [sic], learned antiquarian romance about Corwen A.D. 499." The article confirmed him in what he called his "own instinctive method." The 22 August letter to Boyne Grainger is in the ms collection of Colgate University Library.

8. H. J. Massingham, *Downland Man* (New York: Doan and Company, n.d.), p. 49.

9. John Cowper Powys, *Porius: A Romance of the Dark Ages* (London: Village Press, 1974). Typescript references are to the Colgate University typescript that I have collated with the holograph ms at the University of Texas, Austin, and are cited parenthetically by page number.

10. A summary of the excised passages and chapters included in the typescript is provided in Joseph Slater's "Porius Restauratus: A Summary of the missing third of *Porius*" in *The Powys Newsletter* 4 (1974–1975): 22–44. There also is a discussion of the unpublished text by Denis Lane in "Elementalism in John Cowper Powys's *Porius*," *Papers on Language and Literature* 17, no. 4 (1981): 381–404.

11. Powys writes that Porius discovers "for the second time on that day of stubble-coloured mist and of south-west wind what it meant to take *ravisher's* possession of yielded virgin soil." But he distinguishes between the two occasions: the taking of Morfydd "had been rendered easy by the girl's gallant and heroic passivity," whereas the "*rape* of the last Gawres of the Cader was rendered difficult by the goddess-like creature's own overpowering passion" (517; italics mine).

12. Sigmund Freud, "Civilization and its Discontents," in *The Complete Works of Sigmund Freud* (London: Hogarth Press, reprint ed., 1960), p. 122.

13. Jeffrey Gantzell, *The Mabinogian* (London: Heinemann, reprint ed., 1982), p. 106.

14. D. H. Lawrence, *Fantasia of the Unconscious* (London: Heinemann, reprint ed., 1961), p. 8.

15. W. B. Yeats, *On the Boiler* (Dublin: Cuala Press, 1938), p. 22.

Ultimate Questions: Powysian Answers

G. Wilson Knight

If I were asked why the three Powys brothers were so outstanding among literary figures, I should say that they have together concentrated with unique insistence on man's final problems. They variously treat of sex-love, idyllic and lustful; of nature, sweet or terrifying; of human cruelty; and finally, and often overpoweringly, of death. Religion is a background, but devotion is withheld. For social affairs and politics we must look elsewhere.

Their names are significant: John Cowper; John the Beloved Disciple, and Cowper the eighteenth-century poet, to whom they were related. He alone of the three shows a recurring Platonic sense of idealized youth; as Jesus had for John (as I have noted in *The Christian Renaissance* [1962], revised ed., Epilogue). Also his vast output merits the literary reflection. Theodore, the next; well, he is throughout God-tormented, writing of "the moods of God" in relation both to the Deity and to himself. Llewelyn, besides his writing, has left a record of courage that was heroic and deserves the name of the Welsh prince Llewelyn, who fought to preserve the independence of Wales.

We start with Theodore. His reading of existence is highly original. His novels and short stories are the result of what Llewelyn called his "mordant genius" (*Love and Death* [1930], XIX, 175). Death and graves dominate throughout. Human faults abound, rising to acts of sickening cruelty, and lustful excess. Within his purview are, however, too many truths for us to discount it: much applies to us all.

His novel *Kindness in a Corner* (1939) is refreshing for its light touch and humorous appeal, as also for its positive approach to the grave. *Mr. Weston's Good Wine* (1927) is universally praised for its compact treatment of his main interests, with love and death as the two wines, death the better. Here the allegory is neatly handled, with Mr. Weston as God, accompanied by the Archangel Michael,

236

and the clocks all stopped during the action, to signify Eternity. I think *Unclay* (1931), with its clever personification of Death, both as man and symbol, runs it close and at choice moments attains power. Power is not Theodore's normal aim; events and actions are dispassionately recounted all on one, impersonal, level. Terms such as "ironic," "caustic," "humorous" arise in the reader, but the author's feelings are left unstated; this is true, too, of moral criticisms.

In the short stories, there is a telling use of allegory, aligned with a showing of life and reason in natural objects; in animals, trees and waves; and also in human artifacts, a clock, a rope, a sock. These may converse and even engage in theological discussion. His handling is strangely effective; we accept it, either with humor or as serious metaphysic, in terms of animism or pantheism. So primed we may the better appreciate his preoccupation with graves; if stones and bones live, then body-death has new features. Death is, however, for the most part read in simple terms without any acceptance of human survival.

We are to accept death as a good; this is often stated. Also suicides are frequent. His whole-hearted acceptance has affinities with Buddhism and its hope for Nirvana; in the story "John Pardy and the Waves" in *Fables* (1929), men are as waves, which rise and break, and some essence may be cosmically perpetuated.

In his dispassionate overview of human behavior, scrambles for money inevitably appear ugly, if not deplorable; clerics are seldom much better than nonentities; those that come off best are the outsiders, simple people who do not compete.

We naturally wish to know more, and this we find in his early book *Soliloquies of a Hermit* (1916, reprint ed. 1918) a statement of personal philosophy, wherein he sees himself figuratively as a "priest" or "hermit"—actually living in, and caring for, a cottage and garden, with a hum-drum, uneventful life, true of him throughout—controlled by "the moods of God"; which are also his own moods, though he lacks theological devotion. He does not expect, or want, survival, but is content with day-to-day existence in the present.

He breaks free from his limitations in speaking of Christ:

The most wonderful idea that has ever come to man came to Jesus. It came to Him, silent, subtile, and like the lightning.

This was "a vision with no everlasting deadness about it," "without beginning and without end," possessing him in a "moment"; and this vision of "true life" coming and going with "lightning rapidity" (XIV, 89) he was ready to understand and assimilate.

"Life in a moment" is again contrasted with our deplorable thought of "everlasting years," with time (XV, 91). "One flash" from "that other place" sent a "new wonder" into Jesus' "old immortal stuff," striking dead "all his immortality" (XVII, 96).

Theodore condemns personal survival, his view summed paradoxically in the words "the more dead anything is the more it lasts" (XIV, 88). So Jesus has ended "the stagnation of immortality" and our Hermit longs "to live a moment" with Him in "freedom" (XXII, 113). He concentrates on "the moment," the "now" (XXIII, 115), while deploring "the greed of living for ever" (XXIII, 115, 117), our "cringing to time" (XXIV, 118).

Objections inevitably arise, aroused by the equation of Jesus' gospel with a denial of immortality. This comes from the questionable alignment of "immortality" with "living for ever." The one simply counters death, the other asserts time; and these two are not the same. We need to consider "timelessness."

Timelessness cannot be thought about for long and still less rationally expressed. Theodore can write that for children "every moment is an eternity," and "every hour" is "a life everlasting" (XXIII, 117); and this certainly points us on; for the rest, "timeless" thinking can only be expressed symbolically, and I doubt if Theodore ever found the right imaginative method. His concentration on graves we can accept, but his suicides pall. Though the behavior of his normal people can be revolting, his record of human viciousness—cruelty to animals especially—has an unswerving honesty beyond that of any authors I have read. This we must praise; but what of the more positive qualities? Theodore in his *Soliloquies* can enjoy "just living," "the joy of things as they are" (X, 57–61), and this may represent a much diluted, provisional, mysticism. But his narratives have not, or very rarely, succeeded in sanctifying the trivial; though entertaining, their regular treating of trivialities leaves them in danger of themselves appearing trivial. Imaginative "atmosphere" is weak. *Mr. Weston's Good Wine* contains the only instance I recall of a symbolism adequately expressing timelessness—in the clocks stopped during the action.

In conclusion, we can say that the promise of *Soliloquies* is not matched by the fictions. His view there of Christ as one daring to pit his powers against God and the terrors of the created universe has an electric impact (XXIII, 117). This small book compacts a large wisdom, and was well assessed by a character in Louis Wilkinson's *Blasphemy and Religion* (1916), as likely to be read in "a hundred years."[1] Yes. And perhaps longer than that. In it his pin-pointing of the mystic "now" or "moment," probably the most important theme of my present discussions, is more sharply defined than by his brothers.

Llewelyn is by contrast with Theodore always bright and vigorous, at his best detonating. He worships life as surely as Theodore worships death. He sees life raw; most often as beautiful but also as terrible. He shares with his two brothers a horror of cruelty, not only in objective thought, but admitting his own guilt; and not only in man, but in nature's voracity, the beasts wonderful in grace and destruction. The key is his acceptance of the life-wonder, in nature and in himself. In *Ebony and Ivory* (1923) and *Black Laughter* (1924) and the essay "Africa's Wisdom" in *Damnable Opinions* (1935), I, his pattern is clear.

His philosophy is based on the senses (*Damnable Opinions*, "The Poetic Faith," XI, 89–91), and Epicurean. As philosophy it is almost unanswerable if we take no count of extra-sensory intimations. The unmoral powers of Africa, its vast vegetation and predatory beasts point us to the first thrust of creation. In "Immortality," in *Damnable Opinions* (X, 81), he says:

Last Autumn I came upon a wounded partridge, and being hungry and no pot on my fire, I hunted it down and wrung its neck. Who gave a thought to its soul? Yet it had a sensitive eye, the eye of a tender mother; it had lungs that breathed, and a heart that beat. . . .

In the chapter "The Epicurean Tradition" he says (XII, 100):

Our wisest course may well be to enjoy our hour of sunshine without thought or plan. All life is carried along in this perpetual flux . . . Flies he never so high, the eagle comes to earth at last, a sorry bundle of unbuoyant feathers. Ox and ass, mouse and man, none escape. The very planet itself, for all its encircling tumbler-pigeon flights, is doomed.

Our true religion is to worship life's miracle, though bound for death.

Passage after passage, whatever is under discussion, is illuminated by transfixing side-glances of natural observation. Reviewing Llewelyn's *Somerset and Dorset Essays* in *The Yorkshire Post* (28 November 1957) I wrote:

Natural life is present in vivid, often fierce, dramatic detail. We watch a gull rashly engaging battle with three ravens, fox-cubs at play, the stoat on his blood-lust path. Unlike the circuitous and sweeping manner of his brother John Cowper, Llewelyn's style tended to concentrate its power in the revealing phrase, the stab of insight: as in fishing, from the fishes' view, as a 'treacherous pastime'; the 'tiny polished crystals' of a dead herring-gull's eyes; cows with horns that 'gleam in the moonlight'; pieces of rock as 'morsels' of 'tangible eternity'; a gipsy youth 'lithe as a weasel'.

His strength is in such gems of insight and description.

He writes from personal experience. He is a brilliant essayist, and in longer works autobiography dominates. His one objective story is *Apples Be Ripe* (1930); though based partly on personal experience, it succeeds as a novel. A young schoolmaster is repelled by smug conventions on all sides and breaks free from his marriage into farm labor; meets a girl he loved in boyhood; is dying from exposure; has one great experience of consummated love on a hay-rick; and dies. It covers his life-view with ease, the better for its fairness to the other side, contrasting with much elsewhere that is intolerant.

In *Love and Death* (1939) fiction and personal fact are rammed together without complete success. The book's power is in its idyllic and passionate love rhapsodies and, as usual, in natural evocation. Once sensory experience is all but raised to a mystical awareness. The passage occurs in *Earth Memories* (1934), "Natural Worship" (1983 reissue, 99):

> In the highest moment of love, thought itself dissolves away like hoar-frost in the sun. The mind becomes as nothing, the body as nothing, the whole of our being caught up, translated, until it is as one with the incomprehensible mystery that lies behind matter, at one with that incalculable dynamic that is nowhere and yet is everywhere, and through whose agency the star clouds stream across the firmament, the daffodil lifts its head, the swallow chitters, and the ground-ivy delivers up its soul to the ditches.

Through "the agony and ecstasy of corporeal love" mortals may draw near to "the quivering secret of life."

Much of his time was spent in battling against his recurring consumption together with other ailments. His "gospel" of life-worship persisted despite severe troubles. He had courage; sheer physical courage. He took risks in cliff and mountain climbing in Dorset, Switzerland and Canada. As for Africa, to be forced to take control alone for four years of a large farming area after he had been in a sanatorium; to live in danger from fierce beasts and native riots; to do this, and make himself efficient at it, was a striking achievement.

It would be wrong to regard Llewelyn as a licentious and revolutionary person. As a man he was cautious, and advises an Epicurean refusal to embrace present happiness at future cost. Conventional morality, as usually understood, he certainly repudiates; his own declared morality consists primarily of a vigorous condemnation of cruelty to all sentient beings.[2] Despite his atheism, he was instinctively religious and visited the Holy Land, writing well on Biblical history; and indeed many of his essays touch normal religion with sympathy.

His personality, even at the end, was radiant: Ethel Mannin wrote, in *Privileged Spectator,* of his "charm that kindles the senses like sunlight," and his Swiss doctor of his shining out "as a bright star" from dull humanity.[3]

We are nevertheless forced to register a criticism. He—fortunately for us—shows little sign, except for the incident of black magic told in *Black Laughter* (XXIII), of getting beyond his brilliant sensory experiences into the extra-sensory realm. Religious "faith" is regularly discounted, and as for Spiritualism, he writes in *Glory of Life* (1975 reissue, 19):

It is most sure that when we are dead, we are dead. When our heart has given its last beat, when we have taken our last breath, then all is at quits.

This is a tenable view; many of us, in some moods, hope for such a death. His continuation is not tenable:

If this were not the truth, the whole truth, and nothing but the truth, we would most certainly be able to find some reliable evidence to the contrary. There is no such evidence worthy of the consideration of a wise man, and there never has been. How can we put the tittle-tattle of parlour spiritualism against the verdict of the ancient centuries?

Faith may certainly be rejected by reason; death may be annihilation; but no past spiritualistic evidence that has ever deserved consideration by wise people?—that is a staggering factual blunder. As for "the ancient centuries," I point to my brother Jackson Knight's *Elysion* (1970). In this passage the author's eagle style crashes miserably. "Tittle-tattle" conforms to a set fashion only too usual among those, mainly journalists, who attempt spiritualistic mockery.

In conclusion, Llewelyn was not by nature a novelist, but an essayist and autobiographer. What he has to offer is his style, and also his "personality."[4] With such a style and such a personality, we may be glad of this; glad too even of his spiritualistic ignorance. For, despite all limitations, his overall life-view is powerfully convincing. If impercipient Nature, with its cruelty and slaughter, its earthquakes and tornadoes, and prairie fires, is God-less, as Llewelyn again and again drives home to us, common sense may submit. All this he reiterates; it is the price we pay for his splendid sensory perceptions. I lay primary emphasis, not on his stylistic periods, but on his *exact and detailed miniatures*, so stamped on the living page that he becomes, at these choice moments, a voice of Life Itself, so entrancing and transfixing that I doubt if, in this particular regard, our literature can provide its equal.

2

John Cowper ranges more widely. In common with his brothers he opposes cruelty and sadism, with a yet keener purpose, as in his Confessions in the *Autobiography* (1934), the psychological study of Mr. Evans in *A Glastonbury Romance* (1933; 1955), and the sadists' "Inferno" in *Morwyn* (1937). These concerns I here pass over, together with what may be grouped under the heading of "symbolism" and "elementalism," while confining myself to the ultimates of other-dimensional categories, involving the occult and possibilities of an after-life. With these, Powys's contribution is varied and enigmatic.

His most vivid picturing of spirit-life is in *Morwyn*. Here we are climbing a mountain, as in Powys's poem "The Ridge," before a "premonition" called "as psychic as it was electric" heralds a "crack" in the natural order and we are plunged down to the earth's centre and thence into some new dimension which I describe in *The Saturnian Quest* (1964, V, 65):

> Our hell is well realised through concrete descriptions of non-physical existence. Talk is silent, almost telepathic, yet not always wholly distinct from language. The setting is half-lit by phosphorescent luminance; snow may be black and air electric; the sky is a solid roof; impressions of adamant, metal and volcanic stone are weighty: colours are brown, dark green, blue-black. There is a subterranean sea. Smells may be sickening. Solidity can be dependent on mind or desire; everything is simultaneously half mental and half material. The realisation of an astral or etheric state is expert.

This helps our understanding of Powys's *fear*, on occasion, of spiritualistic engagements; other dimensions may not be pleasant.

This is Powys's most exact delineation of another order. For close psychic earth-plane insights, his best book is *The Inmates* (1952). The hero John experiences direct clairvoyance into the "millions of little clock-cells" in another's skull, "ticking and tinkling and turning their tiny wheels on their electric pivots," reminding us of the psychic X-rays in *Morwyn*. This may be, on Powys's part, a fictional reconstruction of some clairvoyant experience; John's reading of the man's thought follows. So does his sight of the etheric body: "the insubstantial and yet not quite immaterial soul-covering or soul-skin which is the half-way house" between "the visible and the invisible." He sees "a cloudy shape in the form of a man, composed of semi-transparent mist, the colour of a puddle of dirty water upon which has just fallen some dark purplish shadow." He also visualises the body-soul connection, like a "living eel," seeming to be distinct from both spirit and flesh in the way "it quivered and shivered," with "rippling vibrations" (XIV, 258–59). The descriptions of the etheric body and the silver cord, both psychically authentic, appear to be too realistically exact to be indirect, fictional, presentations, and supposedly may be derived from the author's own clairvoyance. (For "the silver cord," see Ecclesiastes, XII, 6.) These two works, *Morwyn* and *The Inmates*, contain Powys's two most incisive descriptions of occult categories.

Soul or astral projection is a recurring concern, as in Geard's unique ability to encompass "the astronomical universe" in *A Glastonbury Romance* (XV, 468–69 or 453–54), or Owen's powers in *Owen Glendower* (1942, XXI, 954–56, 913–14). *The Mountains of the Moon* (1957) has a Welsh lady who regularly visits the Moon in sleep (188–89). In the *Autobiography* Powys claims similar powers for himself (VII, 276; IX, 409), and they are incorporated in the teaching of *In Spite Of* (1953), with the silver cord noted as "the invisible navel-string" connecting the traveling consciousness with the body left behind (VII, 218), though he notes that the body's senses in one place are being used for activity in another: he is apparently recording his own experiences. We have direct evidence of his abilities. W. E. Woodward in *The Gift of Life* (1947) reports an instance of Powys's appearance to Theodore Dreiser from a considerable distance; an extract is quoted in my *The Saturnian Quest* (IX, 128–29). Powys would never explain or discuss it.[5] Probably Powys did not fully understand the matter, nor even wish to.

From his early years he thought of himself as a "magician" (*Autobiography*, VIII, 352; XI, 548). He engaged in spiritual healing, sending out thoughts "like coloured angels"; they are called "coloured" yet they are "invisible" (VIII, 373, 630, 638). He thought he had disturbing malignant powers that could, if given rein, lead to disasters (*Autobiography*, VIII, 352; IX, 408; X, 516–17).

His stories are often spiritualistically suggestive. In midcareer, *A Glastonbury Romance* is crammed with occult and numinous happenings. Spirit powers overwatch the human drama. We start with an extended description of the Rector of Northwold watching the funeral and subsequent events; John Crow prays to his parent's spirit (III, 79 or 95), as do other heroes in *Wolf Solent* and *Maiden Castle* (1936); Philip Crow's mother tries in vain, as is spiritualistically normal, to get his attention, acting from the "etheric envelope" existing beyond our material "dream-world" (XXI, 700 or 672). Geard, in the powerful chapter "Mark's Court," appears to come to him from the distant past (XV, 458 or 443); he can, as we have recorded, project his soul infinitely far (XV, 468–69 or 453–54), has the gift of spiritual healing, directing "arrow after arrow" from his mind against a cancer with "deadly force" (XXIII, 740 or 709); and even, at one point, appears to be able to raise the dead (XXVII, 933–35 or 893–95). His final address asserts the immortality even of insects. At Tom Barter's murder the novelist steps forward to say that whether any, or how much, of his personality survives after the first few moments, he cannot tell us (XXIX, 1100 or 1051); at Geard's own death we are similarly told that his consciousness is in "suspension," but whether this suspension is permanent or not cannot be stated (XXIX, 1172 or 1118). That the author should in these two instances break his fictional omniscience reflects his concern.

In *Maiden Castle*, the cast of characters lists "the Spiritual Presence of Mona Smith, ten years deceased"; it seems that she actually, though dead, can inscribe her name on paper (VIII, 382 or 394; IX, 405 or 417, 430 or 442).

Powys's novels have instances of precognition, as in *Ducdame* (1925), in which the hero's son, now grown-up, appears, a happening probably unique in serious fiction; and as in *Owen Glendower* with its Shakespearian "ghost out of the future," speaking Hotspur's lines (XVII, 663). His mind-adventures make contact with the Hindu Kundalini Serpent. Tibetan associations are insistent, in *Weymouth Sands* (1934) and with Morsimmon Esty in *The Inmates*. Kewal Motwani called him "a great yogi."[6]

In *Porius* (1951) there is less in this vein but a similar magic is within the great conception of Myrddin Wyllt and his tumultuous and all-embracing personality; his telepathic communication with animals, and mind ranging through the ages. In *The Brazen Head* (1956), Peter Peregrinus's sexual magnet wields a terrifying malignant power.

Powys's last fantasies are spiritually engaged. Though the end

of *Up and Out* (1957) shows the expected new dimension as nonexistent, *The Mountains of the Moon* is more positive. The title suggests
the traditional abode of departed earth-spirits and the story has earth-
links, in the Welsh lady who visits the Moon in sleep and in the
collection of "terrestrial milestones" from key-moments in human
history. After that, we have *Real Wraiths* (1974), *Two and Two* (1974)
and *You and Me* (1975). They treat of bodiless mind and the living
dead, of ghosts and immortality, and again of souls visiting the Moon
in sleep. *Real Wraiths:* well, the title speaks for itself, indicatively.
In these stories Powys seems to be playing with all the random
possibilities and impossibilities of bodiless life beyond death. His
gaming reaches an extreme at the conclusion to *Two and Two* where
a living Jesus appears stating that he is now quite dead and that
everyone else will be likewise.

He could nevertheless regard a corpse as merely a "cast-off shell"
that "has no connection at all with the indestructible spirit we have
lived with and have loved" (*Owen Glendower*, XX, 865–66; and see
Wood and Stone [1915], XXIII, 596–99).

Throughout his career Powys remained undecided regarding survival. He could write in positive terms and with considerable impact
in its favour, as when, in *A Glastonbury Romance*, he imagines a
spirit victorious above the material order, "over which, when the
process of decomposition commences, it spreads its contemptuous
wings" (XXIX, 1080 or 1032). But he could also think very differently. Our firmest personal denial occurs in the Preface to the 1961
edition of *Wolf Solent:*

> Whatever death may mean, and none of us really know, I have come
> to the conclusion for myself that when I die it is the complete and
> absolute end of me. I am now satisfied that when I lie dying I shall
> be feeling a perfect contentment in the sure and certain knowledge that
> no consciousness of mine will continue after my last breath. (vii)

Powys told me that, though he used to believe in survival in arguments with Llewelyn, yet now, after Llewelyn's death, he did so
no longer. Perhaps he felt that he should have had psychic contact
with Llewelyn, had his brother's consciousness still existed.

The desire for complete extinction is, as one grows old and tired,
eminently reasonable if only because, as Jim Bleasdale's fine poem
on death puts it in "Dog Saturday":

> We have no means of finding out
> The truth of Hamlet's fearful doubt.[7]

Will survival be pleasant? Our personal desires are irrelevant. In the extended discussion in *Maiden Castle*, Dud No-man insists on clarity: "Either we do survive or we don't survive" (VI, 223 or 235). There must surely be a cosmic law, one way or the other, despite the thought of the philosopher Om in *The Mountains of the Moon* who states that it will be a matter of choice.

Spiritualism comes off badly. *In Spite Of* speaks of "those doubtful, plausible, specious, spiritualistic, telepathic, Yogi-ish" pursuits "which have done more to confuse and bewilder and side-track people with a nervously alert and sensitive intelligence like ourselves than any traditional belief has ever done" (IX, 293). To me, in a letter of 25 April 1955, he wrote:

> . . . But beware of the occult! my dear friend *O beware of it!* You and I have enough of the Demonic in us *without that!* Its *effect on us* is a weakening one and a blurring one and *not* an enlightening one. Beware! Beware! Beware O maestro mine!

A strange equation of the spiritualistic with the "demonic"; perhaps it is clearer from his remark that for himself religion, and for many others spiritualism, lead into "a whole dimension of strange, unruly, disorderly forces that can be very dangerous to our natural peace of mind and to our normal human activities" (*In Spite Of*, IV, 94).

He had apparently had experience of a spiritualistic séance which was disturbing.[8] In his early philosophic treatise *The Complex Vision* (1920), he urges that the desire for personal survival is superficial and the question unimportant. Our supreme moments concentrate only on love (XIII, 314; Conclusion, 368). We have a careful analysis but no exact conclusion is established. Powys's attitude toward the spiritualistic, and to death's mystery, resembles J. Middleton Murry's in an imagined argument with William Archer in *Things to Come* (1931, 66–77).[9] Powys's recently published play *Paddock Calls* (1984; composed 1922) engages the occult, both in its title (from *Macbeth*, I.i) and in an enigmatic séance towards the close.

In this mass, or morass, of incertitudes we do well to hold in mind two events depicting a reasonably calm dissolution: the first is in *Rodmoor* (1916), where we have a powerful description of death blending into cosmic peace by the sea (XXVII, 456–58); and the second in *After My Fashion* (1980; completed 1919) where annihilation is a positive joy. In both, dying is accompanied by a loved one's voice, as though that somehow existed within the death. These Nirvana-like descriptions have a strange authority. A central statement occurs in *Mortal Strife* (1942, VII, 113):

When we are dead, life and death, according to this present dimension, cease; and something else substitutes itself for them. Of the nature of this something else it is not only now impossible to obtain the faintest clue; it must of necessity always be impossible, simply because Time and Space *get in the way*.

A similar view is expressed at the conclusion to *The Art of Growing Old* (1944).

We have somehow to break through the time-space barrier; this we shall now attempt, with especial reference to Powys's poem, "The Ridge" (1963; reprinted in *The Powys Review* 13 [1983–84]: 47–48).

3

In "The Ridge" we have a mountain climb, like that in *Morwyn* which there precedes the cataclysmic descent to a subterranean Inferno; and even more like that in *The Mountains of the Moon*, climbing a height also termed a "ridge" (as at 177, 180, 187, 190, etc.). During our ascent in "The Ridge" we have (1) a mystic glimpse of a mysterious "tint" related to a golden superlative beyond man's "hope," and (2) this is followed by a concentration on the present moments of the climb itself, which may conceivably, though it is not stated, be regarded as influenced by (1).

The first may be related to a strange passage in *In Spite Of* (VII, 207) suggesting that there are "moments" when the personality can know itself "outside the radius" of even "planetary disaster," immune to any dangers beneath the "celestial floor of the most god-like empyrean"; this realised in "one single flash of unholy recognition," even while expecting "annihilation" and quite apart from any belief in the supernatural or divine. The suggestions are so worded as to appear paradoxical, but the central meaning is clear.

Such experiences are not to be regarded so much as an extension of time as outside time. For a classic example, we can turn to *King Lear*, to Lear's speech when going to prison with Cordelia in a state which I always define as a sort of "second childhood"; a state welcomed by Powys as a state of wisdom.[10] These are the *King Lear* lines:

> Come, let's away to prison,
> We two alone will sing like birds i' the cage:
> When thou dost ask me blessing, I'll kneel down,

And ask of thee forgiveness; so we'll live,
And pray, and sing, and tell old tales, and laugh
At gilded butterflies, and hear poor rogues
Talk of court news: and we'll talk with them too,
Who loses and who wins; who's in, who's out;
And take upon's the mystery of things,
As if we were God's spies; and we'll wear out,
In a wall'd prison, packs and sects of great ones
That ebb and flow by the moon.

(V.iii.8)

They are, though "in a wall'd prison," beyond the temporal "ebb and flow" of world affairs. We may call this an "eternal" recognition. Note that the poet side-steps difficulties by using the vague "wear out" to avoid becoming involved in a metaphysic of time. This corresponds to Powys's thought of being beyond a "planetary disaster," and perhaps to the mysterious "tint" of "The Ridge."

We are entering a difficult, though not uncharted, territory. In his recent *The Mystics Come to Harley Street* (1983), Basil Douglas Smith writes: "Mystics feel themselves (for good or ill) to be outside space and time, and to be in touch with Infinite Mind" (20). He gives a collection of subjects' experiences. One records, "It was a state of consciousness in which I knew All, in which I was All and in All - and yet was Nothing"; another, "I understood everything in a transcendental ecstasy of joy, knowledge and love"; another, "Afterwards I wanted very much to regain that state where all seemed timeless, unsubjected to the world of change" (45, 46). We could compare such statements with Keats's "Knowledge enormous makes a god of me" in *Hyperion* (III, 113), and with the hero's final consciousness as described in my recently published novel *Klinton Top* (1984, XXXV, and Epilogue).

Such records are not unusual. The best record I know of a mystical experience is J. Middleton Murry's in his book *God* (1929, Part I, 35–36). Others are collected in William James's famous *The Varieties of Religious Experience*, one of the prime influences on my early work, which probably affected my thinking on timelessness in my 1928 unpublished study *Thaisa* (now in the Birmingham Public Libraries), in *Myth and Miracle*, *The Wheel of Fire*, and *The Christian Renaissance*. Afterwards I wrote less in this vein, since extended "timeless" thinking is unfruitful. In "The Ridge" we have a mystic sight of a something quite beyond man and next a concentration on the present climb as less a second-best than a necessary extension, or expansion, existing, as I write in my interpretation of "The Ridge," in the ever-present "Now" of actuality.

We are becoming involved in the mystic "Now," a word occurring often in mystical reports. In Carlyle's *Sartor Resartus* (I, vii) God exists in an "everlasting Now," "Space" and "Time" being repudiated as unreal. My poet-friend Frank Grimley has a long poem entitled "Now: for Maria. On a Birthday." "Now" is said to exist in a new dimension "higher than high," compared to being on a church steeple and, as in *King Lear*, God's sight. So (Section 14):

> Now is the wonder
> now is the sun,
> Whatever the blunder
> whatever the plan
> . . . . . .
>
> Yes, Now is totality.
> Nothing is else
> in the flow to the sea
> in the flow to the pulse.

"Blunder": does this, as God admits in Powys's *Up and Out*, suggest some fault in creation? Anyway, this Now is the self's "integration" creating from "sensation" a totality. Whether the "integral me" is permanently fixed, we are told, does not matter; just to be at the "heart of living" is gladness. As with Powys, there is the feeling oneself, quite apart from any thought of survival, outside the radius of a planetary disaster; or as in Powys's *The Complex Vision* (IV, 78), it is the "eternal" which can be realised in "a single moment" dispelling all thought of "survival." This corresponds to Theodore's view of Christ struck by a "lightning" vision of true life annihilating the everlasting deadness, a vision burning him up, inducing wildness and self-immolation; "life in a moment" to be contrasted with all temporal thinking of the "everlasting" (*Soliloquies of a Hermit*, 14 and 17; 15).

But what of the two main positives of "The Ridge," the mystic, gold-brown, enchantment and the final climb? Even though we dismiss survival, we may ask whether the Now and Time are to be regarded as utterly distinct or whether one includes the other. This is hard, if not impossible, to decide. Theodore's miraculous "lightning" insight and John Cowper's mysterious "tint" and "golden drop that's beyond all the hope of man" in "The Ridge" are not susceptible to human analysis. In the careful and even "academic," or "scholarly," analysis of *The Complex Vision* the all-important "apex-thought" at moments of supreme insight is more clearly defined. In it one is aware of spirit-companions, that is, of guardian spirits or guides (IX, 216), and it resembles "the vision of the immortals" (VIII, 168); he does not say "God." Past and future are not so much nonexistent as "irrelevant" within the "eternal Now," which nevertheless contains "memory" and "hope" (IV, 97; XIII, 314). In this most elaborately worked-out and coherently presented of all Powys's philosophic studies, we have adumbrated a possible fusion of the mystic "Now" and rational thought, including temporal extension. In the New Testament, "eternal life," as at Matthew, XIX, 16, translates *zoen aionion*, "life through the ages."

In practice, we may be supposed as always striving, even the criminal, within time for what is given by the timeless experience. Under temptation nothing else seems worth while, as I think Powys says somewhere, compared to the immediate delight. This raises issues outside my present enquiry, suggested however by the stanza on "Night-Mare Life" in "The Ridge," which succeeds sight of the mysterious color.

The problem of a "sudden illumination" and "the point of intersection of the timeless with time" ("The Dry Salvages," II, III, V) is handled throughout T. S. Eliot's *Four Quartets* (1943). The "now" is here emphatic: "And all is always now" and "Quick now, here, now, always" ("Burnt Norton," V). But it has somehow to blend with motion, "the still point of the turning world," without "fixity," a kind of "dance" ("Burnt Norton," II). Or again it may blend with the spatial, as do the "patterns" of words or music and the "Chinese jar" moving "perpetually in its stillness" ("Burnt Norton," V). To be fully "conscious" is to be independent of a world moving "on its metalled ways of time past and time future," and yet time is needed for memory of the "moment in the rose garden" ("Burnt Norton," II and III). A final blend of the inspired "moment" with time can only be realized by saintliness and a "lifetime's death in love"; for others, the inspired moments only, and afterwards continual "trying" ("East Coker," V; "The Dry Salvages," V). The aim is

> Not the intense moment
> Isolated, with no before and after,
> But a lifetime burning in every moment . . .
>
> ("East Coker," V)

So the counsel is to "fare forward" ("The Dry Salvages," III). The change from timeless insight to practical action in time corresponds to the final climbing in "The Ridge."

Eliot's poetic thought in *Four Quartets* has other correspondences with Powys. Here I note that its passages on the dead in "East Coker" (III), "O dark dark dark. They all go into the dark," recall Theodore; as too does the theological part-bitter and part-humorous view of life as a hospital "endowed by the ruined millionaire" (IV). Though, as I note later, there is also powerful thought on survival.

In "The Ridge" we watch the climber towards death passing from his mystic "enchantment" to concentrate on the present moments of his climb poetically—this is stated and important—accompanied. These we may call a series of "transitions," a concept of wide significance. My thinking on transitions derives from Rudolf Steiner's statement that the spiritual significance of music resides less in the notes than in the *transitions* between them. The essence of an aeroplane's flight is best felt in the transitions, involving danger, of its take-off and landing. Commenting on my transitional researches, the mystic and sculptor Norman Yendell wrote to me on 21 November 1983, "It is precisely this which is my 'Now', between times past and future, the instant which is outside time and inside Eternity," to be related to "the Divine Love": which implies a fairly clear distinction between the "Now" and temporality. But, as he puts it in a poem "The Heart Child," time may be simultaneously both dismissed and expanded:

> And Love is NOW, neither past or future,
> but immediate; which is Eternity
> lasting forever.

To resolve our paradoxes we may perhaps suppose Powys's poetic climb in "The Ridge"—it is called poetic—succeeding his intuition of the golden drop "beyond all the hope of man," to be diluted, as he climbs on, into a succession of semi-golden moments; Eliot's "trying."

Certainly "gold" is often used in poetry to symbolise such higher insights as we have been discussing. The phrase "the golden mean" is itself significant. In Byron's *Manfred* the hero, while scorning philosophy, says that he has nevertheless felt "the golden secret, the sought 'Kalon', found and seated in my soul"; thinking that, though it did not last, it was anyway worth while to record that there had been "such feelings" (*Manfred*, III, i). Nietzsche in *Thus Spake Zarathustra* has as his highlights the Lady Eternity ("The Seven

Seals," III, 16) and "the Golden Wonder, the boat of freewill and its Master"; that is "the Nameless One for whom the songs of the future will first find names," the mystical insight outreaching our present intellectual equipment ("Of the Great Longing," III, 14). Nietzsche writes of "a mellow brown drop of golden happiness" in "At Noontide" (IV, 10). "The boat of freewill" corresponds to Eliot's sense of "right action" as freedom from past and future, being driven no longer "by daemonic, chthonic powers," in *Four Quartets* ("The Dry Salvages," V). Strangely *Four Quartets* contains no reference to gold though in *Ash Wednesday* (1930, IV) we have the fine death-countering line, "while jewelled unicorns draw by the gilded hearse."

Our argument may appear dangerously discursive. Our central concern is still "The Ridge"; it describes a quest, going up a hill or mountain, with expectance presumably of death or some equivalent at the summit, with fear of what may befall there. The climber's solution is to concentrate on living, the "now" of his striding, poetically accompanied. He has temporarily enjoyed the enchantment of intuiting the "golden drop"—as in Nietzsche—"that's beyond all the hope of man," and climbs on, with a transitional suggestion of what I have called "semi-golden" moments till the poem stops, unfinished. Meanwhile he has at least obeyed the counsel of the *Four Quartets* to "fare forward."

Lured on by our recurring thoughts of gold we turn next to James Elroy Flecker's *Hassan* (1923) and its "golden journey to Samarkand." This, rather strangely, helps us to define all three Powys writers. Flecker's use of Samarkand corresponds to Coleridge's Kubla Khan and Xanadu and Yeats's Byzantium, the poets using a renowed historic place and giving it a new impact. "Samarkand" is peculiarly valuable for its resonating sound.

What happens is this: Hassan and Ishak have watched the lovers, Rafi and Pervaneh, buy one night of love at the cost of torture and death, and we have watched their spirits dissolve, Pervaneh counselling the unborn that Life is sweet in the manner of Llewelyn Powys, who insists on life's transcendent glory while not forgetting its fearful end.

Our play within the play is over, but we are immediately jerked up, awakened, to a new consciousness. The middle action is now as an unhappy dream framed, as Ishak recognizes, by his twice finding Hassan unconscious by the Fountain; there is much talk, during the trial, of life as a delusion. All that has gone, bells sound, preparing for the Journey to Samarkand. Prose dream gives way to the higher actuality of a sharp and resonant poetry. The theatric nightmare of love, torture, and dissolution gives place to a new daylight, close-up immediacy, an awakening. This is not an answer to the terrors we have endured but something of an entirely different order, or dimension, in the "Road to Samarkand," as different as waking from a dream.

The bells are ringing. The journey is to start. We remember Eliot's counsel to "fare forward" and Powys's climb. The rich merchandise is beautifully described. Then,

> But who are ye, in rags and rotten shoes
> You dirty-bearded, blocking up the way?

The words do not suit Hassan and Ishak, but do, strangely, fit the frequent social outsiders of the Powysian world.

> We are the Pilgrims, master; we shall go
> Always a little further; it may be
> Beyond that last blue mountain barred with snow
> Across that angry or that glimmering sea.
>
> White on a throne or guarded in a cave
> There lives a prophet who can understand
> Why men were born; but surely we are brave,
> Who take the Golden Road to Samarkand.

I suggest that this may be regarded as a neat designation of the three Powys brothers. The first signifies Llewelyn, as imaginative lord of creation. We might expect him to be characterized by the "golden," but, though in his last and reasonably indicative book, *Love and Death*, there are normal "gold" references, they are forcibly outnumbered by the word "white," which occurs continually.

Then the darker personality of Theodore. His central philosophic book bears the title *Soliloquies of a Hermit*. He lived a hermitlike existence and would have been content in a cave, and except for his passing but evanescent intuition of Christ, he leaves us a simple gospel of death-as-the-grave, and in *Unclay* a gripping personification of this Death.

These two leave precise answers. One loves life and deplores death; the other embraces death, almost as a Nirvana, but with his "mordant genius" more dark than that. Neither will have any sympathy with thoughts of survival. They exist in the order of clear answers to the ultimate issue. Are these reliable? Or indeed possible? Our Samarkand poem continues:

> We travel not for trafficking alone;
> By hotter winds our fiery hearts are fanned:
> For lust of knowing what should not be known,
> We take the Golden Road to Samarkand.

"Should not"? Or "can not"? It makes no difference. Either way we are refused facile answers. In *The Art of Growing Old* (XII, 218), Powys says that the final reality, if revealed, would be utterly incommensurable with our present understanding.

Let us return to our earlier lines. After the two prophets, we have the Golden Road; the quest. The difference between John Cowper and his brothers lies in their unchanging certainties throughout and his own lifelong wrestling with ultimate issues; with occult powers, with problems of survival, with all conceivable contradictions and ambiguities and uncertainties. While they deal in "yes or no," logical, extremes, he is marginal; in *The Art of Growing Old* (XII, 215) he says that "a feather's weight" turns the balance in favor of survival. He is always balancing and the total result may be called the golden mean of Keats's "negative capability" (To George and Thomas Keats, 21 December 1817). Gold is certainly a recurring symbol. The central positive in "The Ridge" is "a golden drop that's beyond all the hope of man"; the Age of Gold occurs in its fifth line, and is ubiquitous in Powys's imaginative thinking elsewhere; there are the gold buttercups that denote an ultimate solution in *Wolf Solent;* and so on, continually.

Following our two prophets, we have in the Golden Road to Samarkand, instead of prophecy a questing; a trying as in Eliot, a plodding on and up, as in "The Ridge." Our answer, if there is one, will not be in concepts but in living, in what I have called the "semi-golden" transitions. After the life-prince, Llewelyn, and the grave-hermit, Theodore, we have the greater insight and courage—"but surely we are brave"—for it needs courage to dare these hidden (occult) profundities, of John Cowper's undying and indomitable quest.

4

It might be thought that my essay is concluded. But we have to face the awkward fact, which appears to negate any value my analyses may have had, that in 1963 John Cowper was apparently transmitting a message to me through a medium in the Exeter Spiritualist Church, as reported in Appendix 3 of Powys's *Letters* to myself. If he survives, it might be supposed that our main questions have been finally answered.

I hope my readers will not feel inimical to this quite normal happening. Whatever we make of them, such messages are usual and certainly obey some natural law. The evidential quality of this one was high. Within the brief time at her disposal, the medium (Miss Frances Horsfield) was aware of a Wales association, described Powys's appearance, face and hair, accurately, and delivered messages exactly appropriate to the occasion with no errors. She stated that he was aware of occult realities and the after-life and, most important, she said that the power of his personality, as we should expect, was in excess of any she, as an experienced medium, had ever known; she was afraid that he would take over control, which she would not allow. My original account was a little more full and even better than the published version.

If we recall what we have heard of Powys's occult powers—the dangers of his malignancy if given rein, his spiritual healing, his astral travelling, his clairvoyant descriptions in *Morwyn* and *The Inmates*, and his dervish-like and mesmeric powers as a lecturer (as described by Henry Miller in *The Books in my Life*, London, 1952, VII)—we shall not be surprised at the medium's fear of further engagement. The knowledge of extra-plane communication on this side is always said to enable adepts the more powerfully to communicate from the spheres beyond; it is because the Red Indian race was already so well attuned on this plane that they are so often guides on the next. To the American Indians, whom he called "the most original and formidable race among all the children of men," Powys felt himself especially close (*Autobiography*, XI, 548; XII, 635). Modern spiritualism started in America, and may even be supposed to have derived from the Red Indians: Powys, in his healing, appears to be aware of a contact.

Powys's uncertainties we have already discussed, and in view of his occult expertise, his after-life communication is not strange. What then are we to make of our long story of his anxieties, skepticism, in-and-out assurances? Especially of "The Ridge"? Was it all waste of energy? Having written the main part of my essay, I feared that my analysis of his tumultuous and fascinating engagements would be discounted by the publication of this post-mortem witness. Then one day the answer to my problem came, in a flash, during a later service. The answer is simply this: *there is no conflict.* For we may assume that Powys is still advancing.

Let us consider death as once handled in my *Atlantic Crossing* (1936). We are in a liner, going down the St. Lawrence River in Canada and approaching a bridge. By an optical illusion, it appears that our mast cannot negotiate the passage. My text runs:

'Look, Mother—can you see?' The bridge looks very low, the mast terribly high, and the nearer we get the more impossible it seems. 'It can't possibly,' she said, enjoying the fun. 'Don't talk nonsense.' Now the mast springs up, taller, taller, and the whole ship's speed seems to increase second by second, the mast leaps higher, swiftly towards disaster, just twice as high as the bridge, like a man instant by instant approaching death, which, as he sees it coming, spells necessary dissolution - and next, smoothly, easily, serenely, the masthead glides beneath with leisurely assurance, many feet to spare, and the big ship sails queenly down the river as before.

(I, 27)

I appear to have been writing from what may be a valid intuition, which my later spiritualistic knowledge tends to ratify. We are told that Death is normally an easy transition.

Are we still skeptical? As literary students we should remember that spirit-survival has been accepted, as is indicated throughout my *Neglected Powers*, by the most renowned poets of our century; by Yeats, by Masefield, by Eliot. *Four Quartets* is empowered by such intuitions, as in the ghosts of "East Coker," and the wisdom of the psychically described "compound" spirit in "Little Gidding." The belief is compacted in the lines

And what the dead had no speech for, when living,
They can tell you, being dead; the communication
Of the dead is tongued with fire beyond the language
of the living

(I)

Again:

We die with the dying:
See, they depart, and we go with them.
We are born with the dead:
See, they return, and bring us with them.

(V)

Poetically, Eliot's finest immortality statement is surely his *Marina*, where the celebration of death's insubstantiality is related to the

finding of the speaker's own part-creation, a daughter; or we may
say, creation in general. Eliot's poetic treatment of survival in full
consciousness directly after death is noted in my *Neglected Powers*,
XIII, 397.

Dying may be supposed less a reverberating cataclysmic change
than a necessary and easy progress; we are the same after it as
before, as Eliot assumed. So the climb of "The Ridge" was not
to result in annihilation, but is simply part of an advance toward
the higher and ever higher planes, as purportedly described by
F. W. H. Myers in spirit, through Geraldine Cummins, in *The Road
to Immortality* and *Beyond Human Personality*. (See also *The Return
of Arthur Conan Doyle*, ed. Ivan Cooke [1963]. These are central
books of cosmic suggestion.)

Every phrase of "The Ridge" and all Powys's quest and questioning
is accordingly still valid. The problems of evil and suffering known
by life on our plane may still be with him. I hope nothing in my
essay is taken to claim that such problems have been answered.
In *The Complex Vision* we hear that the soul's desire is not absence
of evil but the continual *process* of its overcoming by love (XIII,
314); and that presumably is not easily ended, nor soon. I can do
no better than quote from Alexander Pope's *Essay on Criticism* the
passage starting "A little learning is a dangerous thing" (215) and
continuing:

> Fir'd at first sight with what the Muse imparts
> In fearless youth we tempt the heights of Arts,
> While from the bounded level of our mind
> Short views we take, nor see the lengths behind;
> But more advanc'd, behold with strange surprise
> New distant scenes of endless science rise!
> So pleas'd at first the tow'ring Alps we try,
> Mount o'er the vales, and seem to tread the sky.
> Th'eternal snows appear already past,
> And the first clouds and mountains seem the last;
> But, those attain'd, we tremble to survey
> The growing labours of the lengthen'd way,
> The increasing prospect tires our wandering eyes,
> Hills peep o'er hills, and Alps on Alps arise!

(220–32)

That may well be true of the greater reality; we are still to "fare
forward." "The Ridge" was only, as its name implies, a "ridge,"
the term used also for the similar crest in *The Mountains of the
Moon*. With what wisdom Powys used the term "ridge," and with

what cunning he or his inspirers—for any serious literary exegesis should always take these into possible account—left the poem unfinished.

Notes

1. Malcolm Elwin, *The Life of Llewelyn Powys* (London, 1946), VII, 128 note.

2. *Confessions of Two Brothers* (New York, 1916), 200; *Damnable Opinions*, VII, 65; IX, 75; XI, 89; *Love and Death*, XXIV, 235–36.

3. Elwin, XV, 261, 270.

4. Elwin, VIII, 143; IX, 154; XI, 183.

5. If we wish to know more, we might turn to F. W. H. Myers, *Human Personality and its Survival of Bodily Death*, (abridged ed., London: 1927) VI Sensory Automatism, 158–86, especially 181–86 on "Phantasms of the Living"; or to Andrija Puharich, *The Sacred Mushroom*, (London: 1959); or Robert Crookall, *The Study and Practice of Astral Projection*, (London: 1961).

6. Derek Langridge, *John Cowper Powys: a Record of Achievement* (London: 1966), 57.

7. James F. Bleasdale, *Dog Saturday and other Poems* (London, 1975).

8. Maurice Brown, *Too Late to Lament* (London: 1955), XII, 205; discussed by Glyn Hughes, *Two Worlds* (London), No. 3842, March 1964.

9. See G. Wilson Knight, *Neglected Powers* (London, 1971), XII, 358–61.

10. *Powys to Knight* (London, 1983), letters of 14 January and 27 February 1957; see also his *Letters to Nicholas Ross* (London, 1971), 10 and 16 July, 1957.

11. Rudolf Steiner, *Eurhythmy as Visible Speech* (1944; reprint ed., London, 1961), XI, 49–50; VIII, 98; XV, 197.

Contributors

MICHAEL BALLIN is Associate Professor of English at Wilfrid Laurier University. A specialist in British literature of the period 1880 to 1945, he is particularly interested in the work of Hopkins, Lawrence, and Powys. He is editor of *D. H. Lawrence's "Women in Love": Contexts and Criticism* (1982), and has contributed to *Vital Candle*, ed. John S. North and Michael D. Moore (1981), and *The D. H. Lawrence Review*.

PETER G. CHRISTENSEN teaches English at Marquette University. He has published articles on John Cowper Powys in *The Powys Review* and has contributed to the special Powys issue of *Plein Chant* and to a forthcoming collection of essays on *Wolf Solent*, edited by Belinda Humfrey. His other published work includes articles on Marguerite Yourcenar, Lawrence Durrell, and D. H. Lawrence.

H. W. FAWKNER is Senior Reader at the University of Gothenburg and is currently finalizing criticism on Shakespeare, which will be published in 1990. His publications include *Animation and Reification in Dickens' Vision of the Life-Denying Society* (1977), *The Timescapes of John Fowles* (1984), and *The Ecstatic World of John Cowper Powys* (1986). He has contributed several articles to *The Powys Review*.

BEN JONES is Professor of English at Carleton University, Ottawa, Canada. He has published several articles on John Cowper Powys and has coedited *Fearful Joy: Essays on Thomas Gray*. He has also coedited a collection of essays on Nietzsche, *The Rhetoric of Nihilism*, to appear shortly. He is now working on Frances Gregg's autobiography, *The Mystic Leeway*.

G. WILSON KNIGHT (1897–1985) was Emeritus Professor of English Literature at the University of Leeds, and Honorary Fellow of St. Edmund Hall, Oxford. Commencing with *The Wheel of Fire* (1930), he wrote no less than nine studies of Shakespeare. Described by George Steiner as "our most esemplastic critic," Knight also wrote major studies of Byron, Ibsen, and, in *The Saturnian Quest* (1964), of John Cowper Powys.

DENIS LANE is Associate Professor of English at John Jay College of Criminal Justice, the City University of New York. He is the coeditor of *Modern British Literature*, vol. 5 (1985) and of *Modern Irish Literature* (1988). His writing on John Cowper Powys has appeared in *The Antioch Review, Papers on Language and Literature, The Powys Review*, and *Modern Fiction Studies*. He is Executive Secretary of the Powys Society of North America and serves as editor of its journal, *Powys Notes*.

CHARLES LOCK received his B.A., M.A. and D.Phil. from Oxford University, where he was Exhibitioner and Senior Scholar of Keble College. His doctoral dissertation was the first at Oxford to be devoted to John Cowper Powys. He taught English literature at the University of Karlstad, Sweden, from 1980 to 1982 and since 1983 he has been at the University of Toronto where he is now Associate Professor of English, Erindale College. He has published numerous articles on the Powys family and their circle and is presently working on the biography of John Cowper Powys. He has also published articles on Hardy, Hopkins, Bakhtin, Tolstoy, and others.

ANTHONY LOW is Professor of English at New York University. He is the author of a number of seventeenth-century studies, including *Augustine Baker* (1970), *The Blaze of Noon* (1974), *Love's Architecture* (1978), and *The Georgic Revolution* (1985). Modern literature has long been a second interest, including the novels of John Cowper Powys, which he first encountered at Cambridge during sabbatical leave in 1974–75. He is a charter member of the Powys Society of North America and serves on its advisory board.

RICHARD MAXWELL is Associate Professor of English at Valparaiso University, Indiana, and has published essays on nineteenth-century literature in *Comparative Literature, ELH, Romanic Review*, and other journals. He recently finished a book on Dickens, Hugo, and the novel of city life. He is presently thinking about relations between novels and history, especially in the decades after World War I. He is a member of the Executive Committee of the Powys Society of North America.

MARGARET MORAN is editor of *Is Modern Marriage a Failure? A Debate by Bertrand Russell and John Cowper Powys* (1983), and coeditor of

Intellect and Social Conscience: Essays on Bertrand Russell's Early Work (1984). In addition she is the co-editor of *The Collected Papers of Bertrand Russell*, including volume 12, *Contemplation and Action* (1985); and volume 13, *Prophesy and Dissent* (1988). Two of her essays on aspects of the writing of John Cowper Powys have appeared in *The Powys Review*.

The Reverend PATRICK SAMWAY, S. J., is literary editor of *America* magazine and adjunct Associate Professor of English at Fordham University/Lincoln Center; he received his Ph.D in American literature from the University of North Carolina at Chapel Hill. Father Samway is the author of *Faulkner's "Intruder in the Dust": A Critical Study of the Typescripts* (1980), and is coeditor of *Stories of the Modern South* (1981), *Faulkner and Idealism: Perspectives from Paris* (1983), *A Modern Southern Reader* (1987), and *Stories of the Old South* (1989).

A. THOMAS SOUTHWICK is currently a student at Columbia Law School. He has taught at Grace Church School, New York City, and at Barnard College. He earned a Ph.D in English from Columbia with a dissertation on J. C. Powys, and he was the recipient of Columbia's Christo-Loveneau Award for his master's thesis on R. L. Stevenson. His articles have been published in *The Powys Review*, *Powys Notes*, and the *Harvard Education Review*.

Index

263